EDITORS, SCHOLARS, AND THE SOCIAL TEXT
EDITED BY DARCY CULLEN

An academic book is much more than paper and ink, pixels and electrons. A dynamic social network of authors, editors, typesetters, proofreaders, indexers, printers, and marketers must work together to turn a manuscript into a book.

Editors, Scholars, and the Social Text explores the theories and practices of editing, the processes of production and reproduction, and the relationships between authors and texts, as well as that between manuscripts and books. By bringing together academic experts and experienced practitioners, including editorial specialists, scholarly publishing professionals, and designers, *Editors, Scholars, and the Social Text* offers indispensable insight into the past and future of academic communication.

(Studies in Book & Print Culture)

DARCY CULLEN is an acquisitions editor at the University of British Columbia Press.

EDITED BY
DARCY CULLEN

Editors, Scholars, and the Social Text

UNIVERSITY OF TORONTO PRESS
Toronto Buffalo London

© University of Toronto Press 2012
Toronto   Buffalo   London
www.utppublishing.com
Printed in Canada

ISBN 978-1-4426-4104-4 (cloth)
ISBN 978-1-4426-1039-2 (paper)

Printed on acid-free, 100% post-consumer recycled paper with vegetable-based inks.

Library and Archives Canada Cataloguing in Publication

Editors, scholars, and the social text / edited by Darcy Cullen.

(Studies in book and print culture)
Includes bibliographical references and index.
ISBN 978-1-4426-4104-4 (bound).   ISBN 978-1-4426-1039-2 (pbk.)

1. Editors.   2. Editing.   3. Scholars.   4. Criticism, Textual.
5. Transmission of texts.   6. Books.   I. Cullen, Darcy, 1974–
II. Series: Studies in book and print culture

PN162.E45 2012   808'.027   C2012-900211-9

University of Toronto Press acknowledges the financial assistance to its publishing program of the Canada Council for the Arts and the Ontario Arts Council.

   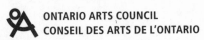

This book has been published with the help of a grant from the Canadian Federation for the Humanities and Social Sciences, through the Aid to Scholarly Publications Program, using funds provided by the Social Sciences and Humanities Research Council of Canada.

University of Toronto Press acknowledges the financial support of the Government of Canada through the Canada Book Fund for its publishing activities.

à PsM
de moi qui t'aime

Contents

Foreword

HELEN TARTAR

This is the best book on publishing I have come across, the one that begins to convey something of what publishing feels like, of why it caught my passionate loyalty and has held it for what is now approaching forty years. There are other good books about publishing, of course.[1] But the best ones basically offer advice on how to become part of the publishing process – aka get your book accepted – and so are largely written from the viewpoint of the gatekeeper, the acquiring editor, giving only sketches of the rest of the process.

That word 'process' is key to what makes *Editors, Scholars, and the Social Text* so powerful as an exploration of publishing. It concludes with a meditation on the book as process, and it itself instantiates the process of publishing – not just as a handbook giving access for one's own purposes (normally, acceptance of a book one feels oneself to have authored or to be in a position to author), but as a way to release the voices and thoughts and activities at work in creating the book, however invisible they may be in the final product. Throughout this book, this process is named in a particularly apt and provocative phrase: a social dynamics.

So, what makes this book so good? Let me mention just three of many things. First, it is a multi-author volume – it adopts a scholarly genre well suited to helping a reader experience its topic as an interplay of different voices.

A second virtue lies in the choice of contributors – the virtuosity point in any multi-author book. One apparent predecessor, *Editors on Editing: What Writers Need to Know about What Editors Do*,[2] says it all in the title and subtitle: only 'editors' and 'writers' are named, and in that book, only the former are contributors. The present book opens up what Darcy Cullen terms the 'middle' part of the publication process, the place where the manuscript's metamorphosis into book occurs (Introduction, 3). This means that in it you will hear the voices of those who, if their work is well done, traditionally disappear from the book as the reader encounters it. These are, of course, the press's editors – developmental editors, copyeditors, production editors – but here two important further inclusions have been made, crossing two divides that are seldom breached.

One divide is that between writers (editors and authors) and designers, the people responsible for the decisions that result in the physical layout of the book. The designer of a book's cover is the only person besides the author actually named in it, apart from the author's acknowledgments. But the author rarely even knows the name of the text designer, to enable even that recognition.

Another divide, perhaps a surprising one, separates editors from scholars, the pool of individuals from whom, at a university press, 'authors' are usually drawn. What, let an actual author write an essay for a book about publishing? Why, when I first tried to write about what I do as an editor, a press objected to the very fact that I cited scholars in footnotes, thereby admitting that I had thought, or at least tried to think, about what they said. Unlike *Editors on Editing*, in this book the word 'editor' is not taken solely to refer to people who work for a publisher but is interpreted in a broader sense, to encompass people who might be named as 'editor' on the cover or title page of a book (i.e., scholarly editors). Then, through the choice to privilege the material object, a distinction is drawn between 'book' (in a narrow slice of its traditional definition, meaning the object publishers offer for sale) and 'text,' specifically 'social text.' 'Text' enables us to focus on the writing per se (which includes its materiality – and digital files are every bit as material as printed books); add 'social,' and one factors in the immaterial emotive bonds that are as much a part of the book medium as are paper, ink, or, for a computer's hard disk, aluminum, glass, and ceramic substrate.

Within these pages, the voices of scholarly textual editors thus bring what publishing editors and designers think about day to day into dialogue with the most provocative theoretical and artistic explorations of the status of the author, the text, and the book now available: Barthes's 'The Death of the Author,' Foucault's 'What Is an Author?' Joyce's *Finnegans Wake*, Allan Ryan's *The Trickster Shift*. And that dialogue is by no means forced. It may be a bit more obvious for textual editors, who, like press editors, are in hands-on contact with the various social, material, and historical forces shaping the guises from within which the text reaches out to readers. Yes, when we are working at our most self-aware and creative best, what we editors do is quite consciously in dialogue with the contents of the books we sponsor and with the principles that guide them (not just those of accuracy and scholarly precision but also attentiveness to a basic questioning of what a text is, what an author is, etc.). Speaking even of something so seemingly automatic as the rules applied by copyeditors, in her introduction Cullen writes: 'Questioning of the rules is to be expected, after all, as university presses are places of important social change' (18).

I've been talking for some time now about what is a third virtue of this book: Darcy Cullen's vision as volume editor. She sees, and she shows us, how the everyday social dynamics of publishing connect with the contemporary dynamics of knowledge: those concerning historical and material textual production, including what social patterns come into view as a result of technological change.

I have often said that, in subsidizing a university press, the parent institution is subsidizing more than just the content of new knowledge, even if that is the primary thing it is subsidizing – and with it the notion that there is such a thing as new knowledge, that it can be created, and that to do so is the business of university professors (in short, the idea of the research university). It is also subsidizing the skills and devotion – the profession, in the strong sense of the word – of the various people associated with the university press whose business it is to disseminate that knowledge, whose work contributes to the 'authoritative social complex,' in Peter Shillingsburg's words,[3] that validates a book. This volume is a rare and remarkable testimony to their work. Read it yourself – but then, when and if you are in the right situation, don't forget to bring its message to the attention of your chairperson and your administration, to those who control the shrinking budgets of university presses.

I myself first became interested in the social dynamics of scholarly publishing in the 1980s. An anecdote from that time can help show just how far our thinking has progressed – and start to ink in some of the chiaroscuro attending the term. The book that galvanized my attention was named *Writing Systems* (*Aufschreibesysteme* in German; it was translated as *Discourse Networks*), by the German media scholar Friedrich Kittler.[4] I actually first came to his ideas secondhand, through a riveting lecture by Klaus Theweleit on the composition of an Orpheus poem by Gottfried Benn.[5] What stuck in my mind was the image of a poem composed between two men – the poet and his friend/archivist – across a necessary but silenced and excluded third: Benn's wife, the poem's nominal inspiration as Eurydice. During the closing months of the Second World War, Benn had sent her away to safety to escape the advancing Russians, who were raping German women as they came, while he stayed behind. But he didn't send her quite far enough, so, whereas he emerged unscathed from the invasion, she turned out to have killed herself in terror. How intentional, conscious or otherwise, the lecture asked, was that 'not quite far enough'? What was her social and mediatic role in this textual production between men?

I was listening to this lecture during the relatively early years of the current wave of feminism, at a time when the editor, however massively she may have rewritten a book, was widely viewed, in Cullen's apt term, as a 'contaminant' (Introduction, 10). I had come to editing by accident, as so many others do, and it suddenly occurred to me to attempt to think such elision positively, to think in an enabling way a social role encoded 'feminine' – indeed, to think it in a way that could be occupied, without losing its feminine coding, by powerful men.

So now I come to my anecdote. In the first lecture/workshop on editing I ever attempted, I therefore tried to crystallize such a social dynamic in a story about my former boss at Stanford University Press, Jess Bell. Jess was a towering and very masculine figure, the epitome of the heroic editor who emerges from some of the pages of *Editors on Editing*. At the press, he bore simply the title Editor; he literally wrote his own rule book;[6] he regaled the entire house with his marvellous letters to authors (back in the good old days, carbons of everyone's letters circulated weekly); and he had even coined the name for his favourite field of scholarly acquisitions, 'late imperial' China.

One day, however, after reading one of my letters to a faculty author whose book I was copyediting (something we then did in-house), Jess called me in and said that I had worded my letter too strongly. I should, remembering the respective roles of author and editor, have been more tentative in my phrasing. 'All editors are little girls,' I recall him saying. 'I'm a little girl, you're a little girl.'

When, at the suggestion of one of my colleagues, I submitted the piece containing this anecdote to *Scholarly Publishing*, then and perhaps still the only journal devoted to scholarly publishing, it apparently created something of a furore. How could someone everyone knew as so powerful and masculine a figure have said such a thing about himself?[7]

Well, many male editors at that time and since have feminized both their own role and that of the author by referring to the editor as a 'midwife.' (Note that they never refer to the editor as a 'gynecologist,' a role coded masculine for the same process of birthing.) As I recall (and to the extent that, being then so junior, I could have known), it was a point of pride for Jess and other editors of his generation to cut their own names out of an author's acknowledgments. I never asked the rationale for this act, seemingly so humble and yet so covertly violent, as if in a final assertion that the editor controls what gets published, even in that sanctum of the author's voice as private human individual, the acknowledgments. Was it modesty? Was it a notion of 'professionalism' as an anonymous though highly principled mask behind which a skilled worker, like a surgeon, takes refuge? Was it a recognition of a fact whose name they, being staunchly anti-Marxist, would not have enunciated: that they were engaging in alienated labour, that the fruit of their efforts was quite literally owned by someone else, namely the institution that had hired them, and thus might at any moment be torn from them and their role in it denied? Or was it a dedication to the ideology of the author's individual voice, tellingly revealed in the anecdote with which Rosemary Shipton begins her chapter in this book?

Jess has been a role model for me for many decades, but I remember him most for openly acknowledging, at least in those closing years of his tenure at Stanford Press, what was apparently then unthinkable to the editors at *Scholarly Publishing*: a positive joy in the social dynamics of his role as an editor, or, as he put it another time (and here I can only paraphrase, since the exact words escape my memory): people may think you're crazy, but you spend all your life making it so that other people will have written a book. Or, as the thought has come down into my own statements about my work: to give voice to others, keeping none for yourself. What I myself took from that previous generation was this thought: in my own life as a functioning organic individual, I am dependent at every moment on myriad unacknowledged social dynamics – someone I don't know made the pencil (yes, I'm that old-fashioned) with which I am drafting this foreword; someone made the clothes that I am wearing; someone picks up my garbage – and so an honourable way to live my life, in acknowledgment and gratitude to those people, however anonymous, is to offer my own efforts and work in a similar way. I can offer them only to the others who can benefit from the skills I happen to have and the situation I happen to be in. And those others are scholarly authors.

But times change, and now, in this book, you can hear the thoughts and concerns of people who live their lives in this way – such as Richard Hendel's instructive remarks from a designer's point of view – which otherwise you could have heard only in the corridors of the publishing house in which you might have been lucky enough to get a job.

In this, scholarly publishing reflects a larger social process. The coincidence of my own initial awareness of a social dynamics of scholarly publishing with a newly reshaped feminism is hardly happenstance – once you let the girls start talking, who knows where you'll be able to stop? I take great joy in the portions of this book that reflect how even our basic institutions of authorship, such as copyright, tremble when one listens to, opens space for, the voices of First Nations people. And I will, if I may, gratefully borrow the phrase 'in collaboration with' for my own current author who wants to list on the title-page spread the young South African informants whose voices enabled her to write her anthropological account of their lives.

How is it that we have come to see all this social dynamics, when fewer than thirty years ago it was considered a scandal to quote a powerful man referring to himself in the subordinate role of a little girl? The solidus in the title of Kittler's *Discourse Networks 1800/1900* marks a technological as well as a sociohistorical break – the difference between the media worlds of authors who wrote in longhand script (the province of men, even as clerks) and authors whose work was presented to publishers typed on a typewriter (often by women), as those worlds came into view when authors starting writing on a computer. I feared – and still do fear – that the computer enhances and globalizes our dependency on networks of faceless and anonymous others, while concealing them behind a strident media mythology of individual empowerment. But perhaps things are happening otherwise, as the medium quietly asserts itself, and the multiplicity allowed by, say, the digital textual edition is loosening the bounds of containment between the author and everything else, whether social or technological (and might we even one day re-admit the divine?) that enables the artifact 'book.'

But let me conclude with a glance back towards the author function, indeed, the author as 'genius' (which does, after all, refer to something impersonal, a tutelary spirit). Given my intellectual generation, conditioned not least by a fixation on individual genius in my father's before me, in my professional life and in the work I have overseen I have tended to lay emphasis on a historicizing of the author, on how recent a role this is, and on the previously unacknowledged social conditions for the production of the book, the social text.

But during my latest workshop, it struck me suddenly out of the blue how very old is the impulse to attribute a text to a named author. I was thinking of ancient Chinese philosophical texts: the *Mencius*, the *Xunzi*, the *Guanzi*, the *Zhuangzi*, most famously, perhaps, the *Laozi*. One need not look far to find something similar in Greek or Judeo-Christian culture: in the Christian Bible, all the Gospels bear a supposed author's name. This impulse is not universal: no author, so far as I know, has ever been claimed for the *Gilgamesh* or *The Egyptian Book of the Dead*.[8] But in none of these instances does Foucault's argument about the author function as a locus for adjudicating responsibility and blame seem to hold.

Take, quintessentially, the *Laozi*, also known as the *Daodejing*, the 'Classic of the Way and Virtue.' Why postulate for this collection an author who apparently everyone may well always have known never existed? Granted a biography as a court archivist, Laozi rapidly metamorphosed into an immortal, then a deity. And what about Homer? Why, in a situation that has been demonstrated to be an oral formulaic tradition, create such an 'author'? We know one answer that has been given to the authorship question – that in Foucault's 'What Is an Author?' But what if he had written that essay during his *History of Sexuality* period, when he was preoccupied with ancient texts, some of them, like their Chinese cousins, bearing the names of specific individuals as 'authors'?

To see a book as a process is a very important insight. In that image, like the figure indeterminately duck or rabbit, comes into view not just the current social nexus of publishing but the historicity of the individual whose name will grace its cover – indeed, of the book itself. I habitually invoke the notion of book as process to soothe authors worried about the polish of a manuscript, or indications towards one, they are putting into my hands for evaluation. Just last week, for instance, I assured an author that it didn't matter that, in the time between sending her prospectus and delivering the manuscript for outside readings, she had divided one chapter into two. I assured her that, given the processual nature of the book, it would certainly still be in flux until after the readers had commented, since the assumption that she will be given the opportunity to revise in response to outside readers' suggestions is an integral part of the reading process. Indeed, I ended with my usual example to prove that flux: the typo the author notices the moment she opens the first copy – and hopes to fix in a second printing.

But everything is process – at least, so many philosophers and ways of thought have said: Whitehead, Bergson, Heraclitus, classical Chinese cosmology. A book and its consolidation in an object represents a special sort of process, one that is susceptible to being attributed to an author. And at least in certain circumstances – as in the novel since the eighteenth century (visible, perhaps, in the frequently adolescent feel of its heroes and heroines) – it has served as a template for subjectivity, for the separation that eventuates in individuation. The *Laozi* is a description of the world as process; it is itself a process (one that probably had its origin in a 'philosophical school' and is ongoing today, in myriad translations and potential archaeological discoveries); but it is also a *project*, a set of aphorisms on which one can model one's thinking and behaviour. This is no doubt because books involve language, the basic medium of all human social life, which is both im- or trans-personal. I'm fond of saying that each word carries in it not only traces of every time it has ever historically been used, but of every time in the future it ever can and will be. Language calls out to us from a specific someone, a location. Perhaps it will be a project for future scholarship not only to carry forward the work of opening up the social dimensions of the text but also to ask precisely when and why we feel the urge to close them up into a single name, a single voice that we imagine speaking to us.

Cullen begins this book with separation and intimacy, the 'space between the text and the reader' (Introduction, 3). Let's return to the imagery of birth. The quintessential moment of separation from what later becomes an unimaginable intimacy begins there, with a baby's first cry, considered proof that it has been born alive. The space of separation exists both as a part of growing and as the inability ever to coincide with being a grownup. Most of us still long for the fantasy enunciated by Shipton's dentist (like a doctor, a practitioner of a professional intimacy that I often use as an image for that of the editor), for the moment when 'you don't need someone else to help you with it.' That is the fantasy not just of individuation but of virtuosity, an individuation so complete it takes on the quality of genius, something we know a human has done but that is so very beyond our conscious powers that we must enter into an agon with it for our individuation not to be entirely overwhelmed.[9] Or, in the words of Dee Mortenson, acquiring editor in philosophy at Indiana University Press and a virtuoso lace knitter, speaking of the first lace shawl she knitted and blocked: 'Did *I* make *that*?'

Meaning is made between the reader and the text – and in many ways. The virtuosic is one – an explosion of wonder or an experience like Emily Dickinson's famous comment about feeling that the top of one's head has been blown off. But one of the most productive is a simulacrum of conversation. And when we personalize ourselves and the text as we read, we hold that conversation, insofar as we address it to 'someone,' with that phantasm of individuation, the author. Though it could also, for a moment, be with any of us, whether scholarly editor, textual editor, or designer, who might for a moment assume in whatever way that mantle of author – as this book gives us the opportunity to do – and still our own normally busy fingers in quiet thanks for the gift of other people's work in weaving it.

NOTES

1 I most often send authors to William Germano, *Getting It Published: A Guide for Scholars and Anyone Else Serious about Serious Books* (Chicago: University of Chicago Press, 2001) and *From Dissertation to Book* (Chicago: University of Chicago Press, 2005). Also of note is Beth Luey, *Handbook for Academic Authors*, 5th ed. (Cambridge: Cambridge University Press, 2009).

2 Gerald Gross, ed., *Editors on Editing: What Writers Need to Know about What Editors Do*, 3rd ed. (New York: Grove, 1993).

3 Peter L. Shillingsburg, 'An Inquiry into the Social Status of Texts and Modes of Textual Criticism,' *Studies in Bibliography* 42 (1989): 56; quoted in Cullen, Introduction, 16.

4 Friedrich Kittler, *Discourse Networks 1800/1900*, trans. Michael Metteer, with Chris Cullens, foreword by David E. Wellbery (Stanford: Stanford University Press, 1990).

5 Klaus Theweleit, 'The Politics of Orpheus Between Women, Hades, Political Power, and the Media: Some Thoughts on the Configuration of the German Artist, Starting with the Figure of Gottfried Benn; or, What Happened to Eurydice?' *New German Critique* 36 (Autumn 1985): 133–56.

6 Wilfred Stone and J. G. Bell, *Prose Style: A Handbook for Writers*, 3rd ed. (New York: McGraw-Hill, 1977).

7 Someone at the University of Toronto Press, the journal's publisher, apparently contacted Jess in an attempt to verify the story. He said he couldn't remember, but that he was more likely to have said that acquiring editors needed little girls to pick up after them. But it amounts to the same thing – at the time of the story, I was a copyeditor, a role with which Jess very much

identified, even though at that time he had for years shaped the press's list via his acquisitions.

8 The Jewish sacred texts of the Talmud and Midrash constitute a special and very interesting case, which one will be able to read about in Sergey Dogopolski's new book about who writes, speaks, and remembers in the Talmud (New York: Fordham University Press, forthcoming).

9 I surprise myself by borrowing here from the vocabulary of Harold Bloom, who was, in a way, my first tutor in the social dynamics of authorship – I audited his seminar on Wallace Stevens at the time when he reported getting hate mail from the general public for even proposing, in *The Anxiety of Influence: A Theory of Poetry* (London: Oxford University Press, 1973), the nowadays minimal-seeming social dynamic that poets have the words and through them the looming presence of other poets in their heads at the time when they are writing, rather than drinking inspiration from an utterly individual genius. *Agon: Towards a Theory of Revisionism* (New York: Oxford University Press, 1982) is the last of the three volumes in which Bloom presents his theory of poetic misprision.

Acknowledgments

I have long understood that publishing takes time and involves a series of steps. I viewed this as a matter of fact as a production editor and with more serenity as an acquisitions editor. Publishing as a volume editor has been an altogether different experience. In this role, my relationship with the familiar elements of publishing was altered, slightly but perceptibly, and I would like to thank all of those who oriented me along the way, offering their advice, support, expertise, and camaraderie.

At the University of Toronto Press, Ryan van Huijstee and Leslie Howsam responded to the book proposal with enthusiasm and ushered it into the press. I thank Siobhan McMenemy for her aplomb and intelligence in guiding me and the manuscript through the peer review. Barbara Porter's and Terry Teskey's professionalism made my task at the later stages of publication a simple and enjoyable one. I must also thank the designer, Ingrid Paulsen, for crafting the perfect cover for this book.

I want to thank everyone at UBC Press; I have been fortunate to work with a group of people whose energy and ideas have shaped a vibrant place of publication. I owe particular thanks to Holly Keller, who entrusted me with new and challenging projects, showed me how publishing is about making things happen, and gave me the space and the tools to grow as an editor. Ann Macklem has been a teacher and a friend, whose wit and acuity I simply couldn't do without. She generously read drafts of my chapters, making insightful comments and giving me boosts along the way, and for this and much more I'm grateful.

I owe a debt of gratitude also to professors Ralph Sarkonak and André Lamontagne in the Department of French, Hispanic and Italian Studies at the University of British Columbia. Their dedication as instructors and mentors afforded me the grounding for my future interests and pursuits. I also thank Alan Thomas at the University of Chicago Press, an editor whose photographic project served as inspiration to this editor. I'm honoured that Helen Tartar, Editorial Director at Fordham University Press, generously agreed to write the foreword to this book.

My family deserve special thanks; their encouragement seems unflagging and its importance to me is immeasurable. My husband sparkles with intelligence, creativity, and humour and to him I owe the greatest thanks.

Ce livre, je l'ai imaginé pendant plusieurs années: il fut une idée au départ, un concept se voulant sculpté, ensuite des chapitres, un manuscrit, toujours un projet . . . Pendant longtemps ce livre, dans cette forme où vous le trouvez, existait dans l'avenir.

Tout cela paraît naturel. Ce sont bien les étapes à suivre. Mais elle sont à *vivre* aussi. Et pour cela, je tiens à remercier tous ceux et celles qui ont participé à son développement et sa réalisation: mes collègues à UBC Press, l'équipe à University of Toronto Press, en particulier Ryan van Huijstee, Siobhan McMenemy, Barbara Porter, Ingrid Paulsen, ainsi que mes anciens professeurs André Lamontagne et Ralph Sarkonak et ma bonne amie Ann Macklem.

Pendant le passage à la parution, ce livre fut nourri de l'encouragement de ma famille. Alice, Gaëtane et Lucretia, je vous remercie pour votre confiance en moi et votre enthousiasme tout le long du chemin; vous m'avez toujours soutenu dans mes projets et mon sentiment de reconnaissance est profond. Aucun ne pourrait nier le rôle important que Marie-Rose et Raymond Lemire ont joué dans ma formation culturelle et je les remercie d'avoir transmis leur amour du savoir et de la lecture à leurs enfants et petits-enfants. De Brian, j'ai gardé le souvenir de la symbolique du livre. À mes nièces et neveux, Bronagh, Simone, Caoimhe, Sé et Cormac, qui m'épatent avec leurs belles et vives imaginations, j'espère qu'on saura partager avec vous la richesse de vos cultures. Enfin, l'amour et l'esprit de mon mari inspirent en moi une vision du monde où tout est possible, où la pensée, le rire et l'imagination sont créateurs.

EDITORS, SCHOLARS, AND THE SOCIAL TEXT

1 Introduction: The Social Dynamics of Scholarly Editing

DARCY CULLEN

The purpose of publishing is to bring a text to its readers. This simple definition emphasizes an important and complex relationship between the two, as it suggests both a separation and an intimacy. In the space between the text and the reader is the meaning yet to be made: the reader is drawn into the text and, through the act of interpretation, participates in its meaning-making. Separation, on the other hand, is produced through the need to *bring* the text to its reader. Publishing can thus be seen as the process that separates and unites the two.

The publishing process is a collaborative one, involving the combined efforts of authors, editors, typesetters, proofreaders, indexers, printers, and marketers, each of which introduces a network of relationships. Generally, though, when we talk about publishing, and in particular the social dynamics of publishing, we focus on two sets of activities: those related to acquisitions and those of sales and marketing.

For a scholar in the humanities or social sciences, a lot is at stake in publishing. The acquisitions and peer review stages can appear as hurdles; they loom large in the imagination of the scholar, whose career may depend on or at least cannot be dissociated from publication. And every author wants his or her book to reach its readers, to be visible, to be available, and ultimately, to be read. Scholars and publishers also have an expectation of quality, in content and in form. Yet the 'middle' part of the publishing process, sandwiched between acquisitions and sales, is often closed from view, or viewed as closed off, even though it is here that the manuscript's metamorphosis into book occurs. The editors who oversee and participate in this transformation of the text into typeset publication were for a long period shrouded in mystery. But contrary to their popular characterization as quiet recluses, manuscript editors are at the nexus of a number of relationships that bear on the manuscript, the text, and the book.

Based on the premise that a text is no longer believed to be exclusively within the purview of the author but produced, rather, through meaningful collaborations between heterogeneous communities of readers and writers, the present volume considers the editor within the frame of the 'social text.' It does not delineate the publishing process, nor does it examine the role of publishing in tenure. Rather, it offers a window into the editor's world. What do editors do? What are their concerns? How does the editor figure in the world of publishing? Once perceived as an invisible figure who must leave no trace of his or her presence or as a taint to be expunged, the editor is today understood as an active participant in the making and dissemination of texts. Although the stereotype persists of the manuscript editor as a lone and quiet figure who obsesses over purely grammatical or stylistic details, this image bears little likeness to those in the profession today. In shepherding the text through the editing and production stages, the academic editor conceives of it as a manuscript, a text, a project, a book, and a product. She maintains distinct relationships between the author, the text, the publisher, and the reader. She edits with the audience in mind and anticipating layout of the page and design of the book.

Textual scholars and book historians, who investigate how texts come to be and how they exist, have over time created various frameworks within which to analyse the role of editors and publishers in the making of texts, manuscripts, and books. Delving into archives to uncover the details to be found in correspondence, estate records, manuscripts, notebooks, newspaper clippings, reviews, and the like, these archaeologists of the book explore its many facets to understand it in its historical and social contexts. They reconstitute for us the book publishing industry, printing methods, literacy and reading practices in different times and different places.

Like professional academic editors, textual scholars and scholarly editors (that is, scholars preparing critical, annotated, or definitive editions of literary works for publication) are also involved in current publishing practices. Preparing new editions of works from past eras, scholarly editors must devise ways of translating or importing characteristics of those works into the contemporary publishing environment. Like their counterparts in publishing houses, they strive for accuracy of detail and display an active engagement with the elements that shape the text, the manuscript, the page, and the book. They engage with various aspects of print culture, past and present. In developing methods for preparing scholarly editions, scholarly editors have theorized the production of text in the context of publishing.

This volume brings together textual scholars and academic editors, whose pursuits overlap and diverge, to situate the editor within a larger set of concerns in publishing. Scholarly editors and academic editors are admittedly very different creatures, and Peter Shillingsburg will discuss some of these distinctions in chapter 2, but they also share many interests, which should permit a cross-fertilization that may have seemed unlikely fifty years ago, when publishers' editors were viewed by textual scholars through a particular lens that has now been refocused, thanks in part to the idea of the 'social text.'

The term *scholarly editor* is used in this volume to refer to scholars who prepare scholarly editions of classic or literary works. Most scholarly editors are also 'textual scholars,' that is, scholars who are interested in manuscript studies and, as Peter Shillingsburg explains, work 'to find and analyze all the evidence of authorship, editing, copying, printing, and distribution for a textual work in order to discover the agency, authenticity, and purpose of textual variation and the significance of variant material forms of textual conveyance. Textual scholarship might result in a history of the text, a newly edited text, or a critical essay employing textual history as evidence influencing interpretation.'[1] Another type of textual scholar is the literary theorist whose analysis centres on the text and who is concerned with text and textuality in relation to philosophical and theoretical questions. Both are found in this volume, and the issues explored in contributions by the textual scholars here cover a spectrum that ranges from the practical and mechanical to the philosophical and theoretical.

The terms *academic editor* and *in-house editor* in this volume refer generally to professional editors working in scholarly book publishing. The terms often give way to more specific titles: acquisitions or sponsoring editor; managing editor and production editor; manuscript editor or copyeditor; substantive or developmental editor, as the case may be. The social dynamics of scholarly editing are perhaps most apparent in the realm of acquisitions, where the acquisitions editor exercises his or her role at the juncture of research and publishing, participating in scholarly conferences and cultivating areas of publication by staying attuned to trends and divisions in the disciplines. They also liaise with campus departments and other institutions and familiarize them with the press's publishing identity and mission while creating, through their list development, new networks of peoples and ideas. This volume, however, will discuss at greater length the role of manuscript, managing, and production editors, as it centres on the specifics of book production.

The Invisible Editor

A number of the academic editors with whom I spoke when I first set out to assemble this volume were reluctant to write about the extratextual aspects of their work. Some insisted they were editors, not authors, and were not keen to switch hats, even temporarily. Most spoke of their work as 'situational,' saying that the answer to many questions formulated during seminars and workshops by students or participants with the expectation of a definitive answer could be only 'it depends,' and welcomed the idea of exploring editorial principles and methods through the lens of the social text. The grey zone of 'it depends' is, after all, largely the result of the social nature of the text. Copyediting manuals rarely broach this aspect of editing, preferring to frame the issue in terms of nuance, judgment, and the value of the trained eye and ear. Exceptions exist, such as Carol Fisher Saller's insightful book *The Subversive Copy Editor: Advice from Chicago*, which suggests strategies for negotiating the various and typical workplace issues and for creating a cooperative work environment.[2] The editors with whom I spoke readily acknowledged that the editor cannot be concerned uniquely with language and style, though this is where their expertise lies; that a good editor not only knows the rules but can 'identify and weigh conflicting opinions, and . . . make an informed decision about when to apply, adapt, or ignore various conventions and rules';[3] and that editing means understanding the relationship between the author and the text, the manuscript and the book, the role of scholarly apparatus, and the impact of the physical aspects of the book on the reading experience. Yet, it seemed as though analysing these dynamics in writing might be construed as breaking a code of silence. Perhaps this has its origins in an older model of training, dating back to when young editors began as assistants, like apprentices, learning 'on the job,' accessing privileged areas of discussion and knowledge incrementally over time, as they moved through the publishing circles. Professional associations complemented the bookcases full of reference works found in every editor's office, but even these forums of discussion encouraged a view of editing knowledge or debate as being 'for members only.' Discretion, however, is not the same as invisibility.

Not to be underestimated is the image of the manuscript editor as reclusive, voluntarily hidden from view: this image has been internalized in the profession and the effects are far reaching. In her study of freelance editors' collective bargaining rights, feminist political economist Leah Vosko argues that the myth of the invisible editor persists because it is a supporting structure for the image of the author as artist or *auteur*:

> Editing work is undervalued by many writers and the publishing industry as a whole, since editors' professional qualifications often go unrecognized. Yet this undervaluation also reflects the fact that freelance editing is a peculiar form of artistic work. Freelance editors are not writers in a conventional sense – nor do they aspire to be – yet their work lies in the sphere of the arts. They contribute to producing artistic works, but their profession rests upon an ethic of invisibility – the notion that the editor should be invisible in the text and should not play a public role in the creation and promotion of the work. While essential to the preservation of their profession, the ethic of invisibility contributes to removing editing work from view.[4]

This ethic permeates the editorial discourse of academic publishing, although here, where the scholarly apparatus (notes, bibliographies, appendices, etc.) and citation styles, strength and coherence of argument, and accuracy of detail are valued, the problem is perhaps less acute. University publishers generally promote copyediting as a 'value-added' feature of the press; but an effort is still required to bring attention to the importance of editing, which has to come from an understanding of what it is manuscript editors actually do.[5] Demystifying the editor can then operate for the benefit of scholarly publishing. Through the lens of the social text, the author's status is not threatened or denigrated by the presence of the editor; the manuscript/text/book takes precedence and its multiple contributors are acknowledged. Throughout this volume, contributors complicate the notions of 'transparency' and 'invisibility' rather than indulge the deleterious clichés.

This demystification is already under way, and the place of the manuscript editor in a broader context of industry and society is open to exploration. In the past twenty years, training for editors has been formalized and institutionalized, and publishing and editing programs are now offered on campuses across North America. Professionals and practitioners may still refer to their sense of judgment, their skilled editorial decision-making, as 'experience' or 'intuition.' But their decisions are grounded in knowledge not only of grammatical rules and best practices but of scholarly aims and conditions as well as relationships within the publishing industry. When the basic rules of editing are taught in the classroom, the context of its practice is absent and must be introduced through an exploration and analysis of the social dynamics of editing. It is hoped that this book will contribute to a better understanding of the editor's role in a network of textual and extratextual (f)actors.

Similarly, the past four decades have seen textual scholars reassess the foundations of their methods and engage in lively debates about the role of editors, publishers, and society in the shaping of literary works. As the editorial method of textual scholarship is layered over previous editorial and publishing processes and decisions, it becomes clear that the circumstances of publishing matter and continue to matter, as new readers encounter and return to old books and schoolteachers and university professors select editions for use in classrooms. In their respective chapters, Peter Shillingsburg (chap. 2), John Young (chap. 9), and Alexander Pettit (chap. 5) touch on the historical contexts of writing and publishing, the impact of a book's production history on our understanding of the text, and the cultural power of 'good' and 'bad' editing.

People and Texts at Work: The Social Text and a Context for Editing

The body of literature on scholarly editing and textual scholarship is extensive. As alluded to above, there are different schools of thought within this field, which has evolved from its origins as academic bibliography, 'the discipline that studies texts as recorded forms and the processes of their transmission, including their production and reception,'[6] to encompass a set of distinct methodological and theoretical approaches – among them the intentionalist approach, where the scholar is interested in what the author intended; the sociological approach, where the text is understood as a collaborative product; and genetic editing, which explores the process by which a text came to be.[7]

The sociological approach is what motivates this volume. It offers a way for scholarly editors who study a text in the social process of its production and reception to have a fruitful exchange with professional academic editors, who experience and shape the social dynamics of text and book production today. Unlike a traditional bibliography 'confined to logical inference from printed signs as arbitrary marks on parchment or paper' or an intentionalist approach to editing, where the Author is given primacy over the meaning of a text, a sociology of texts explores the 'social and technical circumstances of production' and allows for the 'complex interrelationships of those conditions of production and the kinds of knowledge they generated.'[8] It thereby creates a space for practising in-house editors to engage with theories of textual scholarship and vice versa.

As textual scholar Peter Shillingsburg summarizes in reviewing the history of textual criticism, 'Generally speaking, the evolving editorial principles in the mid-twentieth century all assume[d] that the literary work was the product of an author whose wishes concerning the text were to be paramount, and that the work should be edited in such a way as to produce the "established" text.' Up to the 1980s, author-centric approaches were still favoured and widely practised, though 'a few relatively serious but largely unsuccessful attempts were made in that period to legitimize the role of publishing and production crews in the eyes of scholarly editors.'[9] A successor of the intentionalist tradition, James Thorpe defined 'the work of art as merely "potential" until it was published. The effect of this definition was to acknowledge the production process both as an aid to the author in finalizing the work and as a necessary fact of life enabling works of art to be known to readers.'[10] In this formulation, editors exist to help authors carry out their intentions. (There are academic editors, particularly those of the 'non-interventionist' school, who agree with this objective. But an editor's absolute deference to the author is rarely sought by a publisher, for it is considered ultimately unhelpful.) The idea still persisted of the text as belonging to the Author, who shares it with the Reader, though not all agreed that 'the work is an intentional object needing to be tied tightly to the author' or that 'non-authorial chaff is to [be] winnowed away, leaving behind the authorial seed in its unalloyed condition.'[11] Nonetheless, much of the debate during the 1970s and 1980s about the function of the author left some basic assumptions in place.

As D.C. Greetham summarizes the shift in theory, 'a witness that we regarded as "insincere" and "inauthentic" in the 1970s (and thus not fixable with any security on any conventional patrilinear stemma, and therefore "authentic" and "sincere" enough to be cited as evidence of an authorial reading) would under the different textual dispensations of a quarter century later now become by far the most challenging and significant, precisely because it showed a copyist/reader actively intervening in the construction of an early "socialized" text.'[12] The social text not only imparts a different meaning to non-authorial interventions, setting 'the author's productive work and the institutions of reproduction'[13] in a more positive relationship, but it also draws attention to human interaction. As D.F. McKenzie emphasizes, 'a book is never simply a remarkable *object*. Like every other technology, it is invariably the product of human agency in complex and highly volatile contexts which a responsible scholarship must seek to recover if we are to understand better the creation and communication of meaning as the defining characteristic of human societies.'[14] This human agency isn't restricted to the will of the author but extends rather to the full cast of characters involved in the text's making, dissemination, and reception.

The social text is an innovation in the field that is particularly resonant in publishing circles. Scholarly theories of book production and textuality that construct editors and others involved in the making of books are not benign to editors working today. As we have seen, the conception of the author as sole creative agent of a work has had significant impact in the culture of publishing. The displacement of the author, developed in literary theory[15] and recognized in textual scholarship, has helped, for example, to liberate the editor from the status of contaminant (it's a common trope that editors are noticed only when they make a mistake) or handmaiden. Authors and editors share certain goals and during a period of time work in tandem to reach them; yet their objectives are not always perfectly harmonious or synchronous. Each specializes in a different area, and the editor brings to the work a specific set of skills and kind of knowledge. This is a central theme in this volume. The text is released from the boundaries of authorial limits to continue to take shape through the publishing process and the reading experience. But an understanding of the text as a social nexus also takes us beyond the workings of a press and its printers and distributors, to encompass the historical, social, and linguistic codes that exert influence in a work's making. That is, the sociological approach

> sees the production process as a cultural phenomenon without which books do not exist. The influence of production on the book does not begin when the author hands a completed manuscript to the publisher; it begins when the author raises his pen for the first word of a work in-

tended for publication, because of a consciousness of the way books gets published. Publishers, too, are only part of an even larger phenomenon that includes language and usage and everything that forms the sociological context within which authors are enabled to write and can hope to be understood . . . Publishers, therefore, are not primarily handmaidens to authorship exercising helpful servant roles, which they may fail to do well; they are, instead, part of the authoritative social complex that produces works of art.[16]

Academic editors cannot extricate themselves from the institutional forces or socio-political motives and implications of their work. And certainly few editors think it possible to do so, nor do most wish to, despite the fact that it makes the precise work of editing more complicated than some manuals might suggest. This social aspect is explored in the chapters by academic editors Rosemary Shipton (chap. 3), Amy Einsohn (chap. 4), and Camilla Blakeley (chap. 7). While they discuss more directly the social relations between actors – author–editor–publisher and editor–author–designer relations – with respect to textual and book production, they make reference to larger social dynamics influencing these relationships and the way that academic editors work as a result. They describe editorial cultures and economic conditions, consider the impact of technological developments, and comment on the nature of different types of publishing environments. These thorough-going examinations of the deployment of professional relationships in publishing serve as an important reminder that human interaction is a complex element of book-making.

Complementing these chapters are contributions by textual scholars who attach aspects of editorial book production to philosophical and theoretical arguments, as this volume embraces the full implications of the 'social text' and recognizes the complicating influences of the social conditions of textual production and the work of author and editor, past and present. Intertwined in conditions of production are discussions of 'economic and political motive'[17] and power differentials. What does it mean, for instance, to edit in a postcolonial or multicultural context? How do social constructions of identity relate to editorial work? In his 1995 article 'Textual Imperialism, Post-Colonial Bibliography, and the Poetics of Culture,' textual theorist D.C. Greetham recounts his own change of position on 'the traditional posture of the old philological/ old cultural critic *outside* the text (or society or history) he was describing,' which he had adopted over the course of his training as editor and, when pushed to reconsider and ' "come clean" about where I stood,' turned to the 'gender-, class-, and ethnic-based displacements that culture criticism and autobiography now offered, and write my own place into that text.'[18] Similarly, McKenzie's sociological reading of the Treaty of Waitangi admits the political significance of examining the particularities of New Zealand's colonial context as he seeks 'to make some sense of the oral, manuscript, and printed texts in determining the rights of indigenous peoples subjected to European colonization and to the commercial and cultural impositions of the powerful technology of print.'[19]

In this volume, the mechanics and conventions of in-house editing are resituated; academic publishing practices are placed within broader social questions, as contributors investigate and try to locate political and ethical grounds and circumstances. Thus, when Alexander Pettit in chapter 5 talks about the alienating effect of typographic errors as both a marker of cultural alterity and, we are shown, a form of resistance to editing, or when John Young later pauses to consider philosophically aesthetic questions that have bearing on colonial histories (chap. 9), both invite us to confront some of the assumptions underlying the accepted and flexible practices and rules of our profession. At the same time, these chapters engaging the question of minority cultures and ethnicity in the spheres of scholarly and academic editing and scholarly publishing should serve as an impetus to editors who still invisibilize themselves, so that they acknowledge their place and position of influence as it extends beyond the chain of production.

Textual Materiality

Academic editors experience many of these questions as challenges, or as puzzles, sometimes struggling with author and designer, sometimes acting as go-between. In this volume, Camilla Blakeley's case study considers how ideas of ethnicity and power relations in a postcolonial context play out on the physical page of the book. As a practitioner, her interest in the relationship is a practical one. In contrast, Peter Mahon's exploration in chapter 6 of the characteristics of the scholarly text – citation, marginalia, and footnotes – offers a philosophical perspective, presenting the page as a social site, in a case study that performs the social text. That is, like Blakeley, Mahon takes the social text onto the page and considers the bibliographical code; however, his analysis consists of examining the ways in which the text and its form slip away from authorial control in a productive and playful way. It's a careful study of the dislocation of the Author-figure as occupying the centre of meaning – and the centre of the physical page – where the 'citational textual play that cannot be owned or dominated by a centralized voice of authority' (140) can be read as a reinscription of the multiple players who produce a text's meaning. In this way, by aligning theoretical approaches with practical ones, this volume seeks to show how theorizing the social text can provide the tools for understanding and theorizing the academic editor's work differently and in a way that is empowering to her.

The materiality of books threads its way through the volume, as contributors of both stripes refer to the influence of bibliographic codes – the typography, layout, paper, ordering of elements, and so on. Both types of editors appreciate the 'expressive function of typography in book forms.'[20] Some would argue, as does Greetham, that these elements 'are the formalist "envelope" without which the book does not even have existence let alone meaning, and that therefore these codes must be confronted and subsumed into our cognition of the bookishness of texts, no matter what the medium may be or the demonstrable role of the author in controlling that medium. In fact, the only demonstration possible is the materiality of text, for it is the only *remaniement* we are left with. This is as true of the electronic text as it is of other transmissional media.'[21] It therefore seems pertinent to invite into this discussion two book designers. For, as Canadian poet and book designer Robert Bringhurst writes, 'Individual readers and whole societies can and do see themselves reflected in their printing, whether or not they are conscious of it as such. The design and manufacture of books can tell us as much about a people or a culture as the condition of its grain fields, pasture lands, and gardens, the social climate of its streets, and the architecture of its buildings.'[22]

In order to deepen the discussion on bibliographic code, two designers offer their views on the principles of typography and design and the relationship between editing and designing. They emphasize the physical aspects of text, explaining how a designer works best when the editor has understood the physical nature of the text and the material nature of traditional, contemporary, and emerging media. (New media are examined through different lenses in the latter parts of the volume, in chapters by a designer, a textual scholar, and an academic editor.)

I should note that a number of the contributors ground their discussions in specific examples or case studies, and the books that are examined present different conditions of production: in one case, a 1970s activist press affiliated with University of Houston is scrutinized; in another, a contemporary novel published by a trade press is featured; in yet another, the work of a world-renowned writer and subject of an entire scholarly industry, James Joyce, is analysed for its qualities as a modernist text, which are offered as an allegory for the social academic text. In his chapter, John Young takes a trade novel and anticipates its future scholarly edition. It's not unusual for scholarly editors and textual scholars to find themselves with a foot in each camp when it comes to publishing environment. Despite the interactions with commercial publishing contexts, the chapters that follow situate their discussions within or address the unique environment of scholarly publishing and nature of scholarly texts.

The Centre and the Margins, Authorship and Collaboration

Agent Smith: A Social Complex versus the Multiplying Author

In book publishing, one is recognized as an author through juridical and institutional discourses.[23] Canada and the United States each have a Copyright Act, which places the author within a system of ownership that defines an author's rights with regard to intellectual property, royalties, reproduction, quotation, and use of works; publishers confirm this status through author agreements, or contracts.

In academic publishing, new ethical and legal questions relating to authorship have been raised in the context, for example, of research grounded in ethnographic fieldwork, where interviewees or participants contribute to the work, and to community-based research, which is conducted after formal consultation has taken place between the researcher and his or her institution and the community's representatives. Thus, the collaborative nature of *research* can bring into relief the question of book authorship. Consider, for example, *Life Lived Like a Story: Life Stories of Three Yukon Native Elders*, at once anthropological study and collection of life stories, or *When I Was Small – I Wan Kʷikʷs: A Grammatical Analysis of St'át'imc Oral Narratives*, where the life stories of fluent speakers of this Salishan language are analysed by a linguist. In both cases, it is not only the scholar's name that appears on the cover and title page; also included are the names of those individuals who might formerly have been referred to by anthropologists, historians, and publishers as informants, sources, interviewees, or participants. On the title page and on the book cover, the scholar's name is followed by the phrase 'in collaboration with' and then the names of the Elders who shared their stories and contributed to the book.[24] (In the cataloguing-in-publication data for *Life Lived Like a Story*, the title is given with the complete byline, so the names of the Elders are listed in the title field; in the cataloguing-in-publication data for *When I Was Small – I Wan K^{w}ik^{w}s*, the Elders are listed as authors, though not listed in full, since the convention is to use 'et al.' after two names).[25] Increasingly, community experts and participants are recognized in law and in the publishing industry as authors. The two examples I cite, one from anthropology, the other from linguistics, bring into contact Western scholarship and Native voices, an encounter that often serves to destabilize the Author figure.

How is authorship marked, affirmed, or reassigned in the editorial and production process? How do the various, non-authorial figures contributing to the book's production become integrated into and influence the shape of the book? In turn, how does a particular process of production affect the authorial and related roles?

In their introduction to *First Nations Cultural Heritage and Law: Case Studies, Voices, and Perspectives*, volume editors Catherine Bell and Val Napoleon present a detailed and highly informative account of the collaborative methodology employed from the conception of the research project to the publication of that research in book form. The table of contents and the copyright page facing it immediately mark the book with concern for authorship. This was indeed a significant question for the editors:

> A more complicated question is how to acknowledge authorship in a manner that respects oral traditions and reflects a truly collaborative process. The Kainai study addresses this issue by including Mookakin as an author. In other studies, this is dealt with by specifying that the studies were developed in consultation with a specific First Nation individual or organization. For practical reasons, it became difficult to name all people who made oral contributions to this project as authors. However, if requested, we would have been prepared to do this despite the challenges it would have created for publishing and making standard contract arrangements for authors' copies, copyright, and allocation of royalties.[26]

Furthermore, as the study is centred on the preservation and protection of cultural heritage, it was essential that the requests of First Nations participants to retain control over their cultural information be dealt with in a respectful way that considered both Canadian and aboriginal understandings of law. As Bell explains, 'In a typical publishing contract, copyright is assigned to the publisher or retained by authors and [volume] editors . . . In our study, we wanted First Nations partners to have greater control over issues of reproduction and royalties associated with copyright. Consequently, we decided that the copyrights to the case studies would be held jointly by the author, the editors of [this] volume, and the appropriate First Nation partner.'[27]

What we see occurring here is a paradoxical displacement and reinstitution of the Author. Catherine Bell and Val Napoleon, as primary researchers, retain their status as volume editors and thus take over the author function, being presented as such in the book (title page, cataloguing-in-publication data, future bibliographies, etc.) while also granting author status to many of the research participants and partners. This redistribution of authorship points to a hierarchy within the legal realm, and while the parties involved sought, and achieved, formal recognition for differing types of contributions, the process ultimately reinstates the Author figure. For in order to access the benefits granted to an author, a participant must be made an author: only the Author is recognized as having status in this legal formulation. Sophie McCall's *First Person Plural: Aboriginal Storytelling and the Ethics of Collaborative Authorship* engages these questions of authorship in collaborative, cross-cultural projects to conclude that, in challenging 'the author-function and notions of the literary by foregrounding process over product, context over text, and audience over author,' they offer themselves as highly productive sites, in contrast with the 'singular, unmediated, and pure' voice that becomes detrimental when overprivileged.[28] In his chapter of the current volume, Peter Mahon will touch again on authorship and the implications of a legal framework or discourse in writing and publishing.

In the case of *First Nations Cultural Heritage and Law*, the question of authorship in collaborative research is visible primarily at the research, textual, and legal levels. But there is also extensive quoting in the volume. The pattern of block quotes discernible when one flips through the book could also be seen as a manifestation of the work's attempt at a decolonizing methodology, as it seeks to respect a tradition of oral history: the voices of community members who joined the collaborative research project occupy a central place in the text. This pattern in the page layout could be interpreted as a demonstration of the way in which conventions of book production, anticipated by the author, executed by the designer, and part of a deliberate purpose to communicate, are used to particular effect and distinct ends. (Mahon argues that the book follows the typographical conventions rather than disrupt them; see chap. 6). In her chapter on the illustrated book, Camilla Blakeley shows how multiple voices add complexity to book production, explaining how, for *The Trickster Shift: Humour and Irony in Contemporary Native Art,* the author, designer, and project editor worked to produce a book that would 'embody the trickster play that is its subject' and where 'neither quotation nor note should be considered a secondary or subordinate text' (151). This desire to give place to ' "subversive" voice[s]' (151) and to resist the normative hierarchies of discourses, of 'main' text and notes, of authors and editors, is the playful and politicized subject of a whole movement of novelists. And it is not limited to the realms of fiction and literature. As the aforementioned examples demonstrate, both scholarly and academic editors confront these challenges to the styles and conventions that guide their work.

A Matter of Style: House Rules and Hierarchies

> There was nothing particularly new about marginating texts, a habit that had its roots in ancient writing cultures and reached its apogee in the monasteries and secular scriptoria of Western Europe and England between the twelfth and fourteenth centuries. During this period, marginalia lent authority to texts, but that authority eventually came under scrutiny in the case of the secular and sacred texts.
> — *W.E. Slights, 'Back to the Future – Litorally'*[29]

Most university presses have a house style, or a couple of house styles for different imprints or disciplines. They are based on conventions in publishing and those of scholarship; they tend towards maintaining standards while also evolving, incrementally, to reflect or engage with changes and developments in society and technology and within specific disciplines.[30] Some styles exist for purely practical reasons: for example, endnotes are generally preferred by publishers because they are easier to typeset than are footnotes, guard against indexing errors should alterations be made on page proofs, and as a result of both also translate into a cost savings. In this relatively stable setting, it is easy to take for granted the relationship between the main text and the scholarly apparatus (preface, introduction, notes, citations, references, appendices, etc.). Material that is of a 'secondary' nature and supplementary (but not dispensable) is said to belong in the apparatus. An editor is responsible for deciding or advising on what can be marginalized or, on the contrary, highlighted through an alternative placement in the book. At the same time, editors, both scholarly and academic, give as much attention, if not more, to what is in the margins of the text. The appendages are given as much care as the body. And that is because editors understand that the ultimate function of the scholarly apparatus is not secondary: it serves to legitimate, to support arguments, to lend authority. It should be, by its very nature, accurate, authoritative, and credible.

The drive towards accuracy and consistency is a persistent trait among manuscript and production editors. Rules, guides, and conventions both direct and are created by editors, who must also on occasion be prepared to invert the aforementioned textual hierarchy or even dismiss it temporarily. Questioning of the rules is to be expected, after all, as university presses are places of important social change. They have a mandate to publish and disseminate original contributions to knowledge in specific disciplines, to promote dialogue across disciplines, and to disseminate ideas and findings to the larger public. They seek to publish works of scholarship that 'stimulate public debate,' 'extend and challenge prevailing views in the academy and society,' 'contribute an understanding of global human concerns,' and participate in the 'transformation of the intellectual and cultural landscape.'[31] This function of the university press is perhaps most frequently emphasized in the acquisitions realm, understood as a central part of list-building practices, where strategies and decisions are made about which works to acquire, solicit, develop, and nurture. These objectives in fact extend along a much longer continuum, and the editorial-production process contributes to the shaping and expression of a press's lists and the works that constitute them.

In the context of these larger objectives of the press, manuscript editors and production editors weigh the possibilities within current standards, innovations, and exceptions. Challenges to scholarly conventions that at the same time remain within the boundaries of scholarship can be difficult to devise and negotiate. They may include the use of neologisms, insistence on particular spellings or word choice, altering of standard structures or bibliographic methods to reflect or enact an argument. How do we respond to these challenges as editors and publishers? Word usage, diacritics, transliterations – these are all covered in editing manuals, and an editor will discuss with the author how best to create consistency across the manuscript and inform the reader of the method chosen or developed for the book. But style, grammar, and the scholarly apparatus – notes, marginalia, front and back matter – can all be questioned or scrutinized by someone sensitive to the meaning that these confer on the text, and the way in which they situate the author.[32]

Putting Them on the Page

> L'écriture 'marginale' se transforme ainsi en une théorie explicite de la production.
>
> *– Janet Paterson and Marilyn Randall, Introduction to*
> Trou de mémoire[33]

As discussed earlier, the 'social text' displaces the Author to bring into focus the multiple contributors to the making of text, thereby making it possible to explore how texts and the paratext, editors and readers, intersect to create meaning in culture, history, politics, and art. The lowercase author, in contrast, makes frequent, intermittent appearances in this volume. The author figure that emerges is not the capitalized one to which we completely defer, the ultimate source of meaning; and as we will see in what follows, this figure too can be a transgressive or revolutionary presence who slips across the margins to contest discrimination, omission, marginalization. As several chapters in this book demonstrate, the page itself can become a space for decolonization and resistance.

A book that thematizes and theorizes the complex relationship between editor and author, bibliographic code and politics of the page, and eventually the layering of scholarly apparatus is *Trou de mémoire*, a novel written in 1968 by Quebec journalist, writer, and political activist Hubert Aquin (translated into English by Alan Brown and published as *Blackout* in 1974 by Anansi Press). This was a tumultuous time in the province's history: the Quiet Revolution (1960–6) was marked by social and institutional reforms that gave the state more control over areas that had previously been governed by the Church or by private business. Nationalist movements grew active, as the Québécois sought greater protection of their culture and language rights. The federal government's institution of the Bilingualism and Biculturalism Commission, coming during rapid institutional changes and combined with a slowing provincial economy, produced unrest in Quebec.[34]

In *Trou de mémoire*, Aquin sought to 'reveal to the Québécois the oppression of their situation.'[35] The protagonist – a francophone revolutionary pharmacist and writer who murders his English Canadian girlfriend – wishes to display his erudition and cultural knowledge, in order to be legitimated – recognized – by the dominant (English Canadian) society, on the one hand, and Quebec's cultural motherland, France, on the other. But in doing so, he confronts his own cultural identity as a Québécois living on aboriginal land governed by the British Crown. This novel, which thematizes authorship in a colonial context, uses the relationship between the author and the editor, the text and the notes, to illustrate power imbalances in such a society and how they are presented through perceived cultural deficits. The novel is replete with notes by the editor (*Note de l'éditeur*) wherein the fictitious editor validates and invalidates, contextualizes and interprets passages. But the editor does not restrict himself to the margins of the text: the protagonist – 'author' and narrator – discovers that parts of his text are missing, and new pages have been inserted, by an impostor – by the editor, it turns out.[36] Throughout the book, he attempts to prove his worth – or reject a subordinate status – by occupying the centre of the page. But he shares numerous pages with an other, the editor, whose annotations do not always support him. At one point, the editor places himself in the centre of the text by writing as an other, but he is soon displaced by yet others. In addition, the editor's own space of the footnotes is infiltrated, as the murdered woman's sister somehow gains access to the manuscript and joins the game, signing her notes 'Note de RR.'

Through these textual and bibliographic/annotative strategies, the reader is shown just how difficult it is for the protagonist to use the text as a way to display his erudition, lay rest to fears of cultural amnesia, and assert any kind of authority, for he is involved in a constant struggle with the editor and other actors, who hijack his manuscript and question his authority, the accuracy of his statements, and his state of mind (he self-medicates), accuse him of plagiarism (why not quotation?), and so on. The book becomes a site of contestation, a site of struggle over cultural identity and forms of knowledge. Simultaneously, the editor is, if not discredited, at least made less credible, having censured the text and taken a false identity; he is no longer a reliable source of truth or accuracy. Nevertheless, *Trou de mémoire* shows the editor as a powerful figure, who occupies the margins quite strategically. The displacement of the figures in the margins and the centre of the text is employed as a decolonizing strategy; the editorial apparatus comes to serve a revolutionary purpose.

In 1993 Marilyn Randall and Janet Paterson published an annotated edition of the book (published by BQ). The notes of these two editors serve to confirm and deny statements, correct or qualify accuracy of details (factual, bibliographic, literary and other), confirm or correct sources and attributions, and comment on neologisms, typographic errors, inconsistencies and whether or not they may have been intended. This envelope of scholarship that pronounces on the text and imposes itself on it cannot, as one might expect, undermine the revolutionary aims of the book. The reader is throughout alerted to the trust that he or she places in the narrators and to the way he constructs the narrator, author, and editor, the conventional distinctions between them, and the disruptions of these conventional roles. The annotated edition, with its introduction, notes, glossary, and appendices, could potentially be seen as dismantling the disruptive framework by reassuring readers, by telling them when and how they are being misled, by providing background information and intertextual references, but instead it becomes yet another layer in the game that contests the legitimating function of editorial and scholarly apparatus. Like the fictitious editor, who fails to assert himself as ultimately authoritative, the editorial apparatus of the critical edition fails to impose a reading or produce certainty within the text. This is not to say that the notes shed no light or offer the reader nothing; they do provide some clarifications, draw attention to textual references, and generally reduce the amount of leg work required for readers to ascertain whether or not they are being given a false lead – but this asks that we place our trust in the editors. One could hardly fail to notice, moreover, the frequent use of modal verbs and hedging adverbs in the notes section of the scholarly edition – 'semble' (seems), 'probablement' (probably), 'vraisemblablement' (most likely) are peppered throughout, which produces a cumulative effect of uncertainty. The novel, designed to put into question the relationships between author, editor, knowledge, power, and authenticity/truth, anticipates its critical edition. It becomes a 'hall of mirrors, where each layer is a reflection that reflects back and extends continuously and repeatedly, limitlessly.'[37]

Similarly, the text is replete with traps and red herrings, both in the plot and on the page. Word play and neologisms invite typographic errors;

which one is masquerading as the other? Randall and Paterson explain in their introduction that they had to limit their intervention in the text: they could not be sure whether an apparent grammatical or typographical mistake was indeed a mistake or part of the text's language.[38]

The novel, and its critical edition, thus explore the 'textual margins' in both a bibliographic sense and as a form of discourse. The author has returned but no longer asserts dominance over the text and its meaning; the author is a politicized figure who engages with the mechanics of writing and publishing and uses the page and the bibliographic codes. The text is produced by multiple participants; the editor is a figure to be reckoned with; the page is a site of contestation. Scholarly and academic editors cannot dismiss the cultural value and power dynamics that exist in scholarly writing and conventions. Editors safeguard the integrity of scholarship by maintaining standards, but they are also entrusted with the judicious application and bending of these rules. This is a crucial and delicate task. In the chapters that follow, these responsibilities and nuances are broached from a variety of angles, each focusing on the social dynamics of editing. Fortunately, the positions are less adversarial than the ones encountered in *Trou de mémoire*! Whether discussing the ethics of the page or author–editor relationships, they give an account of the way in which principles of editing are assessed and put into practice. And more often than not, the examples chosen are of works that resist conventions; thus are offered ways of thinking through what we may think of (perhaps incorrectly) as exceptions and anomalies but whose challenges provide useful insights. At the same time, the tensions that can be found in scholarly and academic editing are not glossed over. Questions are raised and a response is sought – not from subsequent chapters but from their readers.

Organization of This Volume

This volume considers the human interactions and social environment of editing, as well as the cultural phenomenon of book production, and the way in which this 'social' dimension occurs within the text. Some chapters therefore centre on the relations of editors with other actors and forces, while other chapters explore the social dynamics of text and textuality. Reflecting the variety of questions and concerns of the moment, the chapters also range to include both practical and philosophical preoccupations.

Above I evoked the difficulties and undesirability of rigidly applying house style. Not only are editing guides updated regularly to reflect social changes (as when editing guides such as The *Chicago Manual of Style* added sections on the proper ways of citing Internet and other electronic sources), but in-house editors generally devise or use multiple house styles, largely to deal with the requirements of different disciplines. As presses move into new fields, so will their in-house editors become proficient in the scholarly and publishing conventions of those fields.[39] Yet, each book will present its own particularities. In his chapter contrasting the aims of scholarly editors and academic editors, Peter Shillingsburg teases apart the editorial acts that are sometimes confounded, sometimes ignored. He neatly summarizes the types of editing, their goals and principles, and illustrates the dangers of mechanizing this labour or not acknowledging a manuscript's textuality. He urges academic editors to recognize themselves within a historical context and editorial praxis and, concomitantly, to observe the distinctions of editing traditions. Like Rosemary Shipton and Amy Einsohn in the subsequent chapters, he puts good judgment ahead of rules and insists on the value of clear communication between in-house editors and the authors and scholarly editors with whom they work. By insisting on the value of examining a work's evolution, he makes the case for publishers taking a more engaged role when it comes to scholarly editions.

In their chapters, Rosemary Shipton and Amy Einsohn explain the dynamics of editing from a copyeditor's point of view. It should come as no surprise that these two chapters also offer freelancer viewpoints, for freelancers are an essential part of the university press, performing key editorial and production functions. This is not simply due to salary restrictions. The nature of the work makes the reliance on networks of freelancers a viable working model: It can be advantageous for a press to work with a select range of designers and copyeditors, each of whom can bring a distinct set of strengths or a style to the various projects. This volume thus includes contributions by freelancers, who not only give us their point of view but also recommend ways of improving communication between in-house editors and the professionals they hire. While Einsohn points to the cultures that exist within presses and offers concrete advice for easing common problems, Shipton shows how the expectations and procedures of publishers affect the way authors and editors relate. These opening chapters describe what it is that manuscript editors actually do and where they fit within the network of editors that fill the publishing houses. They offer a clear picture of the academic editor at work.

Despite the mantra of perfection that we hear uttered in the distance, most of us accept that mistakes find their way into the books we have worked so hard to bring to the public, and we cringe when we see the errors in print. In his chapter on 'the utility of error,' Alexander Pettit, through an exploration of the published works of Chicano playwright Luis Valdez, discusses the potentially alienating effect of typographical errors to then consider how the material and linguistic manifestations of cultural alterity – the printed editions of Valdez's plays – can be read in terms of responsible versus 'respectable' editing. This essay weaves its way from the circumstance of reception and the relationship between the text and the audience (alternately anticipated and real, diverse and uncontrolled, sceptical or tractable) to the circumstance of production, the collaborative nature of this production, and the way in which a press's disposition imprints itself onto the text.

In his chapter bridging this volume's Part Two: The Text and Part Three: The Page, Peter Mahon offers a section of James Joyce's *Finnegans Wake* as an allegory for the forces and dynamics at work in the 'social text.' After tracing the dislocation of authorship by Roland Barthes evoked above, and central to the idea of the social text, Mahon considers briefly how this relates to recent trends in Indigenous Studies to suggest how physical textuality offers solutions where legal conceptions do not. Then, through a close reading of Joyce's playful if challenging tome, he examines how the textual surface of *Finnegans Wake* is used to illustrate the social space of text.

The materiality of books is the theme of Part Three. Richard Hendel and Sigrid Albert take this opportunity to invite editors into a conversation about editing and design. As designers, they share their views on the physicality of text and ask editors to think visually. Hendel in particular elaborates a 'theory of anticipation,' entreating editors to think of the words and parts of the text as having *physical* properties and manifestations. Albert, in her piece, considers the editor–designer relationship in an era of transformation in communications media: detailing the way in which editors and designers work in tandem with clearly designated tasks, she contemplates the impact of digitization on this division of labour. Like Albert and Hendel, academic editor Camilla Blakeley calls into question the normative hierarchy implied by editors who hold the notion that the designer's job is to carry out the intentions of the author and the editor. Using a case study, she takes the reader through the process of producing an illustrated book from the perspective of the project editor. How do such projects challenge the way the editor thinks about the physical aspects of the book? How do they change the timing and structure of the process? What additional skills must the editor develop? How does the inclusion of illustrations affect the editor's relationship with the author and with the designer, and the mediation between the two? As well, the chapter explores the potential need for an editor to manage additional institutional relationships.

John Young's chapter is similarly concerned with the practical constraints of textual production. As a textual scholar, he brings a different perspective to the question of materiality and images in book production and reproduction, using as examples the novels of Trinidadian writer Robert Antoni, *Divina Trace* and *Blessed Is the Fruit*. After tracing the vexed production history of each novel and the variant editions produced thereby – a 'mirror page,' for example, appearing on the verso and recto sides in the hardcover *Divina Trace* and an earlier excerpt in *Paris Review*, but only on the recto in the paperback edition – he considers the ways in which an eventual scholarly edition might represent that history. He examines the plastic sheet in relation to its lost cousin and the mirror page in its multiple incarnations as a further lens into the relationship between the practical constraints of textual production and the theoretical problems attendant on representing such histories.

Part Four looks at the electronic edition from two angles. Whereas the impetus for the electronic edition in textual scholarship came from within, the push towards digitization in scholarly publishing has come from outside. University presses were first beckoned to the digital age by libraries and the large corporate entities of book distribution. They have since developed strategies for responding, in turn with reserve and with innovation, to the new demands and desires of communities of book sellers, buyers, readers. The industry is still in a stage of transition and experimentation, and the direction for electronic books keeps shifting. Rather than survey the landscape, however, and assess the success and failure of the various attempts to take the book into its new medium, in my closing chapter I take a speculative position. What do we know and what do we not know as we transfer or translate the printed book to the electronic environment?

Both Yuri Cowan and I, in our respective chapters, consider how virtual navigation through layers and networks of materials online has changed our relationships to books, as editors and as readers. Experiments with electronic editions began in earnest among humanities scholars in the 1990s, which saw a proliferation of publications on the future of the book and the possibilities of hypertextual editions. Hypertext and electronic text projects were launched on campuses large and small: the Institute for Advanced Technology in the Humanities (IATH) at the University of Virginia was founded in 1992 and its broad mission led to the creation of productive partnerships, such as that with the university's Scholar's Lab, which assists humanities and social sciences faculty and students with research, digitization, and online editing, and with the international organization Text Encoding Initiative Consortium, which since 1994 has set guidelines for the encoding of texts (primarily literary and linguistic texts); in 1994 the Center for History and New Media (CHNM) was established at George Mason University; that same year, the Humanities Text Initiative was launched at the University of Michigan as part of its Digital Library Production Service; the University of Maryland's Romantic Circles, a refereed scholarly website that includes electronic editions of literary works, was officially launched in 1996; the Walt Whitman Archives took shape in the mid-nineties, as did a number of textual studies centres.

Literary scholar and textual editor George Bornstein wrote in 2003 that hypermedia book projects 'represent glorious possibilities and to some extent realities, but none has come close to realizing its original ambitions. Indeed, the increasing prevalence of the term *archive* for them suggests a retreat from earlier visions of nearly Derridean freeplay in electronic textuality.'[40] Indeed, when a vast network of supporting materials can be embedded into a work, where does the book end and the compendium begin? The digital books of Rotunda (a digital imprint of the University of Virginia Press), for example, replicate many of the aspects of the 'archives' and 'compendia' that textual scholars have developed as alternative forms of or alternatives to critical and annotated print editions. An instigating question for the digital imprint belies the anxiety surrounding the ambiguous status of the electronic 'book.' David Sewell, who has been involved in the project since its creation, explains that 'the Electronic Imprint of the University of Virginia Press [eventually renamed Rotunda], was established in 2001 to test the proposition that instances of digital scholarship *can* be bounded, completed, and presented for review, sale, and academic consumption in much the way journals and monographs had been for decades.'[41] So is it a book when it has a beginning and an end?[42]

Yuri Cowan argues that the reading experience offered by hypertext editions of digital archives can point 'beyond itself to the book in three dimensions and further to the communication circuit, to the social circumstances of the book's production, and to its reception' (234). He raises the question of reader access and 'control,' which I also touch on in my concluding chapter.

Together, these chapters offer a picture of contemporary editing and book production in a frame of collaborative endeavour. Each actor is shown within a network of participants and meaning-makers. Similarly, the text is explored as a dynamic cultural object and a social space (chaps. 5, 6, 9). Some contributors examine practices and methods, while others explore the theoretical terrain, and each speaks from a distinct position. They are consistent in underlining the importance of good communication; they point to and sometimes illustrate tensions, weaknesses, and problems that exist in scholarly book publishing, with their consequences and repercussions. They also urge, inspire, and recommend. There is a passion for books, their material forms and social and intellectual contributions, that resonates across this volume.

NOTES

1 Shillingsburg, in the Overview section of the Textual Scholarship.com website, http://text.etl.luc.edu/ts/?q=textual_scholarship/overview (accessed September 2010).

2 Chicago: University of Chicago Press, 2009. In addition to providing detailed and practical solutions and sound advice to editors in a range of fields, Fisher Saller focuses on the habits and attitudes of copyeditors to help find ways of creating 'a good relationship with our colleagues and ourselves as copy editors' – ways of 'getting along' with each other (xiv).

3 Amy Einsohn, *The Copyeditor's Handbook* (Chicago: University of Chicago Press, 2011), xi. Fisher Saller echoes this point: 'More than once in these pages, you will read the heretical idea "It's not a matter of being correct or incorrect. It's only a matter of style"' (*Subversive Copy Editor*, xiv).

4 Leah F. Vosko, 'The Precarious Status of the Artist: Freelance Editors' Struggle for Collective Bargaining Rights,' in Cynthia Cranford, Judy Fudge, Eric Tucker, and Leah F. Vosko, *Self-Employed Workers Organize: Law, Policy, and Unions* (Montreal & Kingston: McGill-Queen's University Press, 2005), 140. Some handbooks actively insist on the editor's invisibility without discussing the complexities of the precept. For example, *Editing and Publication: A Training Manual* by Ian Montagnes, former editor-in-chief of the University of Toronto Press, and published by the International Rice Research Institute

in 1991, includes a section titled 'Editorial invisibility,' which simply states that readers and reviewers complain about errors and expect accuracy, and thus 'the editor must be prepared to be invisible' (30).

5 This will be discussed further in this volume. See Pennsylvania State Press former director Sanford Thatcher's article refocusing the Open Access debate onto copyediting: 'From the University Presses – The Value Added by Copyediting,' *Against the Grain,* September 2008, 69–70, http://www.psupress.org/news/SandyThatchersWritings.html.

6 D.F. McKenzie, *Bibliography and the Sociology of Texts* (Cambridge: Cambridge University Press, 1999), 12.

7 For an overview of textual scholarship and definitions of the types of scholarly editing, see the research guide Textual Scholarship.com, http://text.etl.luc.edu/ts/, and Textual Scholarship http://www.textualscholarship.org/index.html.

8 McKenzie, *Bibliography and the Sociology of Texts,* 15, 1–2.

9 Peter L. Shillingsburg, 'An Inquiry into the Social Status of Texts and Modes of Textual Criticism,' *Studies in Bibliography* 42 (1989): 56.

10 Ibid., 56.

11 Paul Eggert, 'Version – Agency – Intention: The Cross-Fertilising of German and Anglo-American Editorial Traditions,' *Variants* 4 (2005): 8.

12 D.C. Greetham, 'Uncoupled, Or, How I Lost My Author(s),' *Textual Cultures: Text, Contexts, Interpretation* 3:1 (Spring 2008), 46.

13 Jerome J. McGann, *A Critique of Modern Criticism* (Charlottesville: University of Virginia Press, 1992 [1983]), 119.

14 McKenzie, *Bibliography and the Sociology of Texts,* 4.

15 Roland Barthes's 1968 essay 'The Death of the Author' marked a radical shift in literary criticism, in its assertion that 'it is language which speaks,' not the author; to write is, through a prerequisite of impersonality . . ., to reach that point where only language acts, "performs," and not "me."' For, '[l]inguistically, the author is never more than the instance of writing.' Although the writer as person continues to exist, his or her dominance in the making and interpretation of meaning ceases: 'Thus is revealed the total existence of writing: a text is made of multiple writings, drawn from many cultures and entering into mutual relations of dialogue, parody, contestation, but there is one place where this multiplicity is focused and that place is the reader, not, as was hitherto said, the author . . .: the birth of the reader must be at the cost of the death of the Author.' Roland Barthes, 'The Death of the Author,' in *Image, Music, Text,* ed. and trans. Stephen Heath (New York: Hill and Wang, 1977), 143, 145, 148. Peter Mahon discusses this at greater length in chapter 6.

16 Shillingsburg, 'An Inquiry,' 62–3.

17 McKenzie, *Bibliography and the Sociology of Text*, 1 ('The partial but significant shift this signals is one from questions of textual authority to those of dissemination and readership as matters of economic and political motive.').

18 D.C. Greetham, 'Textual Imperialism, Post-Colonial Bibliography, and the Poetics of Culture,' interweave (chap.) 18 in *Textual Transgressions: Essays Toward the Contruction of a Biobibliography* (New York: Garland Publishing, 1998), 581–2.

19 McKenzie, *Bibliography and the Sociology of Text*, 5.

20 McKenzie, *Bibliography and the Sociology of Texts*, 18.

21 Greetham, 'Book as Meaning / Meaning in the Book,' in *Textual Transgressions*, 457.

22 Robert Bringhurst, *The Surface of Meaning: Books and Book Design in Canada* (Vancouver: CCSP, 2008), 11.

23 See Michel Foucault's discussion of authorship and penal appropriation in 'What Is an Author?' trans. Josué V. Harari, repr. in *The Foucault Reader*, ed. Paul Rabinow (New York: Pantheon Books, 1984 [1979]), in which he writes: 'Texts, books, and discourses really began to have authors (other than mythical, "sacralised" and "sacralising" figures) to the extent that authors became subject to punishment, that is, to the extent that discourses could be transgressive. In our culture (and doubtless many others), discourse was not originally a product, a thing, a kind of goods; it was essentially an act – an act placed in the bipolar field of the sacred and the profane, the licit and the illicit, the religious and the blasphemous. Historically, it was a gesture fraught with risks before becoming goods caught up in a circuit of ownership' (108).

24 *Life Lived Like a Story*, by Julie Cruikshank in collaboration with Angela Sidney, Kitty Smith, and Annie Ned (Vancouver/Lincoln: UBC Press / University of Nebraska Press, 1992); *Life Lived Like a Story or When I Was Small – I Wan $K^w ik^w s$: A Grammatical Analysis of St'át'imc Oral Narratives*, by Lisa Matthewson in collaboration with Beverley Frank, Gertrude Ned, Laura Thevarge, and Rose Agnes Whitley (Vancouver: UBC Press, 2005).

25 On 25 November 2011, the cataloguer at the X̱wi7x̱wa Library at the University of British Columbia edited the existing UBC Library catalogue record so that it would carry all of the names identified as authors of the book *When I Was Small – I wan $K^w ik^w s$*. This library has developed an 'enhanced MARC catalogue record' system for Aboriginal/Indigenous subjects, which can carry the names of storytellers.

26 Catherine Bell and Val Napoleon, 'Introduction, Methodology, and Thematic Overview,' in *First Nations Cultural Heritage and Law: Case Studies, Voices, and Perspectives*, ed. Bell and Napoleon (Vancouver: UBC Press, 2008), 12.

27 Ibid., 16. See also Blakeley, chapter 7 of this volume, on the permissions issues she encountered working on *The Trickster Shift*.

28 McCall, *First Person Plural: Aboriginal Storytelling and the Ethics of Collaborative Authorship* (Vancouver: UBC Press, 2011), 6: 'By focusing on the
processes of mediation and collaboration, I hope to challenge notions of
"voice" that are singular, unmediated, and pure, thereby questioning the
discourses of authenticity that continue to perpetuate static notions of Aboriginal identity.' McCall's book invites other parallels with the aboriginal
recorded life narrative, such as the 'absent editor phenomenon,' where,
similarly to the aforementioned invisible editor who denies his or her part
in the production of meaning, 'the recorder denies his or her role as lis-
tener in shaping the story, stressing his or her neutrality or objectivity' (6),
yet the 'collector-editor selects, interprets, shapes, and determines the form
of the narrative' (7).

29 Slights, 'Back to the Future – Litorally: Annotating the Historical Page,' in
The Future of the Page, ed. Peter Stoicheff and Andrew Taylor (Studies in
Book and Print Culture Series) (Toronto: University of Toronto Press,
2004), 71.

30 These include, for example, developing standards for electronic citations
once the Internet became (in fact, when it seemed it could become) a common place to locate sources; advising on gender-neutral and bias-free language; including a section on basic grammar in a style guide as a response
to the changing needs and skills of editors.

31 From the mission statements of Yale University Press, Stanford University
Press, Columbia University Press, and NYU Press.

32 I recently worked with authors Gary Kinsman and Patrizia Gentile on a controversial book, titled *The Canadian War on Queers: National Security as Sexual
Regulation*, that exposes how the Canadian state used the ideology of national
security to spy on, interrogate, and harass gays and lesbians during a forty-
year period. Because government agents and documents sought to construct
gays and lesbians as 'threats to society and enemies of the state,' the book
builds on an argument of human rights. The word 'citizen' had to be used
precisely. Long-time activists and gay-rights advocates, these scholars would
replace the word each time it crept into documents, including draft marketing copy, where it seemed natural to refer to 'state – citizen' relations. But
this was erroneous as it excludes those non-citizens – immigrants, refugees,
migrant workers – who were equally affected by the policies and cam-
paigns. The extent to which spelling and punctuation are 'nationalized'
and the degree to which authors identify with writing styles is not discussed at any length in this volume. Academic editors routinely meet with

the objections of authors to a style of punctuation or spelling, and I think most appreciate the fact that it is not only editors who can develop a fondness for these aspects of writing and hold strong views about them. How the author identity is reshaped through what can be regarded as a simple convention in publishing is certainly an interesting question. As textual scholar D.C. Greetham recounts in his article 'The Materiality of Textual Editing': 'in a peculiar combination of imperialist injunction and post-colonial diffraction, my copyeditor at Oxford for *Theories of the Text* has cast all my punctuation back into rigorous British usage (thereby making me more British than I actually am after thirty exilic years), and yet has yielded to American cultural imperialism and normalised the British *–ise* suffix univerally in favour of American *–ize*, even in words like *Americanis/ ze* or *normalis/ze*! So the text of my *Theories* is still mid-Atlantic, but it is mid-Atlantic in exactly the opposite features of my actual current usage' (in *Textual Transgressions*, 561).

33 Paterson and Randall, Introduction to *Trou de mémoire* (Montreal: BQ, 1993 [1968]), xxxviii.

34 Events culminated in October 1970, when, in what is known as the October Crisis, the Front de libération du Québec kidnapped the British trade delegate, James Cross, and communicated its demands to officials. When the minister of labour and immigration, Pierre Laporte, was found dead in the trunk of a car five days later, the War Measures Act was invoked: tanks rolled into Montreal and curfews were set across the province.

35 Marilyn Randall, 'Appropriate(d) Discourse: Plagiarism and Decolonization,' *New Literary History* 22 (1991): 534.

36 The author-protagonist has two sources for his inferiority complex: as a Francophone, he is part of a marginalized group in Canada; as a Québécois, he is burdened by a view of France as the superior or authentic French nation.

37 'La multiplicité des "paroles en miroir" qui le traversent et la parodie du discours éditorial en font un texte non seulement riche et complexe, mais éclaté: sans frontières, ni limites.' Janet Paterson and Marilyn Randall, Introduction to the critical edition of Hubert Aquin's *Trou de mémoire* (Montreal: BQ, 1993 [1968]), 'Présentation,' xliii (my translation).

38 'Les modifications au texte de *Trou de mémoire* se limitent aux coquilles, aux étourderies typographiques et aux erreurs grammaticales, corrections qui ne sont pas signalées' (in Introduction by Paterson and Randall, under 'Note sur l'établissement du texte,' xlv). 'Riche et inventive, la langue d'Aquin pose quelquefois des problèmes dans la mesure où il peut être difficile de distinguer entre une faute typographique et un néologisme. Les

cas ambigus sont signalés dans le texte par un [*sic*] ou font l'objet d'une note' (xlvi).

39 For example, in 2000 UBC Press launched its Law & Society series. Although the press has been publishing the *Canadian Yearbook of International Law* for years, it had published no other books in law until then. The new series would require editors to learn legal citation styles and other publishing conventions; it would also have to devise a style to accommodate 'hybrid' books, as volumes would be seeking to bridge the divide between legal scholarship and the social sciences.

40 George Bornstein, 'Pages, Pixels, and the Profession,' *Journal of Scholarly Publishing* 34 (July 2003): 199.

41 David Sewell, 'It's For Sale, So It Must Be Finished: Digital Projects in the Scholarly Publishing World,' *Digital Humanities Quarterly* 3 (Spring 2009), no. 2: para. 8.

42 Yuri Cowan's reference, in chapter 10, to the special issue of *Digital Humanities Quarterly* – on the theme of 'Done'! – suggests that relying on reaching a 'finished' state may not help us to define the limits of a book.

PART ONE

The People

2 A Slight Conflict of Aims: Scholarly vs. Academic Editing

PETER L. SHILLINGSBURG

Scholarly editing is a specialized branch of academic editing with special interests that contradict in some specific ways the interests of other branches of academic editing. At a fundamental level, of course, *academic* editing shares with *scholarly* editing a desire for intellectual integrity, accuracy of print, and a greater desire to represent ideas and texts clearly than to make money.[1] These basic similarities imply, however, fundamental differences among three types of editing: scholarly, academic, and commercial.[2] Different though they are in audience and aims, academic editors (whether scholars or publishers' editors) share with commercial editors a desire frequently negated by scholarly editing: to get one text fully and accurately and clearly presented in 'a best form,' suppressing all alternative or trial forms in order to minimize any questions about what the text was intended to be. Although academic editing usually deals with texts designed to convey complex ideas, its medium for doing so is almost always a single text. Scholarly editing frequently, perhaps usually, aims for a more complex textual product than does academic editing because its subject includes variant and multiple texts of the same work. This observation is qualified but not contradicted by the fact that academic editing often involves texts that are footnoted, annotated, cross-referenced, and accompanied by illustrations, appendices, and indexes. For such complicated text-mosaics, each component is a single text placed in strategic juxtaposition with another complementary single text, each with a clearly separate function.

That is different from the scholarly edition, which frequently adds to the intellectual complexity the fact that variant texts, each purporting to represent the same work, might exist in ways that appear to have been revised over time or to have developed variant forms directed at different target audiences. The existence of legitimately variant, sometimes conflicting, representations of a single work gives scholarly editing a complexity normally not encountered in other forms of academic editing. Further, scholarly editors have a tendency to call attention to errors in the historical record of text production where academic editors would simply suppress errors and smooth the text.

Another difference that occasionally causes problems in publishing is that scholarly editing usually takes its standards of correctness and acceptable textual practice for the text of the edited work from earlier periods, different cultures, or even individual authorial norms rather than from the standards for academic or even literary writing that prevail at the present time as recorded in manuals of style. Thus, copyeditors trained in current academic writing standards naturally tend to enforce current standards that conflict with the scholarly editor's efforts to retain historical standards and to allow levels of linguistic and textual tolerances unfamiliar in current academic publishing. The differences between current and historical standards are often not clear to either type of editor, each trained to apply conventions appropriate to their usual kind of editing. The problem becomes particularly acute when a publisher's editor applies modern standards mechanically without the exercise of individual judgment or common sense.

The application of vintage and even eccentric standards of correctness to the edited text is, of course, accompanied by the application of the principles of academic editing to the introductions, notes, and critical apparatuses that accompany the edited text in scholarly editions. And so, the clear, accurate, single text representing the best possible expression of ideas and information produced according to current editorial practices sits in a scholarly edition cheek by jowl with forms and practices appropriate to former times and other places.

The distinction thus indicated between the goals and principles of scholarly editing and those of general academic editing might suggest that 'current standards' are conventions found in style manuals and are routinely applied mechanically, but that may be true only in our worst nightmares. Individual judgment in seeking the clearest way to express complex ideas should always take precedence over style manuals, whose function is to provide the standard way for standard situations. And fortunately, that is sometimes, perhaps frequently, the case. Nevertheless, most writers have experienced the woes of copyeditors applying conventions mechanically to the detriment of clarity.

Too frequent are the sad stories of conflicts between scholarly editors and publishers' editors who did not understand the difference between the special requirements of textual scholarship for the text(s) of the work being edited, on the one hand, and, on the other, the writing by the editor that always accompanies the critically edited text: introductions, annotations, lists of variants, and the like. Publishers' editors, in ignorance of the demands of textual criticism, have occasionally assumed that the scholar has simply failed to understand the principles and demands of modern publishing. So, for example, when a scholar editing Mary Shelley's journals was informed that significant extra space in the manuscript denoting, without punctuation, a pause in thought – like a full stop but not a full stop – could not be represented in the printed text by a similar significant extra space, she decided to represent the gaps editorially with spaced en-dashes. These spaced en-dashes were distinguishable from Mary Shelley's dashes, which were represented as unspaced em-dashes. After long discussion the press agreed, but sent the typescript to a copyeditor who either did not understand or was not informed, and who ironed out the distinction, rendering the editor's indications of significant gaps in the manuscript indistinguishable from Mary Shelley's dashes.[3] The scholarly editor then laboriously rectified the unauthorized un-editing or de-editing, wasting much time and energy in the process. Two things seem to have gone wrong here. The first and most important one is that the press's copyeditor did not read or did not understand the textual editor's explanation of editorial principles and list of symbols. The lesson for scholarly editors is to be more communicative and double check with publishing personnel more often during the production process. The second is that the strategy for indicating the differences in the manuscript between significant spacing and regular dashes may have, in any case, been both too unusual and too subtle – not taking sufficiently into account the principles of normal editorial conventions, which tend to avoid over-subtle variations and to abhor innovations. In the typescript the distinction was easy enough to spot: – as a spaced en-dash, and—as an unspaced em-dash. Small point, perhaps, but the story illustrates a fundamental lack of understanding (and communication) that can exist between professionals in the two fields of editing that are so close that each editor believes falsely that he or she understands the work of the other.

The question of whether the means of indicating the distinction was well-designed typographically is a separate one from whether the distinction was worth making in the first place. Perhaps if a 'smarter' system for distinguishing had been used (such as representing significant gaps in the manuscript with significant gaps in the printed texts?), the press editor would not have assumed that careless error was the cause. Equally important, it would have been a good thing if the copyeditor had been attuned to the special requirements of scholarly editions.

It happens also that elements of scholarly editing, representing the results of textual criticism, occasionally invade essays or chapters of books in conventional academic writing, and hence come under the hands of academic and publishers' editors. Textual criticism, as opposed to scholarly editing, is the investigation of the provenance of texts to determine their genesis, revision, and production evolutions and permutations, and to understand the relationships among variant texts. Attempts in a critical essay to see and explain the interpretive consequences of evolving texts require many of the same editorial functions found in scholarly editing. One simple example that plagues American, though not British, copyediting is the question of whether periods and commas should always come before and not after closing quotation marks. If the quotation is an indication of what is in a document and the document does not contain the comma or period, then the quotation must be closed before such punctuation, regardless of what the style manuals say or standard printing practices might be. For example, if three texts vary in the use of the word 'spoiled,' 'spoilt,' and 'damaged,' would one assume that in each text the word was followed by a comma? If not, should it not be printed as 'spoiled', 'spoilt', and 'damaged'? Or if only the last had a comma, should it not be: 'spoiled', 'spoilt', and 'damaged,'? What would your style manual say about that?

This way of looking at the differences and similarities between scholarly and academic editing produces a nagging discomfort at the oversimplification of scholarly editing that it entails. And the presentation issues affecting scholarly editing also crop up in 'textual criticism' even when editing a work is not the aim. In fact, 'scholarly editing' and 'textual criticism' are terms applied to a wide range of research and editorial approaches, some of which are not generally understood in the academic community – perhaps because courses in bibliography, textual criticism, and scholarly editing are now infrequently required in graduate curricula or because such courses sometimes reflect one or another scholarly approach at the expense of all others.

In the editing of complete works of revered authors, for example, many times the 'standard edition' is indistinguishable from commercial or academic editing: the goal was a single text of each title, edited to suit the needs of casual readers and to represent the works as literary works according to the best lights of the editor. So, we have Jonson's *Complete Works* (1616), Shakespeare's First Folio (1623), the *Waverly Novels* (1829), the *Standard Library Edition of the Works of Charles Dickens* (1894), and so on, edited with great acumen and diligence by intelligent editors bent on putting the works of their author in the best light. Sometimes it is difficult to distinguish the editorial acts of such well-intentioned editors from acts of censorship or authorial revision, because the aim is not historical or textual or investigatory but worshipful, respectful, or even of an 'improving nature' as with some of the editions of Jane Austen or Emily Dickinson undertaken by family members with literary ambitions of their own.[4] This type of editing is not scholarly editing, but its goals and its standing in academic circles remain widely respected and considered sufficient by many for critical uses.

In the twentieth century, scholars such as A.E. Housman, R.B. McKerrow, W.W. Greg, and F.T. Bowers over a period of fifty years, culminating in the 1960s, developed what has been variously called the New Bibliography, Critical Editing, Eclectic Editing, and even Copy-text Editing (a particularly inappropriate label, in my opinion). It is now relatively easy to see that, while their new methods were radically different and more stringent than those mentioned in the previous paragraph, they nevertheless aimed at something like the same thing: a single text that best represented an author's work both historically and intentionally. The differences were, first, the new bibliography's focus on historical aspects, involving the thorough collection and reporting of historical data about the evolution of the text; and, second, its focus on authorial intentions, attended to by critical editorial interventions designed to render a single reading representing what the author had wanted the text to be – not what the current editor, family member, or publisher wished the text to be. The difference was both in the thoroughness of the historical textual investigation and in the basic notion of 'best representation.' Such scholarly editors waived 'their personal notion of best text' in favour of what they could infer to be the 'author's notion of best text.' Critical judgment, not accurate representation of the actual texts of historical documents, took precedence in these projects aimed at producing 'a text that had failed to properly see the light of day before.' Of course, even censors exercise personal judgment while following the notion that a censored text will best represent the work for some purpose; family hagiolaters or family cringers are motivated by some notion of a best reputation for 'our ancestor author'; commercial editors are driven, often, by a notion of what text will sell best; and, so also, scholarly editors of the Anglo-American critical editing school were driven by the dual (and sometimes conflicting) notion of a historical text that best represented the author's final (or sometimes original) intentions. Therein lies the trigger for the next revolution in scholarly editing.

Perhaps from that school of editing it can be seen that scholarly editing and academic editing are really brothers – with scholarly editing merely showing the work where academic editing cleans up first. But that would be to misunderstand the purposes underlying the scholarly editing of literary texts, distinguishing scholarly editing from the editing of academic or explanatory texts: that editors of literary texts have always been fascinated by variant forms – even when, as editors, they were striving to eliminate wrong or no longer preferred forms.

In the last thirty years developments in scholarly editing have tended both to diversify the goals of scholarly editing and to focus more attention on the value of variant forms once thought to be expendable and expunge-able. Probably because the attention of scholarly editors was turned for the first time in the twentieth century from classical and sacred works where all manuscripts were scribal to modern works for which much authorial material is extant, it became clear that many works were tailored and re-tailored for different markets or different audiences, and that, therefore, different versions of a single work meant different things or functioned in different ways – intentionally.[5] It also became clear that production frequently made collaborative works out of texts previously thought to belong exclusively to the author. Inevitably disputes have arisen about the authority of different portions of collaborative works. But regardless of what any one scholarly editor might say is the right way to edit a work for which multiple materials exist, it is the case that scholarly editors in general are now much more anxious to present the variant texts of historical documents (manuscripts, proofs, magazine versions, first and revised editions) in juxtaposition than they are to sift through these variant forms in search of the best text of the work, no matter how the notion of 'best' is defined. The main reason is that scholarly editing as a discipline now recognizes that different historical texts function (and functioned) in different ways, each with a bearing on interpretive outcomes today. And so, accuracy in representing historical texts takes precedence over conformity to modern standards or even the exercise of informed judgment by skilled editors. Here again, a press editor imposing routine academic standards would run amuck.

The academy at large has always, of course, given at least lip service to the importance of multiple texts. Witness library acquisition policies, especially for special collections, in which every edition, every printing, and every state of every printing (at least for some usually canonical works) is sought in order to flesh out the collections. Indeed, digital library cataloguing standards are paving the way, through the emerging use of FRBR (Functional Requirements for Bibliographical Records), which allows encoding of a rich complex of relationships among editions and printings of a work, indicating also their social, economic, and 'agential' relationships – as if each instance of a work were an object worthy of study in its own right.[6] In addition, electronic editions and archives are making virtual image representations of documents more widely available, though projects like the Blake Archive, the Rossetti Archive, and the projects associated with NINES,[7] should not be confused with textually irrelevant ersatz publishing endeavours like Project Gutenberg and fan sites posting un-proofed and un-documented texts. Scholarly editing would be impossible or reduced to a speculative endeavour were it not for brick-and-mortar archives or their scholarly virtual electronic reconstructions. But archives can be used in several ways. For example, the multiple texts could be sifted for evidence of the single best form of the work with which the world at large should be presented in the newly edited standard text. Or, the multiple texts in an archive could be compared, analysed, and reported as distinct social, economic, and cultural instantiations of the work in a heritage of literary events. Scholars continue to be interested in doing both.

Commercial and academic editors, except when producing textual criticism and scholarly editions, have little reason to follow the multiple text path. It is expensive, confusing, and disorienting. People (including students, critics, and most academic writers) are used to encountering a work in only one text and taking for granted that it adequately represents the work. Famous exceptions have entered the critical folklore, so that references to two *Hamlet*s or two *Lear*s or different endings to *Great Expectations* are no longer surprising, but that does not keep most students and critics from building their interpretive superstructures on the back of a single text, frequently, alas, a paperback or un-proofed, un-documented electronically transcribed or scanned text, without knowledge of the evolving variant materials, the multiple forms, or the textual faults at their foundations.

And so, the tendency of literary critics and, often enough, of their academic editors and publishers is to ignore or misconstrue the work of textual criticism and scholarly editing and to publish critical essays and books that also ignore textual issues. Just look for scholarly editions of literary works in the 'Works Cited' of most academic publications. It is true, of course, that there is no scholarly edition for most literary works, especially for most recent literary works. I suppose that lulls both the critic and his or her academic editor into thinking that ignorance of the work's textual condition will not undermine the critical edifice. I do not, by the way, mean to disparage paperback editions. The paperback edition of James Gould Cozzens's *By Love Possessed* was revised by the author after a fourth printing and after the hardbacks had lost their general appeal in the marketplace. American editions of A. S. Byatt, Virginia Woolf, and the Harry Potter books are well-known to be significantly different from their British originals. In such cases it might be better if the critic were to do some textual investigation personally by looking at more than one edition of a text.[8] It isn't enough to have a rule of thumb about which might be the best or most reliable text. Scholarly editing and textual criticism are founded on the notion that textual variants, revealed through examinations of the evolution, revision, and production of texts of a work, can have significant effects on intellectual engagements with a work.

It follows that the editorial requirements of scholarly editing are different from those of conventional academic editing, though in all cases the exercise of individual informed judgement is clearly better than the rote imposition of conventions spelled out in the manuals. When precision and clarity and accuracy can be achieved best by violating the rules, they should be violated. But clear communication about styles and standards between scholarly and academic editors at work on any single project must be the starting point if well-intentioned but uninformed interference is to be avoided.

NOTES

1 My understanding of scholarly and academic editing arises from experience rather than research into this subject. In scholarly editing I have consulted for both editors and university presses on major scholarly editions of Carlyle, Twain, Lawrence, Hardy, and Conrad; I have worked as assistant editor on major scholarly editions of William Gilmore Simms and Washington Irving; and I am the textual and general editor of a scholarly edition of the works of William M. Thackeray. In academic editing I have been book

review editor of two journals (*Studies in the Novel* and *TEXT*) and have both edited and typeset issues of two journals (*TEXT* – for ten years – and *Variants*), and I have served as publisher's reader for editions, monographs, and essays.

2 For clarity, I am dividing 'academic editing' into 'scholarly editing of literary works' and 'all other kinds of academic editing' and I am including as 'academic editors' not only scholars who edit journals and textbooks but publishers' editors. (I do know, however, one or two publishers' editors who have produced scholarly editions.) I have little to say about commercial editing, with which I have no personal experience. But it is worth noting that the need to make money, or at least to seek editorial and production solutions that will save money, affects every kind of editing. Here I merely mention my sense that the current links between academic editing and commercial publishing represented by major commercial firms owning the learned journals of academic societies has deplorable (unintended) consequences to the free exchange and spread of ideas.

3 *The Journals of Mary Shelley,* ed. Paula R. Feldman and Diana Scott-Kilvert, 2 vols. (Oxford: Clarendon Press, 1987; reprinted in paperback by Baltimore: Johns Hopkins University Press, 1995; electronic publication by Intelex, 2004).

4 See Kathryn Sutherland, *Jane Austen's Textual Lives from Aeschylus to Bollywood* (Oxford: Oxford University Press, 2005).

5 Of course, scribal copies are also repurposed, but the authority of a scribe to do so stands in contrast to the authority of an author.

6 FRBR is being used spectacularly by the AustLit data base – a bibliography of Australian Literature – but it has yet to permeate the OPAC world of most library online catalogues and serves more as an abstract model of a potential networking system for cataloguing works.

7 http://www.blakearchive.org/blake; http://www.rossettiarchive.org; http://www.NINES.org.

8 See, for example, my essays on J.M. Coetzee and Darwin: 'Textual Criticism, the Humanities, and J. Coetzee,' *English Studies in Africa* 49 (2006): 13–27; and 'The First Five English Editions of Charles Darwin's *On the Origin of Species,*' *Variants* 5 (2006): 221–41.

3 The Mysterious Relationship: Authors and Their Editors

ROSEMARY SHIPTON

Imprisoned in the chair, I was waiting for the expected command 'Open wide,' when the dentist paused.

'I was reading the Trudeau biography last night,' she said, 'and I saw your name in the acknowledgments. So you're an editor, eh? You must really know your grammar.'

'Well, yes,' I responded, 'but that's not the kind of editing I usually do. I'm more involved in working with authors on organizing their books – shaping them, building momentum, crafting the sentences, choosing just the right word . . .'

'I'm disappointed to hear that,' she reflected. 'I thought that was the whole point of being an author. You can write – and you don't need someone else to help you with it.'

That's the rub, isn't it? Readers want to believe that writers are geniuses, or at least have exceptional talent. Authors naturally buy into this dream, and publishers find it advantageous to present their writers as stars. Editors remain a mystery, their work invisible. And, given the cloak of discretion that covers their profession, editors are not about to divulge the extent of what they did on any particular project. In the real world of publishing, however, they work in very practical ways to fulfil the needs of their various employers or clients and to cooperate with their authors in producing the best books they can for their intended readers – all within the restrictions of tight schedules and insufficient budgets. Although we will focus here on scholarly and trade publishing, we will also look briefly at editors working with writers in other areas, to get some idea of the wide diversity and scope of author–editor relations.

Publishers come in many stripes – trade, scholarly, educational, professional – and they all copyedit their books. Similarly, most newspaper and magazine publishers, non-profit organizations, and corporate and government departments copyedit the print and electronic materials they produce. The people who perform this task may be called communications officers or even writers rather than copyeditors, but the result is the same. They focus on the three big Cs – clarity, correctness, and consistency – so fix all the errors in syntax, grammar, punctuation, usage, and spelling and make sensible decisions about capitalization, abbreviations, and how best to handle numbers, tables, and other recurring items. These details have a way of hiding in a manuscript, but once the text is published, they flash in neon lights and proclaim the sloppiness of the firm behind the publication. That's why good copyeditors are so much in demand.

Copyediting is generally a mechanical skill: these editors follow a guide such as the venerable *Chicago Manual of Style* and apply the rules.[1] They need a good eye for detail, a thorough knowledge of the language, an excellent memory, quick fact-checking skills, and a liking for making lists. The more general knowledge they have, the better – to save authors from embarrassing slips about dates, events, names, and idiomatic expressions. Most authors welcome this help with 'the small stuff,' as some of them call it, though there is potential for clashes and stalemates on a few fronts. Renowned professor Jacques Barzun told us all about them in his cautionary article 'Behind the Blue Pencil.'[2] After listing some errors that copyeditors had introduced to his own texts, he went on to rail against the imposition of a 'homogenized' house style and ill-educated editors who are deaf to rhythm and give 'no thought to nuance and rhetoric.'

The most common disputes arise when copyeditors lack training and experience. Many students in university will be satisfied with a B grade, but in copyediting, catching 75 per cent of the errors and inconsistencies in a manuscript is just not good enough. The standard is much higher, around 95 per cent.[3] Once an author realizes that his copyeditor is not up to par – or, even worse, is introducing errors and infelicities to his text – he loses all confidence in her and goes on the warpath to check every change she suggests. Another problem is the arbitrary editor who follows the style guide to the letter but is insensitive to the needs of the particular manuscript she is working on.

Superb copyeditors need good judgment as much as language skills, and they must vary their decisions depending on the author they are working with and the conventions of his particular subject area. If they're working with a cabinet minister who visualizes himself with a capital *M*, there's no point in fighting the lower-case battle, unless a house style demands it. It's preferable simply to make all similar titles, from 'lieutenant-colonel' to 'chief justice,' upper case too. And, if they're copyediting fiction or literary non-fiction, they should allow the author some flexibility. These creative writers tend to savour every word, even every comma. The best copyeditors get into the same groove and have fun with well-placed sentence fragments, careful choice between dashes and ellipses points, and perhaps at times no commas or quotation marks at all. The effects can be exhilarating as the broken sentences, the rush of words, the pauses or interruptions signalled by the punctuation reinforce exactly what the author is trying to do with his words. Without doubt, copyediting can be creative too.

Some publishers require quite specialized copyediting skills – science and technology is one obvious example. Scholarly publishers also need copyeditors who can handle all the academic apparatus of notes and bibliographies in various styles, figures and tables, complex appendices, foreign languages ancient and modern, and, frequently, indexes prepared by authors with no training in this area. They should also be able to understand the arguments in the often difficult text and communicate effectively with their authors. There is nothing more frustrating for a scholar than having an editor who asks dumb questions and obviously doesn't 'get it.' For all these reasons, scholarly presses prefer to hire copyeditors with an academic bent and, preferably, some knowledge of the area in which they are editing. Commonly these editors have graduate degrees themselves, so they are familiar with academic research and conventions and understand scholarly goals. They feel comfortable talking to their authors, and they are able to make helpful comments and ask appropriate questions as they copyedit the text.

In recent decades, most publishers have not had copyeditors on staff. Rather, they develop a stable of editors who work for them on a freelance basis – editors who are familiar with the kinds of books they publish and whose quality of work they can trust. This trust also involves the ability to work within set deadlines and budgets, and the courtesy to keep the managing editor informed immediately when glitches or delays occur. In some houses, the freelance editor does not communicate with the author directly – the managing editor or the project editor acts as the liaison. In other houses, the editor sends the author the copyedited text and, together, they finalize it before it goes back to the publisher to enter the production process. It is preferable for editors who are doing more creative copyediting to deal directly with their authors, especially if they have been involved in the stylistic editing of the manuscript.

In all cases, this editing may be done electronically or on paper, though a preference for the efficiency and speedy communication of the former is rapidly overtaking the latter. For both authors and editors to be comfortable with this system, however, it is essential that editors be adept in using the tracking and comments features available in current software, and that authors be able to respond in kind. Electronic editing has also changed the way that authors and editors relate to each other: there is likely to be far more frequent communication between them as questions are asked and answered throughout the editing process, and – like it or not – as manuscripts are often delivered and edited in sections, with a quick read-through at the end. In this new electronic world, flexibility and multitasking are the keys to survival.

Compared to the legions of copyeditors in all the various areas of publishing, there are relatively few substantive and stylistic editors. Substantive editors (or structural editors as they are also called) look at the shape of the entire manuscript – how it begins, how it ends, and how everything proceeds in between in terms of organization, divisions, pacing, balance, clarity, and focus.[4] They consider the readers who will most likely use the book, and what exactly this publication is trying to do. Has the text met its intended purpose? they ask. Is it geared to the interests and needs of its audience? As substantive editors answer these questions, they must not only define the problems they encounter but come up with solutions too. Myriad changes may have to be made to get the manuscript 'right' – and, in doing so, editors work closely with their authors.

Bestsellers and other fiction and non-fiction books published by trade publishers are usually discretionary reading – no one has to study them to keep a job, and most of them are read simply because people find them interesting or entertaining. It's crucial, then, that the opening pages get readers' attention and propel them into the rest of the book. In all the chapters that remain, the text has to be accessible to general readers, clear and focused, and divided into manageable chunks, with a strong narrative, a good balance between context and front story, and an ending that readers feel is somehow satisfying and appropriate.

When the substantive editor finds there are problems with the manuscript, he (as we will call this editor) communicates them to the author, usually in writing, but in discussion too.[5] If the structure is generally in order, he can annotate the manuscript with comments and queries. When, for instance, the protagonist disappears from the narrative during twenty pages of background information on an event, he can suggest that the context discussion be condensed. When the author refers obliquely to an event, he can say that general readers will not be familiar with the facts, so she should build in a brief description. When the author says that the future prime minister wrote a passionate love letter to his fiancée, he can ask for a quotation from the letter itself, to make the text come alive. When the editor gets bogged down in detail, he can ask the author for a directing sentence or two to introduce him and other readers to the main theme and lead them through the text. In fiction, when a character or an episode turns out to play no real role in the narrative or the resolution of the plot, he can suggest that the author 'kiss her darlings goodbye' – and perhaps save them for the next novel. Or when a needed character seems simplistic or unbelievable, he can help the author to explore that personality in greater depth. And so he goes, page by page all through the text, requesting tightening here, elaboration there, the elimination of peripheral details, the addition of descriptions to build a sense of place, along with some reordering of paragraphs and sentences or the addition of new section breaks – all to make the finished book the best it can possibly be for its readers.

If the manuscript or parts of it have severe structural problems, however, there is no point in glossing it with such remarks. Reorganization and rewriting are required. In these cases it's better for the editor to write his comments for the author in a report, with an introduction explaining his basic criticisms and solutions. He then goes through the manuscript chapter by chapter, section by section, setting out how the text should be reorganized, developed, and balanced. Once the author has considered this advice and come to an agreement with the editor on the revised outline, the author rewrites the text.

Authors are understandably protective of their texts, and it's imperative that the editor's recommendations be presented diplomatically and persuasively, in a way that will win the author's confidence and cooperation. The writer must feel that the editor knows what he is talking about and that his suggestions will really improve the book and make her look good. The editor should be tactful and positive in his remarks and willing to enter into a partnership with the author as, together, they strive to achieve the results they both want. Not all the editor's suggestions will be taken by any means, but it is often sufficient to raise the point that there is a problem. The best solutions commonly emerge out of the discussion that follows between the writer and the editor.

Once the structure of the manuscript is in place, it is time for the stylistic editing – the detailed editing paragraph by paragraph, sentence by sentence, to get the prose clear, the rhythm right, and the whole text a pleasure to read.[6] A little tightening here, the cutting of hackneyed phrases and repeated words there can make a huge difference, as can parallel sentences, concrete words, and a variety of sentence structures and lengths. This work is very labour intensive, particularly when the manuscript needs close work all the way through. Above all, the editor must not take over the project. His role is to assist the author to present her material in the best possible way – even if he does not always agree with the interpretation she gives in the text. He must keep the author's voice no matter how heavy the edit – and the writer must instantly be able to recognize the text as her own. For this reason, it is best if the editor works with the author's words and sentences as much as possible rather than taking the often easier route of rewriting. A successful editor clones the author's tone as he works with what is there – by rearranging sections and paragraphs, condensing, and deleting extraneous events and facts. He also addresses what is not there and, by astute querying, asks the author to fill in the missing narrative or information. The process is rather like taking a fuzzy image and clicking it into focus.

Stylistic editing is frequently done by the substantive editor, usually in a second pass after he and the author have agreed on the overall structure and content of the text. It can also be assigned to a talented copyeditor, who combines the stylistic edit with the usual copyediting tasks. And sometimes it is shared by both editors, as they each make their suggestions to the author on their separate passes through the text. Whatever the particular arrangement, however, if a manuscript is to get a 'full' edit – substantive, stylistic, and copyediting – the three tasks are almost always performed by two editors or by a single editor in two distinct passes, never by three different editors.

The *New York Times Magazine* initiated a vigorous debate in the literary and publishing worlds when, in 1998, it published a revealing article by D.T. Max about Raymond Carver's relationship with Gordon Lish, his first editor. After examining Carver's literary papers and letters, Max argued that Lish often sharpened the short stories brilliantly, but at the cost of completely changing their tone from descriptive to minimalist, with subplots removed, paragraphs rewritten, and endings rendered abrupt. A decade later the *New Yorker* published one of

Carver's stories in its original form alongside Lish's edited version. The contrast was striking – and the consensus held that Lish had gone well beyond the boundaries of the editor's role. Carver evidently thought so too, as, painfully, he broke with the man who had given him his initial break and early success as a published writer.[7]

In the real world of publishing today, how many books get the 'full monty' (as one author described it)?[8] Trade houses are more likely than other publishers to invest in serious substantive and stylistic editing simply because they are in the business of publishing fiction and non-fiction books in relatively large numbers for general readers. As commercial publishers, they make their own decisions about the manuscripts they acquire, and their goal is to publish books that they like, they think will sell well, and they consider timely or of lasting literary merit. Some publishers suggest ideas for books to likely authors almost as often as they receive proposals from authors, but, once an arrangement is made, the author is expected to buy into the project with enthusiasm, as though he had initiated the idea himself. The majority of trade authors are journalists from different media, professional writers, celebrities, and a few scholars and other experts who are willing to write for general readers. Depending on the expected interest in the author and the subject of the book, the initial print runs in Canada vary from three thousand to thirty thousand copies or more.[9] When some of these books do turn out to be a critical or a commercial success, they can be enormously influential.

Most trade publishers know that, to make their books excellent and interesting, to attract good reviews and other media attention, to win book awards, and to get that word-of-mouth buzz that entices readers to buy, they really should edit at both the macro and the micro level. Some authors are naturally talented writers and require little substantive or stylistic editing. Others, however, need heavy editing: journalists, for instance, are trained to write short pieces of prose, not long sustained arguments or narratives; scholars and other authorities are primarily experts in their particular field, not successful writers, and they often need extensive guidance as they try to write for general readers.

Another problem stems from the way trade publishers acquire their books: they frequently sign a contract with a non-fiction writer based on a proposal and a sample chapter, which have probably been shaped to some degree by the author's literary agent. When the book manuscript is delivered a year or so later, it may be incomplete or but a first draft – the result of writer's block or hurried preparation or unexpected calamities in the author's life. By this time the book has been included in the business plan for the season and may even have been announced, so the publisher is loath to delay it – particularly if the topic of the book is time sensitive. The only solution is to put a trusted substantive/ stylistic editor to work with the author – otherwise, the manuscript is simply not publishable.

Trade publishers generally prefer to have their in-house editors do the substantive editing. When the collaboration works well, inevitably authors bond with their editors – they request them for book after book. Good trade publishers want to keep authors loyal to the house over the long term, to help develop their careers as writers to their mutual benefit, and it is usually the senior editors, and often the publisher or the editorial director, who do this level of editing. Not all publishers have substantive editors on staff, however, or, even when they do, they may not have a good match for a particular author and, commonly, they cannot cope with erratic bulges in the schedule as books go through the publication process. To meet this need, a small group of freelancers specialize in this very creative and analytical work – frequently they are editors who once worked inside the firm and clearly understand what is required.[10]

If the collaboration between author and editor does not work well, the author very quickly feels threatened and loses confidence in the editor. Publishers try to repair the damage, reorienting both parties to respect the other's role and begin anew, but sometimes there is no choice but to find another editor better able to work with this particular author. Trust and confidence are essential for the author–editor relationship to succeed, and it really helps if the editor has genuine enthusiasm for the project under way. 'If I had to name an essential ingredient in successful author–editor relationships,' said Jan Walter, a distinguished publisher, editor, and literary juror, 'I would say mutual respect. For the editor, that means respect for the author's ambitions, his hopes and fears, as well as for his ideas or his prose. And the author must have respect for the editor's expertise and a willingness to trust her experience and instincts.'[11]

Yet even in this one genre of publishing it is not possible to generalize – some large multinational trade publishers do a minimum of substantive and stylistic editing, while some small niche houses offer the best, with the dedicated owner or publisher frequently doing the work. This evaluation applies to trade publishers throughout the Western world – Europe, the United Kingdom, the United States, Australia – and, sadly, the commitment to editing seems to be on the decline.[12] The key determining feature is the attitude of the person or the team that makes the decisions inside the house, and whether editorial excellence ranks high among the many choices that have to be made.

Fortunately, in Canada there are still many trade publishers who believe in the value of editing, and standards in these houses remain high. Scott McIntyre, the chairman of D&M Publishers in Vancouver, the largest Canadian-owned trade house in the country, expressed the conundrum publishers face: 'Good editing is, quite simply, the heart and soul of publishing, the essential bond between publisher and writer, and the sacred obligation of any good publishing house. The downside is that careful editing is expensive, and, in a shrinking book market, it is always vulnerable to cuts and the acceptance of lower standards. This conflict puts any motivated publisher on the horns of a most uncomfortable dilemma, particularly in a small and diminishing market such as Canada's. The mantra must remain: a little compromise is a dangerous thing.'[13] But not all publishers share his sensibility. One cynic from a large house was heard recently to say: 'By the time readers realize it's a shoddily edited book, they are well past the cash register.'

Scholarly publishers do not usually do intensive substantive editing – and for many good reasons. Their mandate is to publish books that make an original contribution to knowledge; most of their authors are professors or researchers; the majority of their readers are academics and students; and the number of copies they print of most titles is small – as few as four hundred for some books, with an average in Canada of around eight hundred copies.[14] All these factors influence what academic publishers want from their editors.

Editors working in-house for scholarly publishers tend to fall into two groups: acquisitions editors working under an editorial director, and production editors working under a managing editor. The configuration and the titles vary with the particular publisher and, not infrequently, each 'group' consists of one or two multitasking persons. The roles are clear. Acquisition editors are often responsible for more than one subject area, but are expected to keep abreast of the literature in their fields and be well attuned to trends in scholarship and to methodological and ideological divides. They attend academic conferences and invite submissions from scholars who are actively engaged in research. When they receive proposals or complete manuscripts from authors, they reject the ones they deem unsuitable for their lists and send those that hold promise to two experts to review. They also apply for grants from the organizations that fund academic publishing and present manuscripts at meetings of the in-house and academic review committees that make the final decision to publish.[15] At every stage, the opinions expressed by the peer reviewers are of key significance in determining whether the manuscript will be rejected outright, accepted, or recommended for revision and further consideration.

All through this long process, acquisitions editors keep in contact with their potential authors, encouraging them and passing on the anonymous evaluations and the committee decisions. As Jean Wilson, a highly respected editor at UBC Press in Vancouver for many years, put it: 'Any success I have had as an acquisitions editor has had as much to do with being respectful and in close touch with authors as with being happily engaged in the business of making books.' Some of these editors, depending on their workload and their personal inclination, will also make editorial suggestions as they can, either on the manuscript itself or in a letter. Many academic authors say these comments from their acquisition editors, along with the often quite detailed readers' reports, proved enormously helpful as they revised their books for publication. Given the number of titles these editors supervise each year, however (forty to sixty in various stages of preparation and review is not uncommon in large presses), it is not possible for them to give even this kind of attention to every manuscript.[16] Other acquisitions editors focus more on their heavy administrative duties and seldom offer detailed substantive advice to their authors.

Once the final manuscript arrives in house, it is assigned to the managing editor or a production editor, who then steers it through the production process. The first step is to find a copyeditor for the text. This editor is almost always a freelancer – usually one experienced in academic editing and familiar with all the scholarly apparatus – and the job offer is standard: to 'copyedit' the text. More is usually expected, however, as the editor makes suggestions for titles, headings, prose style, illustrations, appendices, and perhaps reorganization which go far beyond strict copyediting. One managing editor told me: 'I always say copy edit, but I'm really hoping for stylistic editing too, and maybe a substantive suggestion or two as well!'[17] Some scholarly manuscripts are so specialized that they require copyeditors with considerable expertise in the conventions of particular fields of study. Whatever the level of editing, once it is completed the author answers the queries, reviews the editing, and accepts the suggestions – or not. The copyeditor or, in some cases, the production editor in house, then checks that the manuscript is ready to go into production – and the edited text proceeds on through the various stages of proof.

Does it matter that most scholarly monographs never get an in-depth substantive or stylistic edit by a professional editor? Most academic authors write for their peers, not for the general population. They need publications to secure tenure and promotions with their universities, and their job descriptions require them to engage in original research and publish their results. Many prefer to communicate with other specialists in their discipline – the ones they meet at learned conferences and the experts who review their books in the scholarly journals – rather than reach out to a broader audience. They have all been trained in writing dissertations in graduate school, and they are familiar with the thesis format – survey of the literature and the relevant theory, statement of the original contribution to be made, presentation of the research to support that goal chapter by chapter, conclusion to prove that the contribution has been made, and all supported by voluminous notes. Some scholars have got so used to that template that they prefer it to any alternative. As initiates in the academic club, they expect their readers to have considerable knowledge of the subjects they write about, so, rather than describing events or people or theories directly, they tend to comment on them or allude to them. They also know that these readers will understand the specialized jargon and the guarded, often obtuse long sentences in which they make their arguments.

In comparison to manuscripts coming in for editing at trade houses, those arriving at scholarly publishers are generally far better prepared. Authors spend years researching and writing them; manuscripts are completed to each author's satisfaction before they go out for peer review; and they have probably been revised once or twice since then, guided by advice from both the experts and the acquiring editors. All these factors, as well as the small print runs for these books and the few experts who will read them, make it difficult to justify any bigger editorial budget for these projects than they already have. A sound copyedit by an experienced scholarly editor is fine with most academic authors, readers, and publishers.

Scholarly books are valuable for the original research and the probing analysis they present, and, during the long shelf lives many of them enjoy, they will profoundly affect generations of academics, students, and more popular authors. We are all in debt to the publishers that make these volumes available to us. But what about the relatively few books published by scholarly presses that would be of genuine interest to a broader group of readers than academics and experts? Would they benefit from an in-depth professional substantive edit?[18] Without doubt, many of them could be shaped into better books – books that would get more attention in the outside world, sell more copies, and make more impact than they usually do. As the system stands, many peer reviewers are extremely generous in their remarks about the manuscripts they evaluate, suggesting alternative interpretations of some issues, pointing out omissions, and correcting the errors they find. But these comments generally focus on content, not presentation – they come from fellow academics who are expert in a particular subject of study, not in editing skills. Editors, in contrast, are trained in how best to communicate material to make it clear and interesting for its intended readers. Their skills would nicely complement the experts' advice and help scholarly authors to write books that are not only valuable in themselves but also accessible to many more readers.

These same considerations apply to professional publishers who specialize in a particular area, such as medicine or law. Jeffrey Miller, the publisher at Irwin Law in Toronto, described legal publishing in these words: 'The main purpose of legal writing is to interpret a corpus of statutory authorities and judicial pronouncements and through that interpretation to extract the law. To be successful, a piece of legal writing must be clear, it must be precise in its references, and it must be correct on the facts.' The role of legal editors, then, is to help make this happen: 'Most legal authors are professionals but that is not to say that they are professional writers. Whether they are practitioners, judges, or scholars, legal authors are almost always experts in their fields and often assume that those for whom they write (their readers) share their extensive knowledge of the subject at hand.' 'While their prose may be full of legalese,' Miller continues, 'it may also be replete with truncated references to statutory instruments or to case law. It is not uncommon for an editor to encounter statements such as this one: "As the court said in *Jones*, in reference to a s.15 challenge . . ." where it is assumed that every reader knows who "Jones" is and why he or she was fooling around with a "s. 15 challenge." It is often left to the beleaguered editor to find the reference in case law to a case in which one of the litigants was someone named Jones and then to find the statute to which section 15 belongs. Having done that, he or she must verify that the court did in fact say what the author says the court said. And, having done that, the legal editor must then make sure that the legal principle exemplified in the *Jones* case was not overturned or altered by a subsequent judicial decision.' Miller concludes that legal authors are happy to have skilled copyeditors go through their manuscripts to perform all these tasks with care: 'In a world where one's worth is measured in billable hours (at a rate that is probably ten times that charged by the professional freelance editor), writing books is very much a sideline.'[19]

In government, corporate, and non-profit publishing, the relationship between authors and editors faces the unique challenge that there is, frequently, no one author but a committee of different contributors and a unit manager whose role it is to ensure that the document is 'published.' The manager is usually a subject specialist, but may know nothing about the publishing process. Adding to the complexity in many jurisdictions in Canada is the requirement to publish in both official languages – English and French. Jennifer Latham, the director of editorial services in the office of the Auditor General of Canada, has wide experience in supervising her own staff of substantive editors and copyeditors as well as numerous freelance editors: 'It's my firm opinion that the best editors working for government clients are those who are entrepreneurial, with strong interpersonal and public relations skills,' she says. 'When it's clear that the manager in charge of the publication has no understanding of the editorial process, an assertive editor is needed to guide both the manager and the publication through the process. The editor may have to consult with several contributors to resolve problems with the text. It takes diplomacy, editorial skill, and confidence to educate the client, work through the phases of editing, and produce the final draft, all within poorly planned budgets and deadlines.' Latham further explains that 99 per cent of federal government texts are written originally in English and then translated into French, so the French editors bear a particular burden as, under extreme time pressures and a rush of last-minute corrections, they 'review changes with the "author" to ensure that the intended meaning has been accurately translated.'[20]

In educational publishing, the lead editor for a particular textbook or series of books is known as the developmental editor rather than the substantive or structural editor. In this world, provincial or state curricula rule, so the editor's role is publisher driven, not author driven. As Anthony Luengo, a developmental editor with decades of experience, explained, 'We must very closely follow the curricula, which means that our authors must, under our careful direction, do so in turn. Otherwise, we simply don't get on the approved listings and don't sell any books.'[21] Authors, in other words, are hired for their knowledge and their reputation in certain areas, and they are asked to write a particular content to a predetermined length. Commonly the developmental editors make an enormous contribution in filling out the text, finding illustrations, and creating teacher guides and classroom exercises. The big challenge now, Luengo says, is to develop non-print resources for the classroom. Again, the response is being decided by educational publishers and their editors, not by their authors.

Some specialized areas of trade and scholarly publishing are also driven by publishers or editors, not authors. This distinction has a huge effect on author–editor relations. When authors submit proposals to publishers, they, as the creators of those books, have clear ideas of what they want to achieve. They are therefore consulted and treated with due deference all through the editing process, no matter how in-depth the editing might be. When publishers or clients originate a book idea, however, authors are most often hired to research and write the text in the same way that other members of the publishing team are hired. The editor in charge of the project will shape the concept for the book and also be responsible for selecting the writers, designers, copyeditors, and other team members and for ensuring the quality of the final volume.

In the trade world, this latter kind of publishing is generally referred to as packaging, and the books produced tend to be highly illustrated in relation to the text – cookbooks, popular art and history books, books about wine, travel, gardening, or celebrities, for example. The packager gets an idea for a book (preferably one that will sell in multiple markets), develops the concept with the assistance of skilled editors and designers, lines up a suitable author, produces a sample pamphlet or 'blad' – book layout and design – showing jacket, contents page, and selected interior pages, and presents the project to publishers in two or more territories (unless the projected sales in one market seem sufficient). If enough publishers commit, the volume or the series gets produced; if they don't, the project dies. In packaged books, the author is really a writer for hire. No matter how well known he may be, he works within the parameters of the concept for the book and under the direction of the editor in charge.

In scholarly publishing, certain large and usually long-lasting projects that operate under their own sources of funding are also directed by the editor-in-chief, who then selects suitable academic authors to write particular articles or to edit and annotate previously published texts by renowned writers. Most of the 'collected works' projects fall under this umbrella, along with other series. At the universities of Toronto and Laval, the bilingual *Dictionary of Canadian Biography / Dictionnaire biographique du Canada* has been in process since 1959, and a succession of eminent editors has planned the contents of each of the fifteen volumes published to date and commissioned knowledgeable authors to write each biography. Every writer is allotted a certain number of words, and once the article has been submitted, it is meticulously researched, fact checked, and edited (or sometimes rewritten) by the staff editors. Their pace might be slow, but the quality of their work is superb. The authors are consulted on these revisions, but the objectives of the dictionary project will always trump individual author preferences.

The Internet is now opening up opportunities for other kinds of book-publishing projects, some of which have no connection with traditional publishing houses at all. One of the most ambitious was the brainchild of a family foundation in the United States for a three-volume / two-thousand-illustration publication in the decorative arts area that was published simultaneously in two editions – English and German. After extensive consultation with scholars and curators on both sides of the Atlantic, the foundation selected an editor-in-chief in Canada, who in turn chose nine other experts as authors, along with a lead editor for the English edition, translators in both languages, an illustrations coordinator, researchers, and a German text editor – drawn, collectively, from five different countries. In due course, an excellent art-book publisher in Germany was contracted to look after the elaborate design for the volumes, the production and printing, and the marketing and distribution.[22] In effect, every member of the team was hired independently by the foundation to collaborate and make this challenging publication a reality – all within a five-year span from concept to publication. It would not have been possible without high-speed electronic communication. In the same way that authors of encyclopedia and biographical dictionary articles must write as requested, the authors involved in this project had to shape their work to fit the overall concept for the project. The lead editor had to ensure that the various essays blended together to make a harmonious whole, with no gaps and a minimum of repetition, and with full respect for the set word count and illustration numbers.[23]

In reflecting on what she wanted from the editors on this project, editor-in-chief Meredith Chilton, an independent scholar and former curator of the Gardiner Museum in Toronto, said: 'As an academic editor of a complex project, what I expect of an editor is an ability to organize and meld the entire manuscript together seamlessly and to edit text without losing the individual voice of the writer, making it completely accessible for the expected reader. What helps? A collaborative spirit, a complete understanding of the goals of the publication, an intense curiosity for the subject, an "outside" view that brings perspective and balance, great language skills – and, of course, the willingness to work under intense pressure and, in the storm of deadlines, to be a calm yet determined voice, the essential pillar in any publication.' She continued, 'The editor-in-chief and the editors must enjoy working together, have great clarity of purpose and excellent communication, and know that they are members of a team. They need to be well organized, dependable, open, and honest. Once achieved, these qualities will result in a harmonious relationship and truly remarkable work.'[24]

What do authors say about their relationship with their editors? Potentially it is fraught with difficulties, as authors, understandably protective of their hard-won words, narratives, and arguments, may see editors as intruding on their turf, bossily taking over their projects, unnecessarily extending the already long gestation period for their books. Certainly there are stories of poor editing, broken relationships, and unhappy writers. But are they the norm?

Jack Granatstein, a prolific author of scholarly and trade books, has clear ideas about the relationship: 'What do I want from an editor? Someone to catch my stupidities before they are set in stone. Someone to spot the tics in my prose, all too prominent in my writing, and eliminate them or, at least, tame them. And someone who knows enough about my subject to understand what I am trying to say and to help me say it better by making the text clear and accurate. The first two are fairly common among competent copy editors, but the last is what separates the great editors, the content editors, from the good.'[25] Ideally, he seems to be saying, he expects good copyediting, but he would also appreciate excellent substantive and stylistic editing from an editor who understands exactly what he is trying to do in his books.

John English, the acclaimed author of the definitive biographies of Lester Pearson and Pierre Elliott Trudeau, the two best-known Canadian prime ministers internationally, echoes his wish: 'What I expect from editors is a "second look" at the manuscript. This look is best seen as a view through a prism. One beam focuses on the overall effect of the argument, another on the clarity of the writing, while yet another concentrates on the details – spelling, grammar, and facts. After the editor has completed the "second look," the author should consider the entire package, read the manuscript, and then revise in a way that maintains his own integrity while recognizing the new insights that have been brought to the material by the editor. Ultimately, the relationship must be based on a profound trust that obviously needs time to develop.'[26]

Richard Gwyn, who has been a highly successful journalist, columnist, and media personality over many decades and has also written four books, including a biography of Canada's first prime minister, John A. Macdonald, was even more expansive about this delicate relationship between authors and editors: 'Editors are a cross between censorious nanny, protective angel, an old friend with the confidence to be honest, a father confessor, and a partner. The attribute that matters is that of being a partner. For any writer, the experience of being in the hands of a first-rate editor is highly personal. An editor knows all of a writer's vulnerabilities and inadequacies; the writer has to know that the editor knows that all that matters in the end is what it is that the writer is trying to say.' And, he continues, 'The experience can realize its purpose only on the basis of mutual trust. Trust by the writer in the intelligence, sensitivity, integrity, sheer skill, of the editor. Trust by the editor in the professionalism of the writer and that he or she is really trying to say something worthwhile (as well as, of course, to write a bestseller, get rave reviews, win prizes).' He concludes: 'I've had that experience twice in my life. They've been among the most exhilarating in my life, and by now the scars they left on my psyche have – almost – healed.'[27]

In contrast to these three veterans with many successful books behind them, Sarah Jennings, an experienced radio and magazine journalist, had a different vision of the ideal relationship between author and editor when she decided to write her first book: 'What authors are looking for is a "creative producer" – someone who brings out the best of what they have to offer, without imposing their own selves on the process . . . The editor, like a wise shepherd attending his flock, must take into account the writer's skittish and sometimes frightened nature, her tentative – or overwhelming – sense of self and sense of importance about what she has to say. The editor's task is to guide the author through the process in a way that allows the story to emerge. Sometimes that may mean rewriting all of the author's thoughts, but, if the author is a reasonable writer, the editor's task is to sharpen and enhance what the writer is trying to

say.' And so, she concludes, the editor must be a good and honest lis-
tener and reader, a person endowed with enormous tact and genuine
enthusiasm for the subject of the manuscript, and someone able to assist
the neophyte writer to see the overview of the manuscript in a gentle,
step-by-step process. Above all, she says, the editor must remember that
the writer is trusting her, as a partner, to make this book a success.[28]

'To accomplish this special magic,' Meredith Chilton says, 'an editor
must be able to develop a relationship of mutual trust and respect with
the authors. Friendly relations need to be fostered with each author,
as it is a sensitive matter to suggest major changes to writers who are
often protective of their work. This requires a delicacy of touch with
both text and authors, and appreciation of a collaborative approach. A
dash of psychology doesn't hurt, as maintaining a defensive position
would be disastrous and completely counter-productive.'[29] Editors, she
suggests, need not be specialists in the area in which they are editing.
Rather, they need to be top-notch professionals as book editors, able
to empathize with authors' goals and collaborate with them to present
their material in a way that is admirably suited both to their goals and
to their intended readers.

It seems that authors are not complaining about too much editing;
rather, they are asking for more.[30] Literary agents sometimes ask substantive editors to shape promising manuscripts before they submit
them to publishers – they find they get more bidders that way and
bigger advances too. And, as more publishers are cutting back on the
substantive and stylistic editing they do, some individual authors are
hiring editors privately, either before or after they sign a contract with a
publisher, to do the kind of in-depth editing they want for their books.[31]
Writers should be aware, though, that editing is not a regulated profession, and anyone who aspires to the role can hang up a shingle and
claim to be an editor. Authors who are looking for an editor to collaborate with them in preparing a manuscript for publication should make
sure that the editor they choose has sound editorial training and experience with many successful books, particularly in the area in which their
book hopes to find its readers. As John English says, 'The best editors
are like fine wine; they mature well.'[32]

If authors are so desirous of good editing, why is the profession still
cloaked in mystery, and why does editorial work remain invisible? So
long as the editors' contribution to publications in all genres – trade and
scholarly books, professional and educational textbooks, government
and corporate publications – is not given the recognition it deserves,

editors will remain vulnerable to low salaries and, in times of economic downturn, to early layoff. Yet, to do their job successfully, editors have to be well educated, analytical in mind, talented with language, confident of their abilities, diplomatic in their communication with authors, and be team players who also have the discipline to work alone for long stretches to get the job done within the time and the budget allowed. Above all they must be flexible, and, because every book is different, able to work on a wide variety of projects and with authors of all kinds. Editors deserve more open recognition for the work they do – and, it seems, many authors are willing to give them their due. It is the end product that matters – the published book or article or report – and the details of who did what are ultimately of no significance.[33] The time has come to acknowledge that, together, authors and editors can create great books.

NOTES

I would like to thank the many publishers, editors, and authors who have generously shared their experience and their thoughts with me on author–editor relations. In particular I am indebted to Meredith Chilton, John English, Jack Granatstein, Richard Gwyn, Sarah Jennings, Jennifer Latham, Anthony Luengo, Joan McGilvray, Jeffrey Miller, Meg Taylor, Jan Walter, and Jean Wilson.

1 In addition to other style guides published by various academic associations, see Amy Einsohn, *The Copyeditor's Handbook: A Guide for Book Publishing and Corporate Communications*, 3rd ed. (Chicago: University of Chicago Press, 2011).

2 Jacques Barzun, 'Behind the Blue Pencil – Censorship or Creeping Creativity?' *American Scholar* (Summer 1985): 28–30; Barzun, 'A Copy Editor's Anthology,' in his *A Word or Two before You Go . . .* (Middletown, CT: Wesleyan University Press, 1986), 85–91.

3 When my fellow contributor Amy Einsohn read a draft of this essay, she questioned my standard for copyediting: 'I wonder if even 95 per cent understates the case,' she inquired. 'If an author has been a bit careless (or is a bad speller or a bad typist, has shaky grammar or diction, etc.), a copyeditor needs to catch more than 95 per cent of the mistakes in the manuscript, or else the final book will be an embarrassment to all.' When I asked Gena Gorrell, an accomplished editor and proofreader in Toronto, for her opinion, she responded: 'The goal is 100 per cent. A realistic expectation is 90–100

per cent, depending on the complexity of the text. If the copyeditor is expected to work from before breakfast until after dinner in spite of incipient flu to compensate for the fact that the author is a year late because, after getting the advance, he (she) pursued endeavours of more immediate financial reward and lost interest in the committed ms and took up EST, you get what you get.' In giving the 95 per cent goal, I am assuming that the text will also be proofread and that the proofreader will pick up the few errors missed by the copyeditor.

4 I have based this discussion of the responsibilities of copyeditors, substantive editors, and stylistic editors on the categories set out in *Professional Editorial Standards*, published by the Editors' Association of Canada (http://www.editors.ca/resources/eac_publications/pes/index.html). It is useful to have clear descriptions of the myriad editorial tasks, though, in practice, titles and the division of responsibilities often vary, depending on the country and the publishing house. In the United States, for instance, what I have called substantive (or structural) editing is frequently referred to as developmental editing. See Scott Norton, *Developmental Editing: A Handbook for Freelancers, Authors, and Publishers* (Chicago: University of Chicago Press, 2009)..

5 Ellen Seligman, the publisher (fiction) and senior vice-president of McClelland & Stewart in Toronto, is regarded as one of the best fiction editors in the Western world. Her dedication to her authors and their books is legendary, and she numbers Margaret Atwood, Michael Ondaatje, Rohinton Mistry, and Anne Michaels among her stable. In 2008 she edited *Red Dog, Red Dog*, a first novel published by celebrated Canadian poet and memoirist Patrick Lane. 'Beginning in the summer of 2006 – and continuing off and on for the better part of a year – Seligman led Lane through a rigorous edit of his novel: word by word, sentence by sentence, paragraph by paragraph. Over one six-month stretch, beginning in February 2007, they spoke each day for at least three hours. There were, says Lane, some nine-hour sessions. 'Hands-on doesn't even begin to describe what Ellen does,' he says. 'Ellen inhabited my manuscript . . . She entered into the novel in a way that just stunned me.' Mark Medley, 'Mark of an Editor,' *National Post*, 21 February 2009.

6 Francis Flaherty, *The Elements of Story: Field Notes on Nonfiction Writing* (New York: Harper, 2009), and Constance Hale, *Sin and Syntax: How to Craft Wickedly Effective Prose* (New York: Broadway Books, 1999), are both fine guides to stylistic editing.

7 T.D. Max, 'Raymond Carver's Afterlife,' *The New York Times Magazine*, 9 August 1998. Raymond Carver, 'Beginners,' Carver, 'Letters to an Editor,' and 'Rough Crossings: The Cutting of Raymond Carver,' *New Yorker*, 23

December 2007; ' "Beginners" Edited: The Transformation of a Raymond Carver Classic,' *New Yorker* online, 1 January 2008.

8 With thanks to William Kaplan.

9 In the United States, the print-run range is much higher. Most trade publishers there require an initial print run of at least ten thousand copies.

10 Joan McGilvray, the former managing editor of Mc-Gill-Queen's University Press, is highly aware of the need for good author–editor relations but practical in her approach: 'One of the most important elements in the editing process is a good match between author and editor – something that's becoming increasingly difficult as the deadlines for production become shorter, since waiting for the more appropriate editor to become available may not be possible.' Email, February 2009.

11 Email from Jan Walter, February 2009.

12 Thanks to Dirk Algaier of Arnoldsche Art Publishers, Stuttgart, for his comments about the current state of editing in Europe (including the United Kingdom).

13 Email from Scott McIntyre, February 2009.

14 In the United States, too, the typical initial print run for a monograph published by a university press is four to five hundred copies. With digital printing now an option in both countries, the first printing may technically be smaller, to keep the inventory low. The five-to-eight-year projection of sales would still be in the four-to-eight-hundred range. The numbers for trade-type titles published by university presses are considerably higher, varying with the particular book.

15 For an excellent description of the way university presses select the books they publish, see Sanford Thatcher, 'The "Value Added" in Editorial Acquisitions,' *Journal of Scholarly Publishing* 30 (January 1999): 59–74.

16 Jean Wilson told me that, when she felt a manuscript was important but might have difficulty meeting the standards expected by peer reviewers, she would spend a few days working on it in the hope that it would be recommended for publication. 'And,' she continued, 'I've certainly made substantive suggestions to other authors even if I haven't edited and/or read the entire manuscript.' She says that it is essential for scholarly publishers to control the size of their lists and the areas in which they publish: 'There is a fine line between a publisher's being too big for the number of people it employs to do all that they might for a book or an author and being of a size where, even beyond the acquisitions editor, an author feels there is some personal and immediate attention being paid to her or his book.' Email from Jean Wilson, February 2009.

17 With thanks for her wit and honesty to Joan McGilvray.

18 The few university presses that publish a separate list of trade-type books – for example, Yale University Press – sometimes allow for more substantive/stylistic editing by the in-house acquisitions editors for a selection of these titles. The degree of editing depends on the condition of the manuscript and the budget for the book. Even at smaller presses – Penn State, for instance – some substantive editing is done for books that are given a trade discount. In a few cases, the author may be asked to arrange for this editing by a suitable freelancer before the final manuscript is delivered to the press for the standard copyediting. With thanks to Jenya Weinreb and Jeffrey Schier at Yale University Press and an anonymous reviewer for this information.

19 Email from Jeffrey Miller, February 2009.

20 Email from Jennifer Latham, February 2009.

21 Email from Anthony Luengo, February 2009.

22 Meredith Chilton, editor-in-chief, *Fired by Passion: Vienna Baroque Porcelain of Claudius Innocentius du Paquier* (Stuttgart: Arnoldsche Art Publishers, 2009), in collaboration with the Melinda and Paul Sullivan Foundation for the Decorative Arts. The September publication date coincided with an exhibition at the Metropolitan Museum of Art, New York.

23 Editors who work on these collaborative projects must be able to condense essays by 40 to 60 per cent at times, without losing essential information or balance or style, because many authors deliver texts that are well over the word count allotted to them. Editors at the first edition of the *Canadian Encyclopedia* (Edmonton: Hurtig, 1985), for instance, requested a total of 3 million words from its hundreds of expert authors. Collectively, they delivered 10 million words.

24 Email from Meredith Chilton, February 2009.

25 Email from Jack Granatstein, February 2009.

26 Email from John English, February 2009.

27 Email from Richard Gwyn, February 2009.

28 Email from Sarah Jennings, February 2009.

29 Email from Meredith Chilton, February 2009.

30 Internationally recognized author Margaret Atwood welcomes feedback from her favourite editors and publishers in the many countries in which her books are published. Once she had completed the penultimate draft of *The Year of the Flood* (2009), for instance, she met with four of these women in a hotel room in Toronto and presented them all with a copy of the manuscript, each box individually wrapped and ribboned in colours to suit the recipient. In due course they sent her their various comments

and suggestions, and Atwood completed her final draft. Confidential source.

31 See James Adams, 'Publish and Your Book Will Probably Perish,' *The Globe and Mail*, Toronto ed., 7 February 2009; Don Gillmor, 'The Blockbuster Imperative,' *Toronto Life*, March 2009, 37–40.

32 Email from John English, February 2009.

33 Perhaps this recognition is about to come. Beginning in early 2011, the *New York Times Magazine* added the editor's name on the contents page below the author's name for every article published in each issue.

4 Juggling Expectations: The Copyeditor's Roles and Responsibilities

AMY EINSOHN

Copyeditors are jugglers, attending to the needs and expectations of publishers, authors, and prospective readers. These constituencies share some common interests – the desire for an error-free publication, chief among them – but they are not equally concerned about the who, what, when, where, and how of each stage of the publishing process. Additional concerns, and conflicts, arise in academic publishing, where, compared to trade publishing, print runs are smaller, budgets and profit margins are tighter, and intellectual aspirations are more exacting.

As the copyeditor tries to balance contending needs and expectations, each of the constituencies makes an overt or covert plea for supremacy. Usually the publisher is paying the bill – either the in-house copyeditor's salary or the freelance copyeditor's fees – and everyone knows that those who pay the piper call the tune. Most often it is the publisher who selects the copyeditor for the project, defines the copyeditor's assignment, and evaluates the copyeditor's performance. Both salaried and freelance copyeditors recognize that the publisher is also a source for future projects, referrals for work, job references, and other perks. Moreover, like most people in the publishing industry, copyeditors trust that publishers – represented by in-house staff, including sponsoring editors, managing editors, and production editors – have greater expertise than any other party in matters related to editorial style, book design, and production.

But surely, another voice argues, the academic author who has laboured hard and long, whose tenure and promotion prospects may depend on this one book, and whose name will appear prominently on its cover, should command the copyeditor's strongest allegiance. Authors, however, are typically at a disadvantage (unless the author is hiring the copyeditor directly) because the author's relationship with the copyeditor is mediated by the publisher. The publisher's production editor not only sets the terms of the copyeditor's engagement but also frames the copyeditor's introduction to the manuscript and to the author: 'This is a very high-profile, important book for us' or 'We had high hopes for this book, but the author just didn't come through'; 'This author has always been a delight to work with: cooperative, focused, attentive to deadlines, good sense of humor' or 'Kid gloves, please. This author is likely to resent and resist all but minor interventions.' The mediation continues throughout the project, with the publisher deciding whether the copyeditor may directly contact an author with questions or whether the copyeditor is to route all author communications through an in-house editor. The copyeditor's allegiance to the author is also constrained by the industry-wide commonplace that scholars are experts in their subject matter but naïve about the worldly business of publishing. The author's ideas and industry have brought the manuscript into being, but the publishing pros are apt to treat the author as a rookie in matters related to the making and marketing of books.

Also competing for primacy are the prospective readers, those thousands or tens of thousands of inquisitive souls who will come to the text over many years and decades, even after the author and the copyeditor have returned to dust. Certainly these readers, by virtue of their numbers and their perennial diligence, deserve pride of place. But precisely because these readers are so many, so abstract, and so unknowable, the copyeditor's theoretical fealty to them often founders in practice. Although a few academic titles have 'trade potential' or 'course adoption' possibilities, most of these books and monographs are intended for a small elite readership composed of scholars and graduate students. In the humanities, in particular, scholarly communities have become so specialized that even those copyeditors who once attended graduate school in the author's field are unlikely to know about the newest trends, critical approaches, current topics of consensus and of debate, and fashionable allusions and jargon. And how does one begin to predict the reading habits, research practices, and informational needs of future generations? Those copyeditors who aspire to champion the needs of readers may find that their own education and temperament have not prepared them to anticipate the desiderata of scholarly readers.

Other constituencies may put in an appearance. For a translation or a scholarly edition, the copyeditor will hope to honour the original author and that author's work. For a collection of pieces by many hands, the chorus of stakeholders swells yet again. Copyeditors also labour in the presence of benevolent or fearsome ghosts: a high school English teacher, a freshman composition instructor, one or more publishing mentors, and the authors of favourite usage books.

In this essay, I explore some of the problems copyeditors encounter in juggling these relationships. Even when everyone involved has the best of intentions and the strongest of editorial and interpersonal skills, trade-offs are inevitable because resources (time, money, effort) are finite, and yet there is no end to the work that could be undertaken to improve a manuscript. Throughout I use the qualifiers *typically, usually, often, some, many*, or *most* in describing the activities of copyeditors, academic presses, and scholarly authors because practices are far from uniform across the industry. I know of no broad studies or surveys of copyeditors in scholarly publishing, and so my essay relies largely on my own experience and that of friends, colleagues, and students.[1]

What Copyeditors Do

Scholarly authors spend years researching, drafting, and revising their manuscripts and then another year or more locating a publisher who will produce, manufacture, and distribute the final printed or electronic document. Copyeditors always arrive late to the party – long after many key decisions have been made about the book's content, organization, scope, length, intended audience, and marketing plan. After working intensively with the manuscript for four to six weeks, copyeditors leave early, before paging, indexing, proofreading, and other pre-press quality-control activities, months before manufacturing, and long before the reviews and sales numbers come in.

Some copyediting is done by in-house staff and by part-time, retired, or former in-house editors working as freelancers. But most copyediting is done by outside freelancers, many of whom live far from the presses that contract for their services. Now that email has overtaken the telephone as the principal medium of business communication, copyeditors may not even regularly converse with anyone in-house. Those who live nearby and do maintain personal contact are usually privy to only a sliver of the organization's operations, and they meet just a handful of the staff. Some presses make a special effort to train, coach, and acculturate their freelancers, but most freelancers have few opportunities to learn about the publisher's activities, customs, and mores.

Although copyeditors are latecomers to the project and outsiders to the press, they become intimate with the manuscript. Copyeditors spend more time than anyone other than the author wrestling with the final text, devoting ninety or a hundred billable hours to what will become a three-hundred-page book.[2] Complex projects and poorly written or poorly prepared manuscripts require more time still.

What do copyeditors do with all that time? Above all, they read – and they read very, very slowly, syllable by syllable. Often, they appear to be doing little else: it can take just as long – or longer – to decide to leave a sentence alone as to suggest a change in it. Despite the disincentives (productivity! page rates! deadlines!), a conscientious copyeditor may think better of a change made only an hour earlier, and go back to delete or revise it.

When it comes to defining *copyediting*, all of us in book publishing are Humpty Dumptys.[3] *Copyedit* may mean 'impose house style regarding hyphenation' and 'attend to the grammatical infelicities' but also 'prune the deadwood' and 'transmute this jargon into gold.' We discuss levels of copyediting (light, medium, and heavy) and types of editing (mechanical editing, language editing, and content editing). We even have a term – *editorial judgment* – that means 'knowing all the denotations of *edit* and *copyedit* and selecting those most suitable to a given manuscript in light of the schedule and budget, the intended audience, the author's writing ability, temperament, and availability for revisions, the prominence of the title in next season's list, and the standards, shibboleths, and pet peeves of the in-house editor who will review the copyediting.'

Under the rubric of mechanical editing, the copyeditor corrects typographical errors; corrects or queries inconsistencies and variations in spelling, capitalization, punctuation, use of numbers, treatment of abbreviations, styling of lists, and the like; and corrects or queries inconsistencies and omissions in bibliographical entries and reference citations. The copyeditor reconciles the parts of the manuscript by reading the table of contents against the chapters, matching footnotes to bibliographical entries, and checking the alphabetical and numerical sequencing of items. Copyeditors are also expected to coax Microsoft Word and other programs into doing complex tricks related to templates, formatting, paragraph and character styles, global search-and-replace with wildcards, and redlining.

The scope of these mechanical changes – and which mechanical matters are to be left to the author's discretion regardless of house style –

are determined by the publisher. The copyeditor is told which editorial style manual to consult (e.g., *The Chicago Manual of Style*) and is given a supplementary in-house style guide. The shortest of these in-house guides consists of a page or two of additions and exceptions to *Chicago*, but some of the guides exceed thirty pages and include exceptions to the exceptions as well as a prized set of zombie rules.[4] The copyeditor may be supplied with a short sample edit – perhaps the first ten pages of the manuscript – done by an in-house editor.

Academic authors usually appreciate these mechanical interventions, which some have compared to a housekeeper's tidying up or a hotel maid's placing of mints on the pillow. Conflicts occasionally erupt over variant spellings, the placement of commas, or other mechanical minutiae. Jacques Barzun, for example, has protested his publishers' miserliness when it comes to hyphens: 'Never mind the [*Chicago*] *Manual* – it isn't holy scripture; I haven't joined a religious sect and taken an oath to be ruled by a book. My creed is that I put my name only to what I write; I write as I like; and I like hyphens – especially when they make reading easier.'[5] Stets may be hurled at seemingly innocent mechanical changes should an author find the copyeditor to be inconsistent, fickle, or unbearably nitpicky, or if the author feels that the copyeditor is challenging the author's authority or writing skills.

In two other areas – language editing and content editing – the copyeditor ideally does as little or as much as the production editor requests. Some presses have developed detailed descriptions of levels of edit, while others give only very general instructions and trust the copyeditor's judgment. Of course, no production editor can anticipate every problem that may arise in a manuscript, much less provide detailed guidance for handling those problems, and so copyeditors are left to do as much or as little as time, budget, conscientiousness, and conscience permit. Indeed, people new to academic publishing are often surprised to learn just how much may be left to the copyeditor's discretion and judgment.

Language editing may include pruning wordy patches, substituting stronger verbs for weaker ones or more vivid adjectives for blander ones, eliminating gender-biased language, and remediating authorial tics. Few authors pride themselves on being unclear, ambiguous, and incoherent, and most writers appreciate having a copyeditor call their attention to unintentional repetitions or overuse of a syntactical gambit. But some writers are distrustful of the interventions of an anonymous hand. More than any other writer, Barzun has made us aware of the social, economic, intellectual, and aesthetic chasm between the internationally known erudite scholar and the pesky copyeditor, whom he characterizes as a 'laborious mole' whose 'gratuitous tampering' and 'promiscuous depredation' are conducted to ensure a 'perfection in trifles.'[6] His complaints about the rigidity of house style, however, are better levelled at the publisher, who sets the policy, than at the copyeditor who merely follows it.

Content editing includes querying internal inconsistencies ('Population given as 30,000 on p. 45, but 38,000 on p. 92; please reconcile'), some double-checking of well-known facts, and the querying or fixing of gaps in logic and organization. Copyeditors may point out some broader structural problems, such as overly long detours, straw-man arguments, and excessive signposting.[7] They may suggest that the author add definitions, expand explanations, or provide more background information to assist less-sophisticated readers. In non-fiction manuscripts, copyeditors are also expected to call the publisher's and the author's attention to text and images that might pose a legal problem in the areas of libel, invasion of privacy, obscenity, and copyright (e.g., quoted passages that might require permission to reprint). Copyeditors are not expected to render lawyerly judgments about these matters, but they are usually given guidelines for identifying passages to flag for review by others.

As publishing lore has it, there was once a glorious age in which acquisitions editors (also called sponsoring editors) provided exquisite developmental and substantive editing for many of their authors. Whether that tale is true or apocryphal, budget and time pressures long ago forced scholarly acquisitions editors to abandon page-by-page work on manuscripts. Scott Norton sketches this history in his preface to *Developmental Editing* and concludes that in-house developmental editing has become 'a luxurious impulse rarely indulged.'[8] Instead, most presses allocate some developmental and substantive responsibilities to their most-trusted, most-experienced copyeditors.

Some copyeditors are assigned additional tasks, such as applying templates and formatting to distinct elements of the text (e.g., epigraphs, extracts, and headings); double-checking the accuracy of URLs; calling the author's attention to online sources whose permanency may be in doubt; and spotting incomplete and omitted attributions by running suspect passages through a search engine.[9]

Just as no two books are alike, no two copyediting projects are alike. Every manuscript requires the copyeditor to devise a strategy that will serve the three constituencies and that will suit the manuscript (as a piece of writing) as well as the copyeditor's vocational ambitions and personal needs. All of the sentence-by-sentence decisions are made within the contours of this overall vision of the manuscript. Most copyeditors also appreciate the book as a physical object, and they will call attention, for example, to a complex array or table that requires reconceptualization if it is to fit nicely on the text page.

Each project has its own budget, schedule, editorial challenges (read: problems), and cast of characters. Over time, experienced copyeditors develop tactics, tools, and procedures that can be reused or adapted. But the copyeditor's first task on a new project is to survey the manuscript and hazard an educated guess about what kind of work is to be done. The production editor usually states the major objectives and constraints in a cover memo, but much is left to the copyeditor's improvisation and editorial judgment. On first paging through the manuscript, the copyeditor is both assessing the words on the page and imagining the author, forming quick opinions about the author's abilities as a writer, the author's ego investment in the manuscript, and the author's general intelligence, carelessness or carefulness about details, and likely response to queries and to critique. All these assumptions about the author will inform the copyeditor's page-by-page decisions about the manuscript.

Copyeditors' decisions are also shaped by their self-definition of their role. Is copyediting an art, a craft, a profession, or an überclerical trade? Some copyeditors view themselves principally as the guardians of English grammar, syntax, usage, and diction; others speak in terms of providing publishers and authors with value-added or quality-control services. Some conceive of themselves primarily as the author's coach, teammate, or silent pseudo-collaborator. Yet others wear the badge of the reader's advocate. Most copyeditors have heard at least one story in which a copyeditor or proofreader rode in to rescue an author and publisher from a fatal error that everyone else had missed – or they have heard a tale in which a copyeditor failed to ride in, contributing to the recall and pulping of books or to adverse legal action against the author or the publisher. Like other fantasies, the dream of making (or missing) The Great Catch may foster functional behaviour or dysfunctional behaviour.

Flaws and idiosyncrasies in the copyeditor's professional personality exert their effects. A passive-aggressive copyeditor overqueries and overedits, all the while convinced that he is 'just being helpful and careful.' An insecure or defensive copyeditor writes long, tiresome queries that cite multiple authorities for even the most trivial points, in an effort to browbeat the author into submission and forestall any objection. The immature copyeditor peppers the author with queries intended to suggest that the difficulty lies in the author's obscure writing style, rather than in the copyeditor's discomfort with an arcane subject or method. The stylistically anxious copyeditor is likely to hammer down any unusual locution and insist on enforcing all her favourite schoolbook maxims; nervousness about departing from the style manual leads her to make unnecessary changes (some of which introduce errors where there were none). The fretful copyeditor's fixation on trivial incidents and examples may prompt rounds of fact-checking gotcha ('Please supply the date the hangnail was removed').

Publisher–Copyeditor Relations

In scholarly publishing, like any other business, the balance of power between employer and employee (or independent contractor) is unequal. The publisher's dealings with the copyeditor are handled by a production editor, an acquisitions editor, or a managing editor; copyeditors may also have transactions with a designer, a permissions associate, and even a representative from the marketing department. Four chief areas of concern are quality, collegiality, cost, and control.

Quality

Scholarly publishers need copyeditors who are skilled, accurate, and reliable, people who can meet high editorial standards and firm deadlines. Stating deadlines is simple, but setting editorial standards is difficult: Is there an accuracy target (no more than x errors per twenty pages)? A set of unforgivable errors of omission or commission? An overall pass-fail measure? Extra credit for glowing praise (well-deserved or not) from the author?

Copyeditors' uncertainties about what the standards are and how their work will be evaluated feed into the performance anxiety inherent to the work. Copyediting is like taking a surprise English-skills quiz every hour of every workday, with every manuscript bringing unexpected conundrums. In addition, copyeditors strive to remember which usage peeves are dear to which production editors.

A copyeditor whose language preferences are more conservative than those of the production editor may come to believe that she – the proud outsider – is the only one upholding the Grandeur of the language, while others have been misled by expediency, burnout, ignorance, or poor taste. In turn, the more liberal production editor is apt to believe that the conservative copyeditor is misapplying resources – wasting time and money and squandering the author's goodwill – in a crusade to enforce idiosyncratic or antique preferences. Sometimes the roles are reversed: the conservative production editor bemoans the low standards of the copyediting pool, and the liberal copyeditor winces when asked to enforce prescriptivist bosh. Even when the production editor and the copyeditor have similar standards, there is room for disagreement about how to implement those standards and how lightly or heavily to intervene on a particular manuscript.

Broader concerns about quality surfaced after several trade publishers were snookered by authors who represented their novels (or highly embellished autobiographies) to be memoirs. Those authorial deceits focused public attention on trade publishers' rudimentary approach to the fact-checking and vetting of non-fiction manuscripts: If these publishers were unable to detect massive intentional fraud, what could one assume about their ability to detect small or unintentional factual errors?

In academic publishing, errors in an author's facts and assertions may be pointed out by the acquisitions editor, the outside readers (referees), members of the press's editorial board, and those of the author's colleagues who see portions of the manuscript in progress. Some trade and scholarly copyeditors attempt to do cursory research to check easily verifiable, well-known facts when they spot an internal discrepancy in the manuscript or when something strikes them as odd. But the copyediting budget and schedule do not allow for the rigorous fact-checking that the more fastidious magazines conduct,[10] and the boilerplate warranties and indemnities section of a book publishing contract place full responsibility for the accuracy of the content on the author.

Collegiality

Scholarly publishers treasure copyeditors who are good team players, those who do not require excessive hand-holding, who have good 'people skills,' and who understand their role in the publishing process.

Copyeditors who lack the needed measure of professional self-confidence, those who ask too many naïve questions, and those who repeatedly overreach tend to receive fewer projects. The overreaching is not a matter of overediting per se, but a matter of self-aggrandizement or self-importance that may reflect a copyeditor's misplaced priorities, his misunderstanding of the boundaries of the task, or his insecurities concerning his own educational attainment or intellectual firepower.

How a copyeditor responds to criticism also figures into a publisher's assessment of the editor's collegiality. The best copyeditors are always learning new things about the English language, editorial conventions, publishing procedures, and allied matters. Just as important, they are continuously discovering that they must unlearn information that they thought was true or useful but that is not. This body of misinformation may include principles they have misremembered or misunderstood, conventions they mistook for set-in-stone rules, editorial styles that have become passé, and pet peeves that their misguided teachers once presented as gospel.

The mutual respect between in-house staff and freelance copyeditors may be tinged with a dram of mutual jealousy: the staffer covets the freelancer's independence, schedule, and freedom from office politics, and the freelancer covets the staffer's salary, benefits package, job security, and professional status.

Cost

Copyeditors who enjoy working for academic publishers cite the pleasures of working on serious, worthwhile projects and teaming up with dedicated professionals, but most scholarly publishers are hard-pressed to pay their best copyeditors enough to retain them over time. Some publishers try to compensate by offering non-monetary rewards: appreciation and recognition, opportunities for training and development, referrals to authors who are seeking to hire editorial consultants, discounts on software, or guarantees of a specific number of hours of work per year.

Fees may be a sore point even for those copyeditors who are satisfied with the money they earn. Most publishers do not publicize their fee schedules, leaving each copyeditor to negotiate his or her own arrangements. Many copyeditors worry, 'Am I settling for too little? Are other copyeditors getting more?' or they wonder which pricing formula – page rate, hourly rate, or flat project rate – would be best for them.

Academic copyeditors have seen the downward pressure on wages that offshoring has effected in other sectors of the publishing industry, and they worry about pricing themselves out of the market altogether.[11] Veteran copyeditors have seen some publishers transfer the cost and responsibility for proofreading to their authors, and they wonder whether publishers will try to do the same with copyediting. All freelancers worry about how much each new generation of computer hardware and software will cost them (in cash, in down time, and in unpaid hours for training and trouble-shooting) and whether 'smarter' software has the potential to nibble away at their livelihood.

Control

Issues of control, or ownership of the editing process, arise when a copyeditor believes that he has a better understanding than the publisher does of what kind of editing the manuscript needs. Occasionally, the production editor will agree with some of the copyeditor's points, but more often the production editor realizes that the copyeditor is overreaching, overstepping, or overreacting. The production editor, who may be handling six or ten projects at a time, knows that some manuscripts, for whatever reason, are below average and are not worth exceptional investments of time or energy. Or the in-house editors have been warned that a particular author is difficult to handle, on a tight schedule, or confronting serious family or health problems. Unaware of these particulars, the copyeditor may make special pleadings (for a longer schedule or a larger budget) or impose unnecessarily on the production editor's and the author's time.

Disagreements also arise when the copyeditor mistakenly believes that she is the only person other than the author to have thought carefully about the content of the manuscript. True, sometimes a troublesome patch escapes detection by the acquisitions editor, the outside readers, and the editorial board, but often the problem is that a relatively inexperienced copyeditor is straining to prove her mettle by raising an argument about a point that had been discussed (and rejected) earlier in the process. Similar misunderstandings arise when a copyeditor views the author's final manuscript as a canvas for her own re-creation, as a starting point rather than a final stage in manuscript preparation.

Many projects involve a minor tug-of-war over the level of edit, with the production editor specifying less work (lower fees, quicker turnaround, reduced likelihood of complaints from the author) and the copyeditor eager to do more because he has developed a proprietary feeling about *his* manuscript.

Ownership can also be a problem when an author rejects a copyeditor's suggestion and the copyeditor asks the production editor to intervene. Sometimes the production editor will try to persuade the author to reconsider the copyeditor's suggestion or an alternate suggestion. In other cases, the production editor will side with the author, concluding that the copyeditor was making a misguided effort to 'protect' the author from statements that are within his authorial prerogative to make. For example, a well-meaning copyeditor may propose watering down an author's strongly stated opinions under the misimpression that scholarship must be bland and balanced, or that scholarly debate must conform to a journalistic fairness doctrine. Or a copyeditor may go overboard implementing the publisher's policies on bias-free language, revising sentences that contain *he* or *his*, no matter that the particular sentences do not promote sexist stereotypes and do not demean any group in any way.

Author–Copyeditor Relations

In academic publishing, the author may be a newly hooded PhD who assumes that turning a dissertation into a published volume is a quick clerical task; or a young assistant professor struggling to secure one more publication before facing a tenure committee; or a senior professor who has published shelves of journal articles, monographs, and books. Although all of these authors are talented scholars and researchers, some have weak writing skills and others underestimate the number of drafts required to produce a final manuscript. A few readily admit to their shortcomings, but many are either unaware of their weaknesses or are convinced that their doctoral degree and publishing contract testify to the eloquence of their prose.

Articulate and abstruse alike, all scholars have had at least one gruesome experience when someone (dissertation chair, colleague, spouse, editor) commented on a final draft – or they have had perfectly ordinary experiences that they perceived as gruesome.[12] The relationship between draft-writer and draft-reader is an oddly intimate relationship, but an intimacy in which only one soul is bared. Having one's work copyedited can be especially harrowing for the author who is overly defensive, finicky, controlling, or indecisive. Some authors assume that the copyeditor's job is to do no more than 'sprinkle a few commas' and correct the typos. Other authors are eager to have an extended conversation about worrisome passages, alternative wordings, and paragraphs that occurred to them the day before yesterday. When the new text constitutes an improvement, most copyeditors are happy to facilitate the changes, even if they are working on page rates and hadn't priced in the additional time. When the author is tinkering aimlessly, seemingly unwilling to let go of the manuscript, even the most sympathetic and generous copyeditor may become snappish.

Copyeditor–author relations are further shaped by the stereotypes that the parties bring to the project, images that may complement or supersede the parties' life experiences. First-time authors have heard war stories from colleagues about 'that insufferable fussbudget who shredded my work' or 'that extremely diligent perfectionist who helped me vastly improve my manuscript.' Copyeditors who have attended graduate school may have a realistic picture of today's faculty, but almost everyone has been infected by the caricatures of the absent-minded professor, the jargon-sprouting solipsist, the ill-adapted genius, the elbow-patched pedant, and the ivory-tower monologist.

Both authors and copyeditors respond to the social dynamics of the relationship. The parties rarely meet, but they form images and opinions of one another from written documents (the manuscript, the queries, email exchanges, websites) and the occasional phone conversation. Any pairing of men and women may invite some sex-based role-playing or stereotyping. Differences in age, cultural touchstones, and computer literacy may be trivial or significant, but the author is usually better educated and higher on the career ladder and the socioeconomic scale. Other significant differences come to the fore when the scholar is not a native speaker of English.

Conflicting opinions about what constitutes good or acceptable expository writing can be particularly difficult to negotiate. Because any sentence can be rewritten (and arguably 'improved' thereby), copyeditors must learn to resist the impulse to tinker. Ideally, the copyeditor's palate is broad enough to appreciate a variety of academic styles. But some copyeditors cling fiercely to their freshman composition handbooks, to favourite passages from Strunk and White, or to a 'plain English' creed designed for insurance policies and rental agreements, not literary criticism. By nature or by training, copyeditors often value consistency, brevity, economy, and simplicity, but many gifted writers view variety, detail, nuance, and pleonasm as equal or higher virtues. Writing that may strike some as 'bad' – as lazy, careless, or inept – may more charitably be described by others as 'difficult,' which encompasses the experimental, innovative, subversive, philosophical, unusual, and irreverent.[13] Some bad writers, of course, hide behind the mantle of difficulty, and critics have long disparaged much academic prose as turgid, obscure, and impenetrable – whether by design, inattention, or ineptitude.

A perennial complaint from authors concerns the hurry-up-and-wait production schedule, but that is beyond the copyeditor's control. Typically the author hears little from the publisher for months after delivering the final manuscript. A sudden phone call or email announces that the manuscript has been launched, and a schedule is proposed: The copyedited manuscript will be ready for review in five or six weeks, and the press sincerely hopes that the author can turn it around within a month or so, though there is no way to predict whether it will require ten-hour workweeks or thirty-hour workweeks to meet that deadline.

Even as the author starts to clear time for reviewing the copyediting, all sorts of people are vying for attention. The acquisitions assistant, the production editor, the marketing rep, a publicist – everyone is asking for information (lists for review copies, schedule for appearances at conferences) or for a perfunctory approval (jacket design and copy, catalog copy). These tasks are pleasant, and the author is elated that things are finally moving forward.

But the copyeditor breaks the momentum by requiring the author to take what feels like a large step backward. The author must return for one more hard look at the manuscript, a review that invites second-guessing and self-doubt. A chapter that sparkled when the author last read it, now on rereading (for the fifth or fifteenth time) seems dull. The author may be tempted to rewrite a section to take into account a recent book or article, or may seize on the notion of adding new art, not thinking about the time it will take to obtain permissions from the copyright holders.

The author's second-guessing of the manuscript is roiled by the copyeditor's second-guessing of the manuscript. For the first few chapters, the author feels flattered that someone so intelligent and perspicacious has thought about every sentence of the text, and the author reveres the copyeditor who has found and corrected dozens of silly errors. This thrill fades as the author notices how long it takes to think through each of the copyeditor's discretionary changes and queries. The internal monologue becomes tiresome: 'Is there something incorrect or unclear about my sentence, or is it just not the sentence the copyeditor would have written? Is my ego preventing me from seeing the problem? Should I just write *stet*, or do I owe the copyeditor an explanation?

Should I put this aside until I can come at it with fresh eyes? But when will my eyes ever be fresh again?'

No matter how excellent and tactful the copyeditor is, an author will reject at least some of the proposed changes. Ego plays a part ('My name will be on the cover, so the words inside may as well be mine'), but so do time constraints. At some point, most authors realize that nothing good will come from trying to re-revise the copyeditor's proposed revisions.

Other disagreements between scholarly authors and copyeditors relate to the value, placement, format, and length of complex apparatus or commentary. An author, for example, may argue for footnotes (to reduce page turning) in a hearty point size (to reduce eye strain), while the production editor and the copyeditor are thinking about the ease and elegance of page makeup or the cost savings that come from using smaller type to reduce the number of pages allocated to ancillary material. Misunderstandings may arise when a copyeditor is unfamiliar with the range of legitimate scholarly conventions for styling source notes and bibliographies for non-standard materials (e.g., letters, unpublished documents, foreign and antique folios, ephemera, collections of inscriptions), or when a copyeditor does not know the conventions for styling the special elements of a variorum edition. Although time-consuming, these kinds of localized squabbles tend to be productive in that they require authors and editors to exchange information and opinions, re-examine their initial assumptions, and weigh alternative considerations.

Once in a great while, a turf war erupts. Authors, naturally, have proprietary feelings about their work, and some respond badly in the face of queries that have a critical edge. Copyeditors, eager to do a good job, may stumble and substitute their vision of the manuscript for the author's; or unseasoned copyeditors may be so fearful of being accused of missing errors that they mark up passages that were fine as they stood. To ward off overinvolvement, experienced editors often chant what is called the copyeditor's mantra: 'It's not my book.'[14] In the worst of cases, one side or the other calls in the production editor to referee the dispute.

Reader–Copyeditor Relations

Authors and publishers of non-fiction take care not to pitch the work too high or too low for the intended readership; one does not want to confuse readers or bore them or patronize them. For each non-fiction work, decisions must be made about appropriate explanatory material and heuristic tools: how much background information to include, which terms to define, whether to include biographical or geographical annotations, how to handle passages in foreign languages, or whether to modernize the spelling of quotations from primary and secondary sources.

Most scholarly authors keep these matters in mind while drafting and revising their manuscript. But a few surrender to their enthusiasms – or are overwhelmed by their material and their notecards – and lose sight of the reader. Nonetheless, even if it doesn't show on every page of the final manuscript, the scholarly author knows more than the copyeditor does about the needs and expectations of the intended audience. This exclusion from the author-reader dyad can be disorienting for copyeditors used to working in trade non-fiction publishing, where copyeditors usually view themselves as representatives of the intended audience.

Unfamiliarity with the subject matter obviously hampers copyeditors, as does an imperfect understanding of the scholarly enterprise. Most copyeditors can make an imaginative leap to identify with scholarly readers, but some copyeditors find themselves bored by certain kinds of scholarship – frustrated with its painstaking pace, indifferent to its goals, and unhappy with its methods. They project their own impatience onto the readers and campaign for reducing, simplifying, or eliminating portions of the manuscript that strike them as 'needlessly difficult.' Some recommend breaking apart long sentences and long paragraphs; some dismiss all unusual words and unusual phrasing as 'pretentious'; and some suggest deleting much of the 'small-print clutter' (footnotes, bibliographies, tables, statistics) and condensing the front or back matter. In contrast, the wisest copyeditors realize that the intended readers are far better versed in the recondite subject matter than the copyeditor is, and they avoid suggesting changes that give the impression of talking down to the audience.

In the age of Google Books, Kindle, e-this-and-that-ery, everyone in academic publishing is trying to anticipate how technology may affect the dissemination of scholarship and the needs of a new generation of scholarly readers. For example, Kate Wittenberg, former director of the Electronic Publishing Initiative at Columbia University, proposes that scholarly authors and publishers ask themselves, 'Must scholarly narrative necessarily be presented in linear form? Are there new ways to present an "authorial voice" while allowing readers to structure the way in which they encounter a work? Are images and data supplementary evidence for points made in the text, or can they now become central organizing structures of a work?'[15] She urges acquisitions editors at academic presses to view themselves as 'researchers who work with authors in creating new models of scholarship rather than as staff who react to scholarly work once it is submitted in completed form for publication' and advises these editors to 'think more creatively about the organization and presentation of information in terms of how readers encounter their publications.'[16] As these new forms of publication are adopted, authors and all categories of editors will be required to reconceptualize their picture of scholarly readers and to develop new skills to serve them.

Towards Better Juggling

Copyeditors will always be jugglers, and almost everyone engaged in academic publishing could suggest measures that would improve the performance, job satisfaction, and retention of academic copyeditors. Here are three suggestions for helping copyeditors better understand the needs and expectations of academic publishers and authors.

Levels-of-Edit Checklists

Every academic publisher should develop detailed definitions for the various levels and types of editing that its copyeditors might be expected to do.[17] For each manuscript, the production editor would check off those statements that best describe the desired level of edit. The completed checklist would be given to the copyeditor as part of the transmittal memo. The use of such checklists would help copyeditors work more efficiently and with greater confidence that they will meet the publishers' expectations. A disciplined approach to types and levels of edit is also likely to reduce author complaints about meddlesome tinkering.

Sample Edits

Publishers of academic books and monographs should adjust their standard production schedules to allow the copyeditor to present the author with a sample edit of, say, twenty pages; the sample edit would be skipped only in special circumstances. Sample edits are useful for the copyeditor, the author, and the publisher: they help establish trust and goodwill, and they enable all parties to fine-tune their expectations. Sample edits also give the production editor and the copyeditor an opportunity to see how the author responds to editing and queries.

Author's Style Memos

Publishers of academic books and monographs should encourage authors to submit, for the copyeditor's use, (1) a brief memo that lists important or unusual style points and (2) photocopies of short samples of published works that the author used as a model in formatting special elements (e.g., references, variorum text, commentary, headnotes, and other apparatus). The request for such material may, in and of itself, encourage authors to think more carefully about mechanical matters when preparing their final manuscript. Possession of these materials is also likely to save production editors, copyeditors, and designers much needless hand-wringing and busywork.

NOTES

1 Carol Fisher Saller offers a vivid picture of the work life of an in-house editor at an academic press in *The Subversive Copy Editor* (Chicago: University of Chicago Press, 2009), but her book is also based on personal experience. Somewhat dated, but still of interest, are the accounts of copyeditors and manuscript editors in several of the essays in Gerald Gross, ed., *Editors on Editing*, 3rd ed. (New York: Grove Press, 1993).

2 Each copyeditor has his or her own procedures, but most make two complete passes through the manuscript, with additional passes, as needed, to check for consistency in batches of selected items (tables, figure captions, footnotes, bibliographies). After the author has reviewed the copyedited manuscript, either the copyeditor or a production editor will spend, on average, another eight to fifteen hours incorporating the author's responses (cleanup editing) and preparing the final files for the compositor.

3 In chapter 6 of *Through the Looking-Glass*, Humpty Dumpty insists, 'When I use a word . . . it means just what I choose it to mean – neither more nor less.' The confusion is compounded by the use of *copyediting* (also styled *copy editing* and *copy-editing*) in journalism to refer to responsibilities that include

ensuring balance and objectivity; fact-checking; averting libel; writing head-lines, captions, and teasers; and cutting articles to fit the hole budgeted for them. An additional wrinkle: In different eras and in different sectors of the book publishing industry, practitioners have used the terms *line editing* and *manuscript editing*. *Line editing* usually refers to a round of revisions proposed by an in-house editor who is focusing on literary style and a piece's overall structure and shape; mechanical issues (capitalization, hy-phenation, spelling, etc.) are left for a subsequent round of copyediting. In contrast, *manuscript editing* most often refers to copyediting that incor-porates greater attention to language, structure, and shape than 'mere' copyediting.

4 *Zombie rule* is Arnold Zwicky's term for a usage peeve that persists 'no mat-ter how many times, and how thoroughly, it is executed by authorities': 'Five More Thoughts on the *That* Rule,' Language Log, 22 May 2005, posted at http://158.130.17.5/~myl/languagelog/archives/002189.html. Copyedi-tors who work for several presses must remember which zombie rules and kernels of prescriptivist poppycock (another Language Log coinage) each press enforces. One publisher may insist, 'Do not allow *hopefully* as a sen-tence modifier,' while another demands, 'Allow *while* only in its temporal sense, not as a synonym for *whereas* or *although*.'

5 'Dialogue in C-Sharp,' in *A Word or Two Before You Go . . . : Brief Essays on Language* (Middletown, CT: Wesleyan University Press, 1986), 116.

6 These phrases are taken from Barzun's screed against overly zealous copyeditors, 'Behind the Blue Pencil: Censorship or Creeping Creativity?' [1985] in *On Writing, Editing, and Publishing*, 2nd ed. (Chicago: University of Chicago Press, 1986); the 'laborious mole' appears on p. 111, 'gratuitous tampering' on p. 110, 'promiscuous depredation' on p. 112, and 'perfection in trifles' on p. 104. In some classical and neoclassical instances of the trope, the laborious mole is also blind: 'The blind laborious mole / In winding mazes works her hidden hole' (Dryden's translation of Virgil's *Georgics*) and 'Poor, busy, blind, laborious mole; / Still let him puzzle, read, explain, / Oppugn, remark, and read again' (Robert Lloyd's 'A Dialogue between the Author and his Friend,' 1763).

7 *Signposting* refers to the use of phrases that refer the reader to previous or later sections of a work ('as described in chapter 2'; 'as we will see in the next chapter'). Signposts are a standard tool, but the overuse of signposts may suggest a defect in the organization of the piece. In some manuscripts excessive signposting simply reflects the author's lack of confidence, an un-justified fear that the reader will be unable to follow a complex argument. For other authors, signposting is more of a tic or a crutch.

8 Scott Norton, *Developmental Editing* (Chicago: University of Chicago Press, 2009), xi.

9 Lapses in scholars' note-taking and citation procedures is a touchy subject. Copyeditors have always wondered about the passage that did not sound like the rest of the manuscript but that carried neither quotation marks nor a reference citation. Search engines enable copyeditors to identify the source of some passages and to remind the author to add the quotation marks and the reference note. Sometimes copyeditors back into a discovery when they search for examples of a term in hopes of finding authority for how to define, spell, or hyphenate it. Instead, they learn that the manuscript contains language that has been silently copied from the work of another.

10 In a tribute to the fact-checking department at *The New Yorker,* John McPhee recalls that one of his longer pieces (sixty thousand words) required the 'full-time attention for three or four weeks' of the magazine's fact-checker, and he devotes several pages to describing her heroic efforts. In contrast, he notes, book publishers 'prefer to regard fact-checking as the responsibility of authors,' but will happily take 'a free ticket to factual responsibility' when reprinting material that first appeared in a fact-checked magazine: 'Checkpoints,' *The New Yorker*, 9 & 16 February 2009, 59.

11 Since 2006, Teri Tan has reported regularly from India for *Publishers Weekly*. In early 2009, Tan offered a summary of recent developments:

> While the tide of projects from SSTM [scholarly, scientific, technical and medical], k–12, trade and professional publishers sweeping the Indian shores remains unstoppable, the nose-diving global economy has somewhat slowed its momentum . . . Some vendors have broadened their services instantaneously through company acquisitions, while a few others have advanced to a hybrid onshore/offshore operational mode through strategic partnerships. And all are moving beyond basic keyboarding, typesetting and backfile conversion – services that have been commoditized and therefore offer little profit. Nowadays, adding value and becoming an extension of the client's editorial team are critical to success and long-term survival. ('Champions of the XML Workflow: Content Services in India,' *Publishers Weekly*, 30 March 2009, http://www.publishersweekly.com/article/CA6646668.html)

> Earlier articles from Tan, all posted at the *Publishers Weekly* website, include 'Playing to Win,' 28 July 2008, CA6581737.html; 'The Content Crunchers,' 12 May 2008, CA6559361.html; and 'Illustration and Creative Services Outsourcing,' 24 March 2008, CA6543963.html.

12 One very learned octogenarian author asked me, at our first meeting, if I had read the *Commedia*. Yes, I had – in translation I hastened to add, lest he launch into a prolegomenon, perhaps in Italian, about some obscure aspect of *terza rima*. Had I noticed the one serious defect in the *Inferno*? he asked. Realizing that my job was to play the straight man, I said no. He smiled. 'Dante neglected to set aside a circle in Hell for copyeditors!'

A few years later, another scholar thanked me for my work by saying, 'Before I met you, I had ranked copyeditors just below used-car salesmen. You've changed my mind about that.' I did not ask how many levels we had risen in his hierarchy.

13 The Bad Writing Contest sponsored by the journal *Philosophy and Literature* in the late 1990s (http://www.denisdutton.com/bad_writing.htm) sparked considerable discussion of 'bad writing' versus 'difficult writing'; see, for example, Jonathan Culler and Kevin Lamb, eds., *Just Being Difficult? Academic Writing in the Public Arena* (Stanford, CA: Stanford University Press, 2003).

14 This advice comes up frequently on Copyediting-L, an electronic mailing list for English-language copyeditors (see www.copyediting-l.info). Ideally, the copyeditor speaks with equanimity and means 'I see the problems with this manuscript, but I know that is not within my power [talent, purview, budget] to address them. And so I focus on those tasks that are within my power.' (The similarities to Reinhold Niebuhr's Serenity Prayer are intentional.) But in some circumstances the message may be closer to 'That's your problem, Author, not mine. Thank goodness my name won't appear in this publication.'

15 Kate Wittenberg, 'The Role of the Library in 21st-Century Scholarly Publishing,' in *No Brief Candle: Reconceiving Research Libraries for the 21st Century* (Council on Library and Information Resources, Washington, DC, August 2008), 36, available at http://www.clir.org/pubs/reports/pub142/pub142.pdf.

16 Ibid., 37.

17 Perhaps the best-known levels-of-edit scheme is the one devised for technical publications by the Jet Propulsion Laboratory; the second edition of this document (1980), written by Robert Van Buren and Mary Fran Buehler, is available at www.faculty.english.ttu.edu/Eaton/5374/levels_of_edit.pdf. For scholarly publishing, a better starting point might be the simpler scheme I sketch out on page 12 of *The Copyeditor's Handbook*, 3rd ed. (Berkeley: University of California Press, 2011).

PART TWO

The Text

5 Bad Texts: An Eccentric Appreciation (Valdez, Brecht, and the Utility of Error)

ALEXANDER PETTIT

Some readers of this collection may not be acquainted with Luis Valdez. Briefly, then: Valdez (b. 1940) was founder in 1965 of El Teatro Campesino, originally a small amateur collective affiliated with César Chávez and designed to perform short propagandistic *actos* for striking farmworkers in the San Joaquin Valley, and subsequently a professional organization with its own touring company and playhouse. He is recognized as the progenitor of contemporary Chicano/Chicana drama; in my opinion, he is also one of the best American playwrights of the last several generations.

Although scholars of drama are on the whole disinclined to acknowledge as much, plays become books, and books, not performances, enshrine a playwright's reputation. Valdez is on shaky ground in this schema, having risked his reputation by putting his name to editions characterized by typographical recklessness as well as dramaturgical brilliance. His publications for Arte Público Press – most extravagantly *'Zoot Suit' and Other Plays* (1992) – are savaged by error; indeed, I am not aware of any major author who has so often re-upped with a press that has handled his or her work so shoddily.

Valdez's fidelity to Arte Público, a publishing arm of the University of Houston, perhaps advertises nothing more or less than a wholesome accord with the press's avowal of 'cultural sensitivity to its writers and the experiences they write about.'[1] His profession's regrettable sense of written texts as ancillary to the real business of drama may also be a factor. The peculiarities behind Valdez's chosen mode of interface with a reading audience are not, however, presently at issue. My interests are limited to the unintended but rich resonances that error creates in texts that it would seem only to degrade. What might a reader experience, for example, when 'sight' is misset as 'site' in a text by a playwright bullish on the materiality and artifice of theatrical performance? Quite a bit, I will suggest.

Notwithstanding its offensiveness, *ipso facto*, to intention, error abets ideology in Valdez's texts. It does so in a way that points up Valdez's allegiance to Bertolt Brecht.[2] The misspellings and other manglings in Valdez's printed texts promote the alienation, in a Brechtian sense, of the reader from the written text in a way analogous to the more familiar alienation of actor and viewer from the performance 'text.' And they do so in a manner compatible with Valdez's self-consciously Brechtian dramaturgy, for example his stop-action freezes and his habit of creating characters whose rapid-fire alternation of English, Spanish, and *caló* (Chicana/Chicano slang) alienates non-Hispanophone readers and viewers. Coincidentally and not to the credit of Arte Público, error forces the reader into the disjunctive, sceptical relationship with representation (text or 'text') that Valdez, like Brecht, values. As falls go, this one tends towards the fortunate.

The interdependency of bad texts and rich meanings problematizes the 'dialogue' between 'scholarly editors' and 'in-house editors' that informs this volume. In the case of Valdez's texts, shoddy work by the latter discourages intervention by the former. Scholarly editors, after all, are trained to regard textual errors as signs that deviate from an actual (e.g., manuscriptal) or assumed (i.e., lexical) ideal. The recuperation or creation of this ideal is the aim of conventional editing. In the case of Valdez, however, the emendations that would normally define this process stand to weaken the dialectical process on which the author bases his dramaturgy. The contextual inharmoniousness of error – the discord between a faulty form and a 'correct' one – becomes a phenomenon to honour, not to efface. This leaves scholarly and in-house editors no room for collaboration. The collaboration that animates this collection is thrown off kilter, in a meaningful way, I hope.

Brecht's alienated actor famously refuses to be 'transformed' into the character that he or she portrays. 'The verdict: "he didn't act Lear, he was Lear" would be an annihilating blow to [the actor],' Brecht declared in 1945, expressing his dissent from the 'realistic' or naturalistic practices pioneered by Stanislavski in the late nineteenth and early twentieth centuries and dominant since as method acting.[3] The audience participates in the actor's ideologically freighted demurral by declining the Aristotelian-*cum*-Stanislavskian invitation to lose itself in the character of an English king with bad taste in daughters, or, rather, in the performance of an actor pretending to be such a king.

Like many dramatic theorists, Brecht regarded his own theory as realistic, insofar as the term can be loosed from its moorings in Stanislavski, Ibsen, and others. The detachment of actor from character artificially codified an experience that Brecht saw as an 'utterly ordinary' aspect of life. 'The A[lienation]-effect,' he wrote, 'consists in turning the object of which one is to be made aware, to which one's attention is to be drawn, from something ordinary, familiar, immediately accessible, into something peculiar, striking and unexpected. What is obvious is in a certain sense made incomprehensible.'[4] From this position of alienation, one sees flux where one once saw stability and is thus (too neatly, one might object) primed to participate in the Marxist dialectic that informs Brecht's theory.[5] Brecht instances a common wristwatch, unexpectedly seen anew, and a familiar factory, regarded more probingly after it has been recognized as a polluter.[6] I will instance Valdez's printed pages, seen as dialectically potent amalgams of 'correct,' or familiar, and 'incorrect,' or unfamiliar, readings.

By frustrating an 'expectation which is justified by experience,' again to reference Brecht, a typesetter or other agent triggers the alienation-effect every time he or she missets a word.[7] '[H]e or she missets' is an expectation; 'he or she misets' is a frustration of that expectation. Absent the arbitrary congruence of intramural error and authorial ideology, the experience need not mean much. Even in the Arte Público texts, gaffes of the 'it's' for 'its' variety, however frequent, might prompt in a reader nothing but transient moments of pique were they not accompanied by knottier infelicities. A reference to 'the site of Tiburcio Vásquez' rather than 'the sight of Tiburcio Vásquez' in the historical drama *Bandido!* (1982), for example, heightens the reader's alienation due to the delayed recognition of error or a willingness to find wordplay where only error obtains.[8] The substitution of '1973' for '1873' in the same play (111) flashes the possibility that Valdez means to emphasize the contemporary pertinence of his subject typographically as he does in other ways. Again, one is jolted. The accretion of error sometimes discourages the comprehension and thus the interpretation of discrete passages, as when, in *Zoot Suit* (1978), a stage direction notices '[a] *group of batos . . . upstage in a mimetic freeze*' (57).[9] Granted, Valdez's characters, like Brecht's, sometimes 'freeze' in order to disrupt the bond of empathy between character and audience; and 'freeze' (or 'freeze-frame') is common parlance in film and television, two media in which Valdez has long been interested.[10]

But 'frieze' seems a plausible reading as well, more so given the classical origin of the modifier with which Valdez introduces the uncertain noun.

The relative rectitude of these readings is immaterial at present, as is the fact that the Brechtian actor consciously promotes alienation and the typesetter (or other agent) does so either unconsciously or in conscious compliance with an error introduced earlier in the process of textual transmission. What matters is that the reader's inability to trust the text prevents him or her from immersing himself or herself in the experience of reading – a laudable circumstance, in Brechtian theory. More specifically, the perceptual muddle of 'freeze' and 'frieze,' like the flurry of grosser errors, produces a cognitive disruption that wrenches the receptor from engagement with story and character and moves him or her towards the broader historical consciousness that, as Brecht would have it, 'regards nothing as existing except insofar as it changes, in other words is in disharmony with itself.'[11] From this to revolution was but a short hop for Brecht as it was for Marx, at least in theory.

'Zoot Suit' and Other Plays provides the most accessible test case. This volume features the author's best-known and most successful play and presents his most error-ridden texts. In the tabulation that follows, I have presumably not recorded every error in that book, because my status as non-Hispanophone prevents me from understanding except in a crude way the lengthy sections of Valdez's works written in Spanish or caló. Again limiting my comments to passages set in English, and by way of recognizing the pervasiveness of the problems that concern me, I note that Valdez's earliest book with Arte Público – Early Works: Actos, 'Bernabé' and 'Pensamiento Serpentino' (1990) – is also riddled with error, particularly the introduction and the play, Bernabé.[12] A bilingual edition of (only) Zoot Suit (2004), including a translation by Edna Ochoa, and 'Mummified Deer' and Other Plays (2005) are set with more care. The former corrects most of the errors that I will identify in the 1992 edition; and the latter, although rough enough typographically, has a lower incidence of error than the earlier texts.[13] Early Works and 'Mummified Deer' and Other Plays have only adjunctive significance to this part of my argument, although I will notice the 2004 Zoot Suit as occasion demands.

The three texts that constitute 'Zoot Suit' and Other Plays – the title play, Bandido!, and I Don't Have to Show You No Stinking Badges! (1986) – comprise 187 pages with an average of approximately 325–375 words per page. In the volume, I count thirteen indisputable errors in the one language that I am competent to discuss. Seven of the errors are obviously misspelled English words that an editor would normally emend on his or her own authority: 'willl' (62; for 'will'); 'was'nt' (91; for 'wasn't'); 'site' (116; for 'sight'); 'it's' (135; for 'its'); *'climatic'* (186; for *'climactic'*); 'your' (193; for 'you're'); and 'Toture' (209; for 'Torture'). Three errors could be emended on the basis of pro forma intratextual consultation: '1973' (for '1873'; noted above); '38TH' (59; for '38th'); and *'tachuche'* (36; for *'tacuche'*), the last of which I have noticed coincidentally. One would normally emend '38TH' on the authority of correct readings throughout the text. '[T]*achuche'* would be emended on this same authority and on the authority of slang orthography. Emending the date requires a different but no more difficult process. Two of the errors from the 1992 text of *Zoot Suit* – *'tachuche'* and 'was'nt' – are corrected in the 2004 bilingual edition. One – '38TH' – is not. An editor's treatment of a seventh misspelling would ideally include the consultation of precedent states, possible emendations being various and the text itself providing no guidance. In *Bandido!*, a character orders 'two whiskey's' (120). Without assistance from an earlier state, an editor would select 'whiskeys,' recognizing it as the most plausible reading to have generated the error but still perhaps wondering if some typescript, somewhere, might read 'whiskies' or 'whiskys.'

Once, a sentence is skewed by the inclusion of a faulty form; once, an extraneous syllable or word slips into the text. In each instance, emendation would again, ideally, be based on stemmatic analysis. The first instance claims an unexpected structural resonance: in *Zoot Suit*, a presumed error initiates the process of alienation that plays out dramaturgically in that play's sequence of conflicting and indeterminate endings. El Pachuco – the protagonist's doppelgänger whom Valdez calls 'the Jungian self-image . . . the power inside every individual that's greater than any human institution'[14] – introduces a series of divergent narratives about the protagonist Henry Reyna's fate. 'That's the way you see it, ese,' he says to 'The Press' that has tut-tuttingly reported Reyna's imprisonment, addiction, and premature death, 'But there's other way to end the story' (94). Because El Pachuco's power comes in part from his linguistic sophistication – for example, he initiates the play with a short speech in *caló* before *'break*[*ing*] *character and address*[*ing*] *the audience in perfect English'* (25) – we may rule out 'there's other way' as representing Valdez's intention for his character. The 2004 edition of *Zoot Suit* reads 'there's other ways' (82); but readers of the 1992 text will wonder if the author had intended 'there's another way' or, less probably, 'there are other ways.'[15] Less momentously, in *I Don't Have to Show You No Stinking Badges!*, a parenthetical instruction following a speech prefix reads thus: '(em Pulls off cap and glasses.)' (198). Deleting the 'em' without either comment or intertextual authority would be tempting but unsatisfactory, as it may be that an earlier state records an instruction to begin the reading with an em-dash.

Three additional readings are sufficiently ambiguous to befuddle a reader, although in two of these cases the 2004 edition may provide authoritative readings. '[F]reeze' stands in that edition (42), as does an unexpected and perhaps erroneous capital at the start of an interpolated parenthetical clause: '(We have a name now)' (67 [1994]; 53 [2004]). Finally, a run-on reference to 'Mario Moreno "Cantinflas"' in *I Don't Have to Show You No Stinking Badges!* puzzles, rhythmically, the more so for its propinquity to a clearly partitioned and neatly cadenced reference to 'Martin Sheen (aka Ramón Estevez)' (203). A scholarly editor would normally follow the 1992 text in each of these instances and would write textual notes in the second and third.

These typographical disruptions alienate the reader much as audiences are alienated by grander gestures like direct addresses; portrayals of 'freezes' or 'friezes'; polemical or symbolic uses of music, masks, and props; and indeterminate endings.[16] The errors and the ambiguous cases short-circuit the reader's cognition of the physical text. This is the effect that Brecht ascribes to the alienation-effect in quotidian life: the 'familiar' has been 'stripped of its inconspicuousness.'[17] Arte Público has entered Brecht's extrapolated (quotidian) sense of alienation into the textual history of the plays themselves, in effect out-Brechting Brecht.

This interplay vanishes in the 2004 *Zoot Suit* and in the only other edition of *Zoot Suit*, apparently set from the 1992 edition. The text prepared by W.B. Worthen for *The Wadsworth Anthology of Drama* (2007) is suitably responsive to the needs of a student readership that would evince little interest in the correspondences that interest me.[18] '[W]a'snt' and '38TH' are emended silently. Less comfortably, *'tachuche'* remains, and this may imply the presence of more errors in Spanish or *caló*. Worthen has chosen to retain 'there's other way to end the story,' a defensible if timid decision. '[F]reeze' and 'We' are retained as well. Worthen wisely declines to translate the Hispanophone passages, thus preserving the most important feature of Valdez's use of alienation. The gain realized by the appearance of the corrected Arte Público edition and Worthen's text is obvious: we now have two readable texts that by their very neatness constitute an important step in an author's progress towards canonization. And presumably we have texts that better represent Valdez's orthographical intentions than the 1992 Arte Público text had done and that therefore facilitate his advancement of certain themes and ideas.

But my unease with this sort of neatness also claims thematic sanction. By rendering alienation typographically, Arte Público promotes Valdez's interest in the material and linguistic manifestations of cultural alterity. Throughout his career, Valdez has dramatized the alienation, in a non-technical sense, of Hispanophone and polyglot people in an Anglophone culture; and he has often mocked the assumptions that allow unilingual Anglo characters to denigrate his multilingual characters.[19] In a small but significant manner (and, again, one wrought by coincidence), Valdez's marred texts require all viewers and readers to experience language as 'peculiar'; and they invite Anglophone viewers and readers in particular to recognize their uncertain position in works that sometimes portray them as tangential, fluffy, menacing, or idiotic.

Valdez's interest in linguistic alterity renders meaningful 'erroneous' readings of the sort that the later texts of *Zoot Suit* reject, however incompatible these readings might be with the author's presumed intention for his work. A closer look at Valdez's method should clarify the point. Characteristically, Valdez shapes dialogue as a means of sorting through various groups of readers and viewers and investing those who share his fluency in English, Spanish, and *caló* with the greatest measure of recreational delight and interpretive power. His strategies of exclusion often involve blunt, ironic recreations of the confusion experienced by Hispanophone workers in a country habitually contemptuous of their language(s). 'You know I don't speak Spanish,' the strike-busting Sheriff Barnes says in response to an utterance by his informant, the eponymous drug-dealer in *Mundo Mata* (1976), finally published as part of *'Mummified Deer' and Other Plays*. Mundo responds: 'Why not? Sixty percent of the whole county does. Why don't you speak the language of most of the people in the county, carnal? You're a county Sheriff, ¿qué no?' (79). Barnes's linguistic parochialism indicates his stasis-inducing stupidity and stands him in contrast to Mundo, whose dexterous use of words conveys charm and intelligence and correlates to social mobility. This adaptation of the 'wily servant' character places Valdez in a comic tradition that runs from Plautus to Shakespeare to Ibsen and beyond.[20]

Mundo spends most of the play shuttling opportunistically between two linguistic worlds: the Anglophone world defined by Barnes and others who would exploit him, and the multilingual world of his family, Chávez, and the striking farmworkers, all represented in the play.

At play's end, he chooses the latter world. In this way he gains the stable familial (i.e., comic) affiliation that ensures his ultimate moral reformation. But Mundo's reabsorption is complicated by the play's tragic closure. The violent death that codifies his rejection of demeaning linguistic alterity topples the play from its comic substratum and forces the two classical genres into a dialectical relationship with one another. Mundo's *'elevated'* and *'flag-covered'* corpse (129) recalls familiar conventions of European historical tragedy, but the heroizing process itself must remain unfamiliar to non-Hispanophone readers and viewers.[21] The eulogy that marks the terminal triumph of the tragic strain does not memorialize a Caesar whose magnitude has been gradually demonstrated to an entire audience. Rather, to Anglophone readers or viewers, a stereotype suddenly claims dimension. Bullett, Mundo's brother, speaks this passage in English; but it celebrates a slouchy, drug-dealing speaker of slangy Spanish whose development has been obscure to non-Hispanophone readers. Mundo's own death-speech, crucially, is polyglot. Just when genre – tragedy – is supposed to render coherent the discordant data that the play has presented, a non-Hispanophone audience must confront the imperfection of its understanding of character. In the midst of much that is familiar is something mysterious, an Anglophone reader's knowledge of which is shown to have been based on a stereotype. The part of the audience that does not 'understand' now has a chance to learn from its lack of understanding. Brecht could not have done better himself.

Bathetically in one sense but instructively in another, Mundo's transformation from drug dealer to folk hero is savaged by a typographical error in the printed version of the play. Before he delivers the speech during which he is shot, Mundo reconciles with his old friend Flaco, a junkie whom he has been supplying and with whose wife he has been sleeping:

FLACO: (*Clean and strong.*) Give it up, carnal. Let all the shit go. We'll catch you. Ándale. (*There is a tense pause, as* MUNDO *stares at* FLACO. *Then the damn breaks.* MUNDO *breaks out sobbing, falling into* BULLETT's *arms.*) (203)

Valdez places greater stock in emotion than Brecht did, and he relishes the sentimentalist strain here, although we may be certain that the typographical error is not intended.[22] Valdez uses sentimental language in a stagey manner throughout his later work, in order simultaneously to provoke emotional response in an audience and to call attention to the artificiality of the medium of provocation – a deft adaptation of Brecht and a neat reminder that realism does not hold a monopoly on emotive representation. (Beckett's characters convey enormous emotional charge, even though we often don't understand what they're saying, literally. Like Beckett, Valdez is not a realistic playwright.) The stylized and, in conventional terms, unsuccessful love-triangle among Henry, Alice Bloomfield, and Henry's Chicana girlfriend Della in *Zoot Suit* is another case in point, linguistically formulaic at times but not therefore emotionally inert.

The otherwise cringe-inducing '*damn*' thus serves Valdez's usual practice, if not his local intention, quite nicely. None of the tools that actors and directors could employ to ironize or mitigate this almost mawkish but important passage is available to the reader of the printed text. The '*damn*' is an instance of unintended ironic distancing, the accidental textual rendering of a familiar presence in both Brechtian and Valdezian dramaturgy. Valdez is never averse to defusing – thus calling attention to – emotional vitality by emphasizing artifice. In *Zoot Suit*, Henry Reyna and El Pachuco (visible only to Henry throughout the play) argue after Henry is committed to solitary confinement. When Henry looks ahead to his appeal, his cynical double counsels him '[n]ot to expect justice when it isn't there,' adding that '[n]o court in the land's going to set you free.' Henry rejects this perspective '*furiously*,' telling El Pachuco to 'Fuck off! FUCK OFF!' El Pachuco responds: '¡Órale pues! Don't take the pinche play so seriously, Jesús! Es puro vacilón!' He then '*snaps his fingers*' and the scene changes (78). Like El Pachuco's admonition, Arte Público's '*damn*' shatters a mood that need not be sustained in order to be effective.

Valdez uses the 'A-effect' situationally, calibrating his dramaturgy in response to different performance-environments. This allows his work to register differently with different groups: he is playing with – or playing to – the commonplace that circumstance affects reception. Alienating a tired and perhaps terrified worker in a hot field is not alienating a paunchy patron in a comfortable theater, and neither is to be confused with alienating an isolated individual 'legs up with a book and a drink,' far from any theater ever likely to mount one of Valdez's plays.[23] What is familiar to one group need not be so to another. Defamiliarization, therefore, is also contingent; and Valdez makes much of this in his plays. Logically (and usually), ad hoc manipulation ends with publication, when a version is fixed in print and made available, promiscuously, to a diverse and uncontrollable audience. The Arte

Público editions, however, extend the period of receptive flux or situational discrimination. In this way, they accidentally affirm and extend Valdez's commitment to what Michael Vanden Heuvel calls 'the shifting relations between text and performance.'[24]

A scene from *Zoot Suit* helps frame the point. At a dance in his 38th Street Gang's territory, Henry fights with Rafas, who has brought his rival Downey Gang to the event. When Rafas falls down, Henry holds a knife to his throat. El Pachuco again *'snaps his fingers'* and *'everyone freezes.'* 'Qué mamada, Hank,' he says, 'That's exactly what the play needs right now. Two more Mexicans killing each other.' Henry appeals to the audience: 'Don't give me that bullshit. Either I kill him [Rafas] or he kills me.' Before *'unfreez[ing]'* the scene, El Pachuco says, 'That's exactly what they paid to see. Think about it' (46).

Henry does 'think about it,' and so should we. Pondering the identities of the 'theys' who have 'paid to see the play' provides a sense of the contingencies at work in this Brechtian scene as it transfers from stage to page. In my primarily Anglo literature classroom, comprising mainly students whose experience of the work is limited to its printed manifestation, the 'they' is, or are, easy to identify. 'They' are 'we,' or most of us, statistically, that blunt oppositional force that Suzan-Lori Parks calls 'WHITEY' and that she, like the mature Valdez, regards as a rather too easily hittable target.[25] This recognition leads to a productive discussion of the Anglocentrism of commercial theater and radical theater's ability to counter stereotypes (for example, the quick-tempered Hispanic gangbanger) that commercial theater and other popular media often promote.

El Pachuco's 'theys' turn out to be rangier and more fluid in performance than they are in class, due largely to the fact that Valdez's play reached a more diverse audience on stage than it does in print. The bad texts constitute both the refinement and the fulfillment of a process of alienation variously evident in the play's pre-publication history; the hostility to scholarly-editorial method inherent in these texts is therefore best understood in the context of a performance-history that consciously trades in disjunctions of the sort that the text accidentally encodes. More specifically, we would do well to consider the early, intentional manifestations of the situational mode of representing alterity that I find continued unintentionally in the published texts.

Yolanda Broyles-González's overview of the pre-publication history of *Zoot Suit* demonstrates the crucial position that the play occupies in the histories of Valdez and El Teatro Campesino. In the mid-1970s,

Valdez began to move away from the collectivism that had defined the Teatro's early history, laying off old members of the troupe and inviting professionals to audition.[26] The instances of 'they' became 'we' and the instances of 'we' became 'they.' The move proved controversial and has continued to prove so, thanks largely to Broyles-González, whose commitment to a Valdez shorn of the 'accommodationist tendencies' (213) that she disdains in his later work informs her interest in a hegemony of writers, actors, and audiences, collectively in conflict with 'theys' whom she would rather existed only as a propagandist chooses to represent them.

Given her lack of interest in the dialectical basis of Valdez's mature drama, it is not surprising that Broyles-González regards Brecht's influence on Valdez as 'less than negligible' (7).[27] She discounts Brecht's contribution to the early agitprop of which she approves, where it is obvious and sometimes superficial, and ignores it in the 'accommodationist' work that she dislikes, where it flourishes more subtly. Her attraction to the *actos* is presumably rooted in their exclusivity with respect to audience. These skits were presented in what Marco De Marinis calls 'closed performances' that 'anticipate a very precise receiver and demand well-defined types of "competence" (encyclopedic, ideological, etc.) for their "correct" reception.' This mode of performance, De Marinis continues, is characteristic of 'genre-based theatre: political theatre, children's theatre, women's theatre, gay theatre, street theatre, musicals, dance theatre, mime, and so on. In these cases . . . the performance only "comes off" to the extent that the real audience corresponds to the anticipated one, thus reacting to the performance in the desired way.'[28]

This tight congruity of audience and performance is consistent with Broyles-González's sense of how drama should defend itself against the depredations of 'mainstream' culture. In the early works by the Teatro, the bond registers linguistically. Harry J. Elam, Jr, notes that 'the dialogue of the *actos*' is designed 'to appeal particularly to Chicano audiences and to reflect the real speech patterns of their model Chicano farmworker spectators.'[29] The 'theys' of the *actos* stood on the perimeter, livid, locked, loaded, and protected by their linguistic limitations from any dialectical pull that the performance might exude.[30] As they ('they') must be, given the propagandistic nature of the *actos*, they are irremediably vile.

Zoot Suit is another matter, Broyles-González suggests.[31] Valdez drafted the script after having approached Gordon Davidson of the

Mark Taper Forum in Los Angeles with an offer to direct the play in that city using professional actors. The first approved version, commissioned by Davidson and assisted by a Rockefeller Foundation grant, ran for ten days in the 'New Theatre for Now' series at the Taper in 1978. Each performance sold out, and the play was folded into the Taper's regular season before being transferred to Hollywood's Aquarius Theater. Its ten-month run there, beginning December 1978, generated more revenue than any play that had premiered on the West Coast. A five-week run on Broadway (1979) was a failure commercially and critically, although it is notable for being the first Broadway run of a play by a Chicano/Chicana playwright. Each theater was larger than the previous one; and, as Broyles-González demonstrates, the play's script 'went through considerable changes each time it moved to a bigger performance venue' (180). An underfunded film, directed by Valdez, appeared in 1981. Again, the script changed.

Broyles-González faults the pre-performance revision in particular for playing fast and loose with the historical events that undergird the play. She notes that Davidson rejected the original script for being too 'realistic' (181) and that Valdez responded by adding more episodes of 'violence among Mexicans' (182). She finds this 'a diplomatic effort to balance the instances of violence against Chicanas/os by whites' (182) and a triumph of 'dramatic effect' over 'historical accuracy' (183). Discussing the play across versions, Broyles-González claims that 'it is where historical facts are imperceptibly altered or tailored to suit fantasy or marketing needs that the drama is at its weakest and the play's ideological thrust most questionable' (201). A comically detailed collation of the events that inspired the play and their renderings in *Zoot Suit* (201–3) suggests a paradigm that might value the author of a textbook over Aeschylus, Shakespeare, and August Wilson, as well as later Valdez.

In Broyles-González's comments on the reception-history of the play, we get some sense of the 'theys' who El Pachuco supposes would relish a knife-fight. Soundly, Broyles-González posits that the East Coast audience comprised more Anglo viewers than the West Coast audiences had done.[32] She does not notice, however, that El Pachuco's admonition thematizes precisely the concern about voyeuristic renderings of brown-on-brown violence that she herself expresses. One might argue that as the audiences become whiter, Valdez ramps up alienating devices that would have been supererogatory in Delano or even Los Angeles – or that would there have 'they'd' a Mexican-American middle class in a way that Broyles-González perhaps elides when she notes that the West Coast productions 'succeeded in attracting barrio audiences ... in large numbers' (188). Lacking the subtler demographic gradations of the West Coast, the performances in New York could only have identified El Pachuco's 'theys' more clearly and thus in a manner still less comfortable to Anglo audiences. The aborted knife-fight presumably caused ample discomfort in New York, where, as Broyles-González demonstrates, the critical debate was dominated by Anglo critics threatened by the play's treatment of race.[33]

Valdez's situational manipulation of alterity is never more stark or subversive than it is on Broadway, although Broyles-González persists in regarding his decision to bring the play east as a heretical instance of 'mainstreaming.' But the line between 'mainstreaming' and 'infiltrating' is thinner than Broyles-González acknowledges. She takes particular offence at the Henry/Alice/Della triangle, which is present in the pre-performance version, attenuated in the Los Angeles versions, but amplified in the Broadway version, in which 'Alice Bloomfield and [defence lawyer] George Shearer were bigger than life and references to barrio leaders and activists in defence of the *pachucos* had all but vanished' (201). I am not persuaded, however, that either the omission of 'barrio leaders and activists' or the exaggeration of the love-triangle redounds to Valdez's discredit, and I wonder if Broyles-González's reluctance to see Brecht in Valdez hasn't caused her to miss a beat. Might it not be that Valdez withholds historically accurate representations of 'activists' out of a concern that these would play to stereotype – this *was* a time of well-publicized Chicana/Chicano activism[34] – but that he boosts the interracial love-plot in order to confront East Coast liberals with the possibility that their own daughters might be possessed of hearts blind to colour?

In the context of this possibility, and in a city with more Jews and fewer Chicanos/Chicanas than Los Angeles, Alice's Jewishness becomes provocative (*'your* daughter') rather than exemplary of Valdez's fondness for 'white savior characters' (as Broyles-González finds it [203]) or indicative of patronization and opportunism (as at least one reviewer found it).[35] The years between the Broadway run and the publication of Broyles-González's book were marked by a substantial increase in the acceptability of interracial relationships.[36] *Zoot Suit* falls farther, chronologically, from Broyles-González's book (1994) than from now-dusty landmarks like *Guess Who's Coming to Dinner?* and Janis Ian's 'Society's Child' (both 1967) that provided early indications both of a change in public perceptions and of the spasticity of that change.

Change of precisely this sort animates the theory of alienation, the targeted audience of which must be both sceptical and tractable. Alienation requires sentient 'theys,' and these are the 'theys' that Broyles-González does not want. She is critical of the Teatro's post-Delano intention 'to go beyond movement politics and performing to sympathetic audiences' and 'to conquer the hearts of those unsympathetic millions of Americans who are perhaps unfamiliar with what we represent as a people or cause' (172).[37] She therefore dislikes *Zoot Suit*'s eastward migration and, if my argument is valid, the modifications of the script that allowed Valdez to defamiliarize stereotypes precisely where stereotypes were most likely to prevail. The audience of 'theys' that Valdez sought greeted him on the East Coast, inky daggers drawn. Its comparative hostility should not be seen as an indicator of failure. Rather, Brecht's model allows the possibility that the play's least successful manifestation might have contained the greatest potential for success – or might have *been* the most successful of the productions, with success correlating to outrage. Outrage enables dialectic; acceptance does not.[38]

It will be clear from the foregoing comments that I regard Valdez as conscious of the need to shape his message according to the vagaries of audience and as eager to do just this. Although Broyles-González seems to delight in what she sees as the fallow fortunes of the Teatro following the New York run of *Zoot Suit*, the audience for works by Valdez and the Teatro has increased significantly.[39] By my rough calculation, something like 197,000 spectators saw *Zoot Suit* in Los Angeles and New York in 1978 and 1979.[40] These are numbers that most playwrights, especially those labouring under the designations 'regional' or 'ethnic,' would love to be able to generate; but they tell only part of the story. Between the end of the Broadway run in the spring of 1979 and the completion of this essay early in 2010, 70,864 copies of the play have been sold, with about 90 per cent of the sales accounted for by the 1992 omnibus edition and the remainder by the 2004 stand-alone bilingual edition. The press estimates that '80% of sales [of all of Valdez's books] are for the academic market (either for classroom use or school libraries).'[41] Books are transferable and seats at theaters are not, so it is safe to say that the ratio of books to seats (thus, theoretically, readers to viewers) inclines more towards books than these figures suggest. The appearance of the Harcourt/Wadsworth text also refigures the ratio – unquantifiably, given the miscellaneousness of anthologies – by augmenting the number of student-readers. In any case, more people have purchased one of the Arte Público editions of *Zoot Suit* than saw the play at the Taper engagements or during the Broadway run, and all of them have done so since the end of that run. Most of them are students. These editions constitute most of the recent history of the work, with the rest allotted to revivals, some associated with the Teatro, some not.

When plays are printed but not staged extensively (for example, most of Valdez's other published works), the book is often the principal medium through which an audience accesses a work. The 19,202 copies of the *Early Works* that Arte Público has sold to date is notable in this context.[42] Here we have an edition of plays conceived for 'closed' audiences in the 1960s and infrequently staged since. And, like all of Valdez's books for Arte Público, the edition is selling at a respectable clip to a readership comprising principally the scions of the plump American middle-class, neither migrant farmers in rural California nor mature theater-goers in two coastal cities.

Therefore to say, as Jorge Huerta does when he introduces '*Mummified Deer' and Other Plays*, that 'each of these plays must be read with an understanding that they are to be seen and heard, not visited simply on the pages of a book' is naïve.[43] The commonplace is of dubious merit generally, but is particularly unsatisfying where performance-histories have stalled and printed books continue to rack up sales. Regardless of how plays 'must be' encountered, in many cases they *will* be encountered by readers rather than viewers.

Textualists sometimes seem to share Broyles-González's and Huerta's dismissive attitude towards printed texts of contemporary plays. This is understandable to some extent: as editors of early printed drama know, it is extraordinarily difficult to extract a defensible text from a crowded documentary record further complicated by contingencies of revision not analogous to the transmissional histories of more stable genres. Contemporary textual theory, however, does help us conceptualize the problem.

The idea that texts should honour the conditions that resulted in their issuance has moved to the forefront of the discussion since the publication of Jerome J. McGann's *Critique of Modern Textual Criticism* in 1983. As most readers of this collection will know, McGann argued that authorship was collaborative and social, and that accounts of a text's often vicissitudinous progress should attend to the 'close working relationship between the author and various editorial and publishing professionals associated with the institutions which serve to transmit literary works to the public.'[44] 'Final authorial intention' was chucked overboard as the dominant criterion for the selection and emendation of copy-text.[45] The model has stuck, to the improvement of the discipline. Critical editions are now more likely to prefer first editions to later ones, and critical editors are now less likely to regard as contaminants textual oddities that may lack authorial sanction but may nonetheless advertise a broader range of origins and meanings. The post-McGannian edition tends to be more populous, vocally, and thus livelier and more interesting.

This is not to say that McGann would validate boners of the 'mechanical' or unintended sort – the 'was'nts' that textualists have been expunging guiltlessly since antiquity. Peter Shillingsburg's observation that in the McGannian paradigm 'the editor abjures all responsibility except that of collecting the evidence and giving a guided tour' elides the fact that editing at its most basic *is* the rectification of agential error, however agency is construed.[46] McGann's own editorial work testifies to this.[47] Shillingsburg's remark nonetheless provides a framework for appreciating radically flawed, agentially promiscuous, and socially resonant texts like Valdez's. It opens up the possibility that critical editing per se might not be appropriate where these texts are at issue. The post-McGannian chariness about textual intervention seems more reasonable – less fussy – in the presence of Valdez's mottled texts. These may be texts that need not be edited.

Regarding the Arte Público editions as satisfactory or even definitive is an uneasy position to take. With respect to most of Valdez's plays, there is only one edition available, and I am offering a way to make peace with those texts. In the case of *Zoot Suit*, it seems likely that the 1992 edition will continue to outsell the 2004 edition, because it offers more plays for the same price and because bilingual texts will tend to be seen as niche products, at cost to their commercial success. More readers will read and cite the 1992 edition than will read or cite the corrected text, which in any case suffers from some of the presentational problems of its predecessor, most importantly the lack of information about the selection and emendation of copy-text. The anthologized text continues to benefit student-readers but will not and need not be significant otherwise. Those of us who love Valdez's work had best learn to love the mess.

I believe, generally, that responsible editions honour honourable writers and that the preparation of responsible editions of minority authors is important, ethically and bibliographically. Furthermore, honouring Valdez with a 'good' edition could be seen as a significant stage in the dialectical process that animates Valdez's work: having provoked outrage, argument, chagrin, and adulation, Valdez could ride respectably into the lives of the 'unconverted,' there to disseminate ideas sure to survive the application of sound editorial practice. In a limited way, he is doing so now in Worthen's edition. Surely this is a positive development.

But I intend to keep reading and teaching from the Arte Público texts. As an admirer of Ruskin, I profess myself less appalled by the evidence of misplaced trust in individual workmanship than perhaps I should be. And I think that the press's failings, however regrettable, should be considered alongside of its mission, which is noble and has proven viable as well. Casting itself as 'David' to the 'New York publishing industry Goliaths,' Arte Público declares that its 'vision for the role of Hispanic literature in the United States' has allowed it to '[demonstrate] that size (or lack of it) is not proportionately related to success in the commercial book market.'[48] As I have posited, this may be enough to have secured the loyalty of Valdez; presumably he and other successful writers who choose to publish with Arte Público have put their belief in shared ideals over a theorized interest in presentational sparkle that another press might better address. It is not up to me to suggest that their fidelity is misplaced; and I do not hesitate to rank the slaying of Philistines, large or small and past or present, above even than the judicious exercise of typesetting.

In any case, the move towards bibliographical 'respectability' raises certain questions. Might one regard the 2004 text of *Zoot Suit* as a successful synthesis, loosely to invoke Hegel, of flawed (physical) and ideal (theorized) texts? And might not the successful advancement of this textual process constitute a tangible and proud achievement for those who have struggled in the service of this process, thus, in this instance, as an actualization rather than an effacement of dialectical struggle? Might not the 2004 bilingual edition, that is, constitute an exception to my exception, albeit one limited to one play? Surely, one would like to applaud Arte Público for the improvement of its in-house work. Also: is the achievement concretized in the 2004 text put at risk when the agency of textual transmission shifts from a small Chicana/Chicano press to the hefty corporate entity known at various times as 'Harcourt,' 'Wadsworth,' 'Cengage,' and, more antiseptically still, 'Wadsworth Cengage Learning'? And can a textualist in good conscience employ an ideological model simultaneously to discount one witness (the 2007 Wadsworth text) of a flawed archetype (the 1992 Arte

Público text), to praise another witness (the 2004 Arte Público text), and to plead for dignity in the archetype?

I don't know. For now, and limiting my discussion to certain texts by a certain writer, I will venture a tentative 'yes' in all these instances. But, honestly, I don't know.

I have not proposed that a press should eschew sound practice or relish jobs poorly done. But, mindful of McGann, I will say that the bonds between a text and its origins demand respect even when they offend the most fundamental beliefs of scholarly editors and contradict the usual practices of their colleagues at the presses. Tidying-up can be a form of misrepresentation. Valdez never tidies up the human histories that interest him, and maybe we should not be eager to tidy up the texts that record and, however unexpectedly, manifest these histories. Perhaps it is better simply to read them and learn from them, buoyed up, not burdened, by our artifactual interest in texts.

NOTES

Thanks are due to Ashley Brookner Bender, Susan McElwaine (Cengage Learning), Domino Renee Perez, Marina Tristán (Arte Público Press), Jacqueline Vanhoutte, and the exceptionally insightful referees and skilled copyeditor of this essay.

1 Arte Público Press, 'About Arte Público Press,' http://www.latinoteca.com/content/app-information/app-about%20us (accessed 25 August 2010).
2 Valdez has acknowledged Brecht's influence at least since 1966; see Valdez, 'El Teatro Campesino – Its Beginnings' (1966), in *The Chicanos: Mexican American Voices*, ed. Ed Ludwig and James Santibanez (Baltimore: Penguin, 1971), 115, 116–17. See also, e.g., an interview by David Savran conducted 6 May 1987: 'Brecht looms huge in my orientation. I discovered Brecht in college . . . I started reading all his plays and his theories, which I subscribed to immediately. I continue to use his alienation effect to this day' (in *In Their Own Words: Contemporary American Playwrights*, ed. Savran [New York: Theatre Communications Group, 1988], 261; see also 262, 265). Critical discussions of the Brechtian strain in Valdez include Harry Elam, Jr, *Taking It to the Streets: The Social Protest Theater of Luis Valdez and Amiri Baraka* (Ann Arbor: University of Michigan Press, 1997), e.g., 110–11; Jorge Huerta, 'Chicano Agit-Prop: The Early Actos of El Teatro Campesino,' *Latin American Theatre Review* 10 (1977): 47–8; Mark Pizzato, 'Brechtian and Aztec Violence in Valdez's *Zoot Suit*,' *Journal of Popular Film and Television*

26 (1998): 52–61; and W.B. Worthen, 'Staging América: The Subject of History in Chicano/a Theatre,' *Theater Journal* 49 (1997): 101–20.

3 Brecht, *A Short Organum for the Theatre* (1948), in *Brecht on Theatre: The Development of an Aesthetic*, trans. and ed. John Willett (1964; rpt. New York: Hill and Wang, 1992), 193. Brecht's understanding of Stanislavsky was more nuanced than this excerpt suggests; see 'Some of the Things That Can Be Learnt from Stanislavsky' (1952), in *Brecht on Theatre*, 236–7.

4 Brecht, 'Short Description of a New Technique of Acting Which Produces an Alienation Effect' (1940), in *Brecht on Theatre*, 143. See also Brecht, *Short Organum*, 192; and 'About the Part of Galileo,' an undated fragment evidently concerning a post-1942 version of *Life of Galileo*: 'What gives this new historical character his quality of strangeness, novelty, strikingness, is the fact that he, Galileo, looks at the world of 1600 around him as if he himself were a stranger' (in Brecht, *Life of Galileo*, ed. John Willett and Ralph Manheim, trans. Willett [1980; rpt. New York: Arcade, 1994], 120; see 121 for the dating).

5 Brecht's theory is now often regarded as thin, and rightly so. Herbert Blau is the most influential detractor; see *The Audience* (Baltimore: Johns Hopkins University Press, 1990), e.g., 36, 190. My interest is not in Brecht's theory per se, but in its application, naïve or otherwise, by one playwright. Valdez does not share Brecht's fondness for Marx. He recounts a testy discussion in Mexico in which he said, 'the whole of Marxism is alien to this continent . . . Let's get down, let's talk Aztec, let's talk Mayan, talk Virgen de Guadalupe and that's closer' ('A Conversation with Luis Valdez,' interview by José Antonio Burciaga, *Image* 2 [1985]: 140).

6 See Brecht, 'Short Description,' 144.

7 Brecht, 'Short Description,' 144. The term *typesetter* is imperfect in a discussion of texts published after the early 1990s. It will be understood that even in 1992 Arte Público may have worked with word-processed texts that Valdez generated and was likely to have done so for Valdez's later volumes.

8 Valdez, *Bandido!*, in *'Zoot Suit' and Other Plays*, 116. Subsequent references to Valdez's plays will appear in the text.

9 All references to *Zoot Suit* are to the 1992 edition, except as noted.

10 For Valdez on film and television, see, e.g., interview, *In Their Own Words*, 270–1. The most common sort of 'freezing' in Brecht, evident throughout his work, is the stopping of action for song. For less ambiguous substantive uses of the word *freeze*, see *Zoot Suit*, 56, 92.

11 Brecht, *Short Organum*, 193.

12 See Tony Curiel, introduction to *Early Works: Actos, Bernabé, and Pensamiento Serpentino*, by Luis Valdez: 'El teatro Campesino' (3); 'a large does of

corazón' (3); 'subjective, elusive qulaity' (3); 'pre-de- | termined blue print' (4). Twice on one page, words are separated by four millimetres of space (3); 'antithesis' is broken 'antith- | esis' (4). The introduction is not noticed in the table of contents. In *Bernabé*, see *'bosom. hypocritically'* (141); 'All th funny stuff' (146); 'We alerady boozed it up' (153); and *'strenth'* (160). Arte Público's substandard in-house practices occasioned a suit filed unsuccessfully in 1993 by Denise Chávez, rankled by the press's decision to reprint, against her express wishes, an error-ridden edition for which she held the copyright; see, e.g., http://publishing.cdlib.org/ucpressebooks/view?docId=kt5n39q4cc&chunk.id=ss1.09&toc.id=ch04&brand=ucpress (accessed 25 August 2010).

13 Once, a character is found *'Concealing his let down'* (92); once, in a passage that I will discuss below, a *'damn breaks'* (128). An extraneous comma lingers on the second page. A 'county Sheriff' becomes a 'County Sheriff' over the course of several lines (79) – an instance complicated by the fact that the first reading is general ('a county Sheriff') and the second specifies the office ('County Sheriff'). This increases the number of possible emendations.

14 Valdez, interview, *In Their Own Words*, 265.

15 Lacking a table of emendations, the 2004 text has no way of informing the reader if the emended reading represents Valdez's intentions or merely a presumptive intramural correction.

16 Valdez notes that El Pachuco's stopping of the action is 'a Brechtian device' (interview, *In Their Own Words*, 265). Savran, the interviewer, notes that the 'happy ending' of *Zoot Suit* is 'immediately called into question'; this, he says, 'seems very Brechtian' (266). The best-known of Brecht's plays to justify Savran's connection are *The Threepenny Opera* (1928); *The Good Person of Szechwan* (1948); the 'American version' of *Galileo* (1945–7, trans. Charles Laughton; rev. 1953); and, arguably, *The Caucasian Chalk Circle* (1948). In the earliest of these plays, the thief Macheath is pardoned, *deus ex machina*, moments before the play ends. But the curtain-speech by his father-in-law Peachum, on 'the poorest of the poor,' notes that 'in reality their end is generally bad' (trans. Desmond Vesey and Eric Bentley [New York: Grove, 1949], 96). Pointed uses of music, props (e.g., placards), and masks are familiar elements of Brechtian dramaturgy. See also note 10, above.

17 Brecht, 'Short Description,' 144.

18 See Valdez, *Zoot Suit*, in *The Wadsworth Anthology of Drama*, brief 5th edition, ed. Worthen (Boston: Wadsworth, 2007), 737–63. The text also appears in the longer edition of 2007.

19 See, generally, Valdez's remark that 'our *campesinos*, the farmworking *raza*, find it difficult to participate in this alien North-American country' (Valdez, 'The Tale of la Raza' [1966], in *The Chicanos*, 97). For proud multilingualism, see my discussion of *Mundo Mata*, below; and see, e.g., Francisco to the Teacher in the *acto* 'No saco nada de la escuela' (1969): 'You call yourself a teacher! I can communicate in two languages. You can only communicate in one. Who's the teacher, Teach?' (in *Early Works*, 78). Valdez recalls performing *actos* '*todo en español Español*' for 'thousands of campesinos,' overseen by hostile Teamsters ('Conversation,' 129). Valdez once called the Teatro 'a bilingual propaganda theater' ('El Teatro Campesino,' 115).

20 Discussing his formal studies, Valdez says, 'I connected with a number of ancient playwrights in a very direct way. Plautus was a revelation, he spoke directly to me . . . The central figure of the wily servant in classical Roman drama – Greek also – became a standard feature of my work with El Teatro Campesino' (interview, *In Their Own Words*, 261). Mundo has been cuckolding the sheriff whom he pretends to serve but will ultimately unmask. Mundo's martyrdom (he is shot as he proclaims his allegiance to Chávez) subverts the tradition; this indicates not that Valdez has rejected Plautus but that he had come to regard genre as inspirational rather than prescriptive. My reference to Shakespeare is presumably transparent; in Ibsen, I instance Jacob Engstrand from *Ghosts* (1881).

21 Domino Renee Perez notes that the scene also 'calls to mind Angel's return in *Giant* [1956], specifically the flag-covered coffin as it is lifted off the train, the difference being, we stay with the family to hear the fallen son/soldier eulogized instead of watching the Obregon family's silent grief' (email to the author, 25 January 2010). See also the conclusion of *Bernabé*, where Torres and Primo exhume and display the protagonist's corpse (167).

22 E.g., 'there's no underestimating the power of emotional impact – I understand better now how ideas are conveyed and exchanged on a beam of emotion. I think Brecht began to discover that in his later works and integrated it' (interview, *In Their Own Words*, 262). Valdez may have been mindful of *The Caucasian Chalk Circle* and various versions of *Galileo*, although Brecht himself disdained empathetic interpretations of the latter play (see, e.g., 'Praise or Condemnation of Galileo' [1947], in *Life of Galileo*, 126–7). For Valdez on the role of emotion in *Zoot Suit*, see, e.g., Burciaga, 'Conversation,' 136–7. Cf. the young Brecht: 'I don't let my feelings intrude in my dramatic work. It'd give a false view of the world. I aim at an extremely classical, cold, highly intellectual style of performance. I'm not writing for the scum who want to have the cockles of their hearts warmed'

('Conversation with Bert Brecht' [1926], in *Brecht on Theatre*, 14); Willett (16) cautions that the translation is loose. For a mature reconsideration, see Brecht, 'Short Description,' 140; and 'Formal Problems Arising from the Theatre's New Content' (1952), in which Brecht observes that his dramaturgy 'by no means renounces emotion' (in *Brecht on Theatre*, 227). See Blau on Brecht's 'inability to forgo ... the empathy in the Alienation, and with it the lure of emotion in the powers of illusion' (*The Audience*, 245).

23 The spondee and the irresistible anapests appear courtesy of Chris Difford and Glenn Tilbrook (Squeeze, 'Is That Love,' on *East Side Story*, A&M 325, 1981, compact disc).

24 Vanden Heuvel, *Performing Drama/Dramatizing Performance: Alternative Theater and the Dramatic Text* (Ann Arbor: University of Michigan Press, 1991), 68.

25 Parks regards the equation 'BLACK PEOPLE + 'WHITEY' = STANDARD DRAMATIC CONFLICT (STANDARD TERRITORY)' as 'bullshit'; she is interested in '*situations showing African-Americans in states other than the Oppressed by/Obsessed with "Whitey" state*' ('An Equation for Black People Onstage,' in Parks, '*The America Play' and Other Works* [New York: Theatre Communications Group, 1995], 21). Parks's readers will recognize the cultural pride that informs her comment.

26 See Broyles-González, *El Teatro Campesino: Theater in the Chicano Movement* (Austin: University of Texas Press, 1994), 214–35. Subsequent references will appear in the text. Valdez 'regrets' that he didn't jettison a fully collective approach to writing earlier ('Conversation,' 131).

27 Less easy to dismiss is Broyles-González's irritation about the lack of attention paid to Valdez's use of 'older Mexican traditions' (*El Teatro Campesino*, 7). Worthen synthesizes the indigenous and European strains in Valdez, with particular attention to Broyles-González's tendentious remark ('Staging América,' see esp. 107–8).

28 De Marinis, 'The Dramaturgy of the Spectator,' *Drama Review* 31 (1987): 103. A need for solidarity and teleology, not an urge for dialectic or inclusiveness, animated the *actos*. 'As propaganda,' Valdez wrote in 1966, 'the Teatro is loyal to an *a priori* social end: the winning of the strike'; he prefaces the remark by saying, 'this is where Brecht comes in' ('El Teatro Campesino,' 116).

29 Elam, Jr, *Taking It to the Streets*, 119.

30 For violence and the threat of violence at Teatro performances in the mid-1960s, see Valdez, 'Conversation,' 129; and interview, *In Their Own Words*, 261.

31 The account in this paragraph derives from Broyles-González, *El Teatro Campesino* (179–96).

32 Broyles-González notices the Teatro's 'shift away from Chicana/o community audiences and toward . . . unsympathetic white audiences' (*El Teatro Campesino*, 173).

33 See Broyles-González's account of Anglo critical responses to the Broadway production (*El Teatro Campesino*, 189–95). The present discussion is complicated by the fact that the Arte Público editions do not specify the sources of the texts they print.

34 Armando B. Rendon typifies the period when, in 1971, he appeals to Chávez and other foundational figures: 'The success of the huelga [strike] is la raza's success . . . In a very real sense, the predicament of the campesino underscores the predicament of all raza, for if we cannot free the Chicano of the fields, how can we free the Chicano of the barrio? They are one and the same' (*Chicano Manifesto* [New York: Macmillan/London: Collier-Macmillan, 1971], 279).

35 The reliably unpleasant John Simon supposed that Valdez included one 'implicitly' and one 'explicitly' Jewish character 'on the assumption . . . that most of our theatergoers are Jewish and that buttering them up is good for business' (quoted in Broyles-González, *El Teatro Campesino*, 203).

36 Valdez would continue exploring interracial relationships as part of a commitment to expansiveness; e.g., the interracial marriage in *I Don't Have to Show You No Stinking Badges!* 'gets into some realities in our lives, in America as a whole' ('Conversation,' 132).

37 José Delgado, 'El Teatro' (1977), quoted in Broyles-González, *El Teatro Campesino*, 172. Delgado's statement appeared in the program of the 1977 TENAZ (Teatro Nacional de Aztlán) Festival. See also Valdez: 'I really want to start writing plays about America as a whole, okay?' ('Conversation,' 132).

38 Noting that he is often attacked 'from the left and the right,' Valdez says, 'as long as [the criticism] keeps coming from both sides I think it's all right' ('Conversation,' 136). Elsewhere: 'The critics are part of the process' (interview, *In Their Own Words*, 269).

39 See Broyles-González, *El Teatro Campesino*, e.g., 235–9. 'Valdez and the Teatro' here honours the collaborative origins of much of Valdez's work.

40 Assuming seven performances weekly (two shows on Sunday; dark on Monday), the two sold-out runs, totaling ten weeks, at the 739-seat Mark Taper Forum would account for 51,730 tickets; and the sold-out ten-week run at the 1,200-seat Aquarius Theater would account for 84,000 tickets. If all the Broadway performances sold out (which seems unlikely), the forty-one performances at the 1,498-seat Winter Garden Theater would account for 61,418 tickets. The maximum total number of tickets sold would be

197,148; actual figures for the Broadway run would almost certainly lower the figure.

41 The sales figures for Valdez's books have been generously provided by Marina Tristán of Arte Público (email to the author, 12 January 2010).

42 Tristán, email to the author.

43 Huerta, introduction to *'Mummified Deer' and Other Plays*, by Luis Valdez, vii.

44 See McGann, *A Critique of Modern Textual Criticism* (Charlottesville: University Press of Virginia, 1992 [1983]), 34–5. McGann, who builds on this idea throughout the *Critique* (and elsewhere), is particularly interested in 'texts of the later modern periods' (34).

45 See McGann, *Critique*, e.g., 37–49.

46 Shillingsburg, 'Editing Thackeray: A History,' in *Textual Studies and the Common Reader: Essays on Editing Novels and Novelists*, ed. Alexander Pettit (Athens: University of Georgia Press, 2000), 115.

47 See, e.g., McGann's ambitious online *Complete Writings and Pictures of Dante Gabriel: A Hypermedia Archive* (2000), which presents, among much else, eclectic texts of Rossetti's work.

48 Arte Público Press, 'About Arte Público Press.'

6 From Book to Text: Theory of/in the Margins

PETER MAHON

'Text'

As is well-known, the word *text* derives from the Latin *texere* (to weave), which can be traced back to the Proto-Indo-European base **tek*-(make), the same root that gives us the word *technology*. In other words, what we sometimes serenely refer to as 'text' is something simultaneously artistic and technological, literal and metaphorical, and which points to the ancient past even as it turns towards the future. 'Text' is thus – and will always be – a contradictory, multiple, and fragmented thing: there is always more than one text. Not surprisingly, 'text' also calls for different types of textual scholars who have not always existed peacefully together. For example, there are textual scholars – such as Fredson Bowers, Jerome McGann, and Peter Shillingsburg – who, despite some critical differences, study the lineages or genealogies of particular texts; at the same time, there are textual scholars – such as Roland Barthes and Jacques Derrida – who, and again despite some crucial differences, think about text and textuality in more philosophical and theoretical terms; and there are scholars such as D.C. Greetham who could be said to occupy something of a middle ground between the first two camps. There has been, of course, a certain amount of crossover between the various camps; nevertheless, I wish to approach the question of the text and textuality here from a theoretical and philosophical perspective because doing so makes it possible to read James Joyce's *Finnegans Wake*[1] as a playful allegory of the forces and dynamics that serve to make up the social academic text. It is hoped that the reading offered here will invite readers to think about the surprising textual and theoretical crossovers of modernist and academic texts.

Finnegans Wake **Is a Peculiar Academic Social Text**

At first glance, *Finnegans Wake* may seem like an odd text to examine in a collection that explores academic social text. Such an impression, however, would ignore the fact that much of Joyce's writing regularly crosses into the academic or scholarly realm. For instance, the final section of Joyce's *A Portrait of the Artist as a Young Man*[2] focuses on its scholarly protagonist, Stephen Dedalus, as he attends university and creates an academic theory of art grounded in the work of Aristotle and the Scholastics. Stephen resurfaces in *Ulysses* as a teacher,[3] and for almost half the text the reader is subjected to stream-of-consciousness versions of several of his theories of religion, philosophy, and art, which are chock-full of academic writers, thinkers, and scholars. Joyce also famously claimed to have put 'so many enigmas and puzzles' into *Ulysses* 'to keep the professors busy for centuries arguing over what I meant' and thereby insure his immortality.[4] And, since the text of *Finnegans Wake* is crammed with many more headscratchers, posers, riddles, stumpers, enigmas, and riddles than *Ulysses*, it would perhaps be exaggerating only slightly to say that it could well keep armies of professors busy for several millennia to come. The text of the *Wake* itself also betrays an abiding interest in academic discourse: for example, it is as obsessed with citation as is academic discourse and it displays a fascination with what can be regarded as its 'academic sources': the work of the eighteenth-century Italian professor, philosopher, rhetorician, and historian Giambattista Vico, the work of the nineteenth-century French professor, historian, and intellectual Edgar Quinet, and the work of the sixteenth-century Italian Dominican friar, professor, philosopher, mathematician, and astronomer Giordano Bruno. More specifically, Book I, episode 5 features a lengthy commentary by a professor – a textual scholar, no less – who compulsively pores over the manuscript of a mysterious letter in an effort to discover more about its origins and author. However, it is perhaps Book II, episode 2 of the *Wake* that most overtly displays that work's fascination with academic or scholarly discourse through its playful fetishization of the very typographic apparatus and conventions that have come to mark a page as academic: footnotes and marginalia. This concern for academic discourse – its style, its sources, its apparatuses – suggests that Joyce wished for – and foresaw – an academic future for his book. And he was not wrong. Indeed, academia has been so busy reading Joyce's work over the decades since his death that it has given rise to what has affectionately (or not) come to be known as the 'Joyce industry.' And this industry is nothing if not prolific: a quick search on Worldcat shows that more than twelve thousand books have been published on the subject of Joyce. There are also several academic journals – such as *The James Joyce Quarterly*, *The James Joyce Broadsheet*, *The James Joyce Literary Supplement*, and *The Dublin James Joyce Journal* – that are devoted almost exclusively to analyses of Joyce's life and work, and there have been many other essays on Joyce's texts published in academic literary journals not devoted to Joyce. Given all this, then, it is perhaps not difficult to see the *Wake* as a text that not only bears a strong bond with academia and academics, but also as a text that is, in many ways, a peculiarly *academic* one.

At the same time, the *Wake* can be said to be a peculiarly *social* text: Joyce famously taxed his acquaintances, friends, family, publishers, and patrons for help and support while writing; he also routinely extended his composition process well into the publication process, making copious insertions on typesheets and typeset proofs. On many occasions, he incorporated miscommunications and errors that arose from the publication process into the 'final' version of his text.[5] On top of all this, Joyce was plagued by poor eyesight, which was caused by an eye condition that led to his undergoing over a dozen painful eye surgeries in his lifetime. During the recovery periods, Joyce frequently had to rely on various assistants – the most famous of which was Samuel Beckett – to whom he dictated the text of the *Wake*.[6] In other words, without this extensive social network of scribes, copyists, editors, typesetters, proofreaders, the *Wake* would not have been published. As such, it can also be read as an allegory of the forces and dynamics at work in what recent textual scholarship has termed the social text. And, given that it is a text that needs – and is needed by – academia in order to be read, *Finnegans Wake* can also be seen as a playful allegory of the forces and dynamics that serve to make up the social academic text. In other words, it is possible to read *Finnegans Wake* not just as a radical and extreme modernist text, but as an allegory that invites the reader to consider what one of the most famously difficult modernist texts ever published shares with the social academic text, however counterintuitive that might seem.

The reading of the *Wake* that follows is divided into three parts. I first briefly reconsider two very well-known essays on the author – Roland Barthes's 'The Death of the Author' and Michel Foucault's 'What Is an Author?' – in order to outline how structuralist and poststructuralist reconfigurations of the text necessitate a displacement of the traditional understanding of the author. The following section provides a brief overview of the *Wake*'s complex text so as to orient a reader who may not be familiar with its complex textuality. The final section focuses on book II, episode 2 of the *Wake* to suggest how it can be read not just as a rigorous dislocation of the author and but also as an allegory of the social academic text.

The Dislocation of the Author

By the latter half of the twentieth century, structuralist and post-structuralist texts were posing readers in academic settings difficult questions about the place of the author. Perhaps the best known of these texts is Roland Barthes's 1968 polemical essay 'The Death of the Author,'[7] which crystallizes the dislocation of the figure of the author that had already begun in, for example, Vladimir Propp's rigorous 1928 formalist analysis of the folktale, *The Morphology of the Folktale*,[8] and Claude Lévi-Strauss's 1958 structuralist analyses of myth, *Structural Anthropology*[9] (which, of course, was itself indebted to Ferdinand de Saussure's early twentieth-century semiotic analysis of language).[10] For Barthes, 'it is language which speaks, not the author; to write is, through a prerequisite of impersonality . . ., to reach that point where only language acts, "performs," and not "me" ' (143). The author is not, in other words, the originator of the words he or she must use: such words pre-exist him or her. The 'language' that 'speaks' in a written text should not, however, be understood as an aridly abstract or colour-less medium; on the contrary, Barthes notes that it bears the marks of the various cultural situations in which it circulates: 'the text is a tissue of quotations drawn from the innumerable centres of culture' (146). Barthes does not simply argue that a text does not have a 'producer'; instead, he argues that a careful consideration of what constitutes 'text' necessitates the displacement of the notion of the 'author.' In the place of the author, Barthes puts the 'modern scriptor,' a figure who 'is born simultaneously with the text' (145) and thus thoroughly enmeshed in it. And, since the text is a tissue of quotations, the 'scriptor' must also be understood as a sort of 'reader' insofar as he or she is – consciously and unconsciously – engaged in the citation of innumerable strands of culturally marked language.[11] Because the scriptor/reader is never in complete control of those strands of language, she or he cannot provide the last word on the meaning of any text that he or she has generated.

Once the author can no longer be regarded as the sole guarantor of the meaning of his or her text, the reader must also be reconceived:

A text is made of multiple writings, drawn from many cultures and entering into mutual relations of dialogue, parody, contestation, but there is one place where this multiplicity is focused and that place is the reader, not, as was hitherto said, the author. The reader is the space on which all the quotations that make up a writing are inscribed without any of them being lost; a text's unity lies not in its origin but in its destination. Yet this destination cannot any longer be personal: the reader is without history, biography, psychology; he is simply that someone who holds together in a single field all the traces by which the written text is constituted. Which is why it is derisory to condemn the new writing in the name of a humanism hypocritically turned champion of the reader's rights . . . we know that to give writing its future, it is necessary to overthrow the myth: the birth of the reader must be at the cost of the death of the Author. (148)[12]

The Barthesian reader does not share his or her contours with the Cartesian, traditional humanist, or bourgeois subject; she or he does not simply come to know, understand, or consume the text. In other words, Barthes is careful not to trade one domineering and controlling subjectivity – the author – for another; rather, the Barthesian reader is understood as a function of the text, not a personality that dominates it or imposes his or her wilful readings upon it. Insofar as the Barthesian reader is 'born' where the traces of a multiple, multicultural, plural, parodic, dialogic text that is constantly at odds with itself are 'held together,' he or she is, as it were, 'recon-textualized' as a shimmering, flickering entity. The reader cannot be said to be purely 'personal' or individual precisely because she or he is the site or place where the various broader multicultural, plural, and dialogic strands or traces of the text incessantly cross and recross.

Michel Foucault's 1969 essay 'What Is an Author?'[13] also engages with the poststructuralist debate on authorship by considering what he calls the 'author function.' Foucault's discussion, which is more historically oriented than Barthes's, identifies four hallmarks of the author function: (1) texts only began to have authors once they became subject to punishment – that is, once the content of a text could be deemed transgressive. The rules governing ownership of a text that came into being in the eighteenth and nineteenth centuries were thus built on a penal conception of authorship; (2) the author function does not apply to all texts at all times – for example, as Foucault points out, narratives, stories, epics, tragedies, comedies, and certain scientific texts have all done without authors at one point or another; (3) the author function is a more or less psychologized 'projection' of the complex series of operations – isolating traits, recognizing continuities, making exclusions, and so on – performed on a series of texts in order to establish them as the authentic work of a particular author; (4) the author function does not necessarily refer to a concrete individual since, for example, in a novel the speaker is not reducible to the writer at the time he or she is writing (108–13). Although Foucault states that it 'is not enough . . . to repeat the empty affirmation that the author has disappeared' (105), his essay nonetheless starts – and, for that matter, ends – in a place that is quite similar to Barthes: the need to reconceive the author as a function of the text due to a shift in the history of how texts are understood to operate.[14] Thus, while the notion of the author acts as a brake on the 'cancerous and dangerous proliferation of significations' (118), Foucault, like Barthes, also foresees the death of the author function, a death that comes about 'as our society changes, at the very moment when it is in the process of changing' (119). Whatever this social change might be – and Foucault does not specify – it would have to entail a shift away from the peculiar ways in which a state's power to punish is not only tied to – but also extended by – the notion of the author: a notion that makes it possible for the state not only to punish someone for having written a transgressive or offensive discourse but also to punish someone else for having infringed on an author's rights. It was perhaps the first shimmers of just such a social change – announced through, entangled with, and refracted by a newly emerging understanding of language and text – that in 1968 compelled Barthes to announce the death of the author and what it represented legally, punitively, politically, artistically, historically, ethnically, and sexually. Indeed, one might wonder to what extent the considerable resistance that Barthes's essay still provokes amounts to an anxiety about what such social and textual change implies for the ability of the state to punish among those who, for example, rely upon or administer that power.

For Barthes, the death of the author also necessitates a shift from the authorial 'work' to the writerly 'text.' In the essay 'From Work to Text,' Barthes argues that a text, although it is not easily separable from a work, cannot be confined to 'good' literature; a text is caught up in the play of the sign rather than the signified meaning; it is irreducibly plural, and is no longer tied to the father-author's signature; a text is not a product that can be easily assimilated by a consumer culture and it is given over to pleasure (155–64). For Barthes, engagements with text produce, almost promiscuously, yet more text: 'the discourse on the

Text should itself be nothing other than text, research, textual activity, since the Text is that *social* space which leaves no language safe, outside, nor any subject of the enunciation in position as judge, master, analyst, confessor, decoder. The theory of the Text can coincide only with a practice of writing' (164; original emphasis). Barthes's reinscription of the notions of text and writing as that which no longer need a master decoder also links it to other poststructuralist analyses of writing, such as Jacques Derrida's analysis of the power of writing to dislocate the '"transcendental" signified' or animating *logos* (Greek, word, reason, or spirit) that guarantees the distinction between the signifier – or 'sensible' part of a sign – and the 'signified' – the 'intelligible' part of the sign.[15] It should not, however, be assumed that this form of 'writing' is confined to texts that are 'written down' and bound in books; as Derrida carefully illustrates in *Of Grammatology*, even 'speech' does not escape the articulated spacing or unconscious cuts of a more generalized 'writing' (69). As a result, a discipline such as phonology 'must indeed renounce all distinctions between writing and the spoken word' (69). The 'writing' of 'text,' in other words, is already at work in 'oral' narrative, which can be understood as a writing without an author.

Barthes's notion of the text as a 'social space' also opens the way for thinking about what poststructuralist constructions of text share with more recent reappraisals of how books come to be by scholarly editors. For example, as Darcy Cullen points out in the introduction to this volume – and as contributor and textual scholar Peter Shillingsburg has explained elsewhere – the 'sociological approach' to book production

> sees the production process as a cultural phenomenon without which books do not exist. The influence of production on the book does not begin when the author hands a completed manuscript to the publisher; it begins when the author raises his pen for the first word of a work intended for publication, because of a consciousness of the way books get published. Publishers, too, are only part of an even larger phenomenon that includes language and usage and everything that forms the sociological context within which authors are enabled to write and can hope to be understood. Publishers, therefore, are not primarily handmaidens to authorship exercising helpful servant roles, which they may fail to do well; they are, instead, part of the authoritative social complex that produces works of art.[16]

A similar concern for the role played by publishers in book production is also to be found in D.C. Greetham's analysis of the 'agency of publication,' which perhaps has the potential to displace more radically the notion of 'authorship' than Shillingburg's conception of an 'authoritative social complex' insofar as it foregrounds the text as the product of the interaction of linguistic and social forces.[17] One might even wonder if these more recent attempts to rethink authorship through the social text would have been possible without the work of Barthes.

Given that there has been an immense amount of theoretical, scholarly, and historical work done on textuality, writing, and authorship in the wake of the work of Barthes, Foucault, and Derrida (among others) over the last forty-odd years, it is perhaps surprising to see in certain recent academic books dealing with First Nations narrative traditions editors, authors, and researchers still struggling to conceive of First Nations Elders and storytellers as anything other than 'authors.' For instance, if one returns to the earlier example given in chapter 1 of this volume, *First Nations Cultural Heritage and Law: Case Studies, Voices, and Perspectives*, one can see volume editors Catherine Bell and Val Napoleon grappling with the problematic notion of the author:

> A more complicated question is how to acknowledge authorship in a manner that respects oral traditions and reflects a truly collaborative process. The Kainai study addresses this issue by including Mookakin as an author. In other studies, this is dealt with by specifying that the studies were developed in consultation with a specific First Nation individual or organization. For practical reasons, it became difficult to name all people who made oral contributions to this project as authors. However, if requested, we would have been prepared to do this despite the challenges it would have created for publishing and making standard contract arrangements for authors' copies, copyright, and allocation of royalties.[18]

Here is a clear indication that, despite the editors' best efforts, the concept of 'author' has real difficulty in coping with the complexity of First Nations narrative structures and traditions. These difficulties, nevertheless, do not stop the volume editors from effectively imposing the category of 'author' on their 'First Nations partners': 'In a typical publishing contract, copyright is assigned to the publisher or retained by authors and [volume] editors with the publisher. In our study, we wanted First Nations partners to have greater control over issues of reproduction and royalties associated with copyright. Consequently, we decided that the copyrights to the case studies would be held jointly by the author, the editors of the first volume, and the appropriate First Nation partner.'[19] Bell and Napoleon are clearly aware that the research, textual, and legal – 'Western' – conceptions of 'author' are a bad fit for First Nations oral traditions. Unfortunately, their solution effectively ignores what textual scholarship has been saying for the last forty-odd years about text and its power not only to challenge the legal-punitive construction of authorship but also its political potential to displace ethnocentric conceptions of the relations between texts and their disseminators. Instead, their solution risks helping to enshrine, entrench, and extend an outmoded and punitive construction of authorship in law, which only makes it harder to propose alternative understandings of text – producer relations. Thus, despite their conscientious efforts to enact their work's decolonizing methodology, Bell and Napoleon's solution not only extends the empire of an author function that is rooted in and expands the state's power to punish to the type of oral texts that, as Foucault points out, have not always needed an author function; that solution could also be said to prevent the very social change that Foucault imagines would herald the end of that conception of the author function. Bell and Napoleon thus miss the chance to examine what a post-structuralist conception of text may share with the powerful social textuality at work in First Nations oral traditions. One might then wonder if the attempt to attach an author to First Nations oral narratives is either ethical or desirable – or even, for that matter, possible. Instead, it would be preferable to rethink the academic, textual, and legal conceptions of authorship through text. What emerges in the course of this rethinking may look something like either the granting of free software licenses through the GNU Project[20] or the granting of open source licenses through the Open Source Initiative;[21] it may look like neither. Such rethinking will, of course, demand patience and care; it will no doubt be experienced as threatening by vested interests – such as academics and publishers – but only to the extent that such interests continue to rely on the state's power to punish.

A more Barthesian approach – at least in terms of form – to the problems caused for academic discourse by First Nations narrative tradition is perhaps glimpsed in a book like *The Trickster Shift: Humour and Irony in Contemporary Native Art*.[22] As Camilla Blakeley points out in her chapter in this volume, the author, designer, and project editor set themselves the difficult task of producing a text that would 'embody the trickster play that is its subject':

> Quotations and notes are used extensively to disburse the narrative voices and reflect the intertextual nature of the discourse. Neither quotation nor note should be considered a secondary or subordinate text. At various points in the conversation, other voices intersect with the principal narrative . . . Non sequitur, song, poem, prose, and personal anecdote enrich and enliven the discourse. In some instances notes take the form of extended annotation and include illustrations. In this they constitute a kind of hypertext or hypermedia, forms of non-sequential writing and visualizing that until recently were primarily associated with literary studies and computer science. More important, the text honours and participates to some degree in a non-linear process of representation shared by many of the artists interviewed. (151)

Throughout *The Trickster Shift*, Ryan's narrative 'authority' is fragmented, supplemented and displaced by anecdotes, poems, quotations, and interviews with Native artists, which are registered in the text by a shifting typography, while short stories, longer interviews, and artists' statements appear on coloured pages. Thus – on the level of form at least – *The Trickster Shift* invokes Barthes's conception of text insofar as it can be said to be made up of 'multiple writings, drawn from many cultures and entering into mutual relations of dialogue, parody, contestation' ('The Death of the Author,' 148): the 'authoritative' discourse of the scholar is challenged and reinscribed by the 'subversive' discourses of the artists and the visual cacophony of the book's 160-plus illustrations. It is a text that announces itself as text, as a text that offers itself to the reader as text. That said, *The Trickster Shift*'s challenge to academic or scholarly discourse never really becomes anything other than formal: for example, the book's copyright rests with the author, and the high costs of its printing have practically ensured that it will never be reprinted on paper. Nevertheless, the importance of *The Trickster Shift*'s formal dislocation of the scholarly study and the scholarly author should not be minimized; without such formal dislocations – and the commitment and bravery of presses that take chances on such projects – it would be extraordinarily difficult to show the potential a Barthesian conception of text has to transform scholarly discourse and scholarly publishing.

An 'Extreme' Text Case: *Finnegans Wake*

An analogue of the subversive 'indigineity' that disrupts the panoply of scholarly or academic discourse – its subjects, sources, apparatus, methods, and authorship – in *The Trickster Shift* is legible in the complex but playful text of James Joyce's *Finnegans Wake*.[23] As I will argue in the next section of this chapter, this subversiveness comes from the margins of the page in Book II, episode 2, which liberate the usually hidden labour of scholarly production and allow it to haunt scholarly discourse. However, before coming to the *Wake*'s disruption of scholarly discourse, I want to take some time to offer to the reader who may not be familiar with it a brief introduction to the *Wake*'s peculiar textuality. In many ways, Barthes's conception of the text as 'a tissue of quotations drawn from the innumerable centres of culture' is an almost perfect description of *Finnegans Wake*. Perhaps the very first thing any reader who attempts to grapple with the book will notice is that its text, 'however basically English' (116.26), is woven from an odd mixture of portmanteau words, foreign languages, multilingual puns, peculiar spellings, and innumerable mangled citations of the titles and contents of a bewildering variety of sources that ranges from the scholarly, the classical, and 'highbrow' – for example, Vico's *The New Science*, Aristotle's *Poetics*, Shakespeare's *Hamlet*, Ibsen's *The Master Builder*, Yeats's *A Vision* – to the unapologetically traditional and populist – such as 'Humpty Dumpty,' Gilbert and Sullivan's *The Gondoliers*, Moore's *A Selection of Irish Melodies*, Barker's *La Belle Sauvage*, and 'Johnny I Hardly Knew Ye.' Two such mangled citations should serve to illustrate the point: one turns a famous line from *Hamlet* into 'this me ken or no me ken Zot is the Quiztune' (110.13–14) – and the other turns the title of Joyce's *A Portrait of the Artist as a Young Man* into 'a poor trait of the artless' (114.31). This second citation is important because it highlights how in 'Funnycoon's Wick' (499.13), Joyce's own texts are treated in the same manner as texts produced by others. In other words, Joyce had no other choice than to become a reader of his own texts, just as he was a reader of, say, Ibsen or the – anonymously authored – nineteenth-century comedic street ballad 'Finnegan's Wake.'

Tracing how *Finnegans Wake* cites Joyce's other texts also illuminates its radical reinscription of the author in a textuality that is a tissue of quotations. As the *Wake*'s 'citation' of Joyce's other texts – such as the titles of the short stories in *Dubliners* ('A Little Cloud' becomes 'in little clots' [186.23], while 'A Painful Case' becomes 'the painful sake' [187.03]) or *Ulysses*, which becomes 'you are pleased' [154.04]) – makes clear, reading *Finnegans Wake* (the title of which is, of course, already a citation of the street ballad just mentioned) is a constant confrontation with citation. Citation in the *Wake*, however, is not limited to certain – mangled or encrypted – chains of words; it also includes the citation of reading technique. The first page of *Finnegans Wake* can, for example, be read as a series of citations of the reading techniques needed to come to grips with the complex and self-referential textuality of Joyce's previous book, *Ulysses*.[24] Take, for instance, the *Wake*'s first 'sentence': 'riverrun, past Eve and Adam's, from swerve of shore to bend of bay, brings us by a commodius vicus of recirculation back to Howth Castle and Environs' (003.1–3). An attentive reader will likely notice several things here: first, the 'sentence' begins without a capital letter, which suggests that part of it is missing, and is perhaps to be found elsewhere in the text. The next thing such a reader might notice is the citation of certain biblical proper names – Eve and Adam's – while a reader already familiar with *Ulysses* is likely to recognize 'Howth' as the same place where one of the book's major characters, Mr Bloom, proposed to his wife, Molly. This mention of Howth also suggests that the *Wake*, like all of Joyce's major texts, is 'set' in and around the city of Dublin; a quick glance at Roland McHugh's *Annotations to* Finnegans Wake[25] would confirm this suspicion as well as confirming that 'Eve and Adam's' inverts the name of a church in Dublin popularly known as Adam and Eve's (more officially known as the Church of the Immaculate Conception). Another thing that might stick out for a reader of this 'sentence' is the odd phrase 'commodius vicus of recirculation' – in which is embedded the Latin word *vicus*, meaning street or village, as well as the impression that this is perhaps not the 'first' time the text has travelled in a circle: '*recirculation*.' Such an impression might lead the reader to turn to the end of the *Wake*; doing so would allow him or her to locate the 'rest' of the book's incomplete opening 'sentence' and discover that the 'last' lines of the book 'join up' with the 'first': 'The keys to. Given! A way a lone a last a loved a long the [] riverrun past Eve and Adam's, from swerve of shore to bend of bay . . .' (628.15–003.02). A reader already familiar with *Ulysses* will also recognize here a citation of the problematic notion of 'return' that both Stephen Dedalus and Mr Bloom grapple with at various points in the course of their day. The opening sentence-fragment, in other words, cites a great deal of information that would be familiar to a reader of Joyce who has never even cracked the spine on a copy of *Finnegans Wake*: familiar notions of Dublin, rivers, roads, repetition and circularity, all of which bring 'us' – the reader thus already has a place prepared for him or her in the first lines of the text – 'back to Howth Castle and Environs.' Indeed, the prominence of citation in the text can also be seen as one of the first clues to the reader that the *Wake*'s textual technique shares a key feature of academic discourse and style – citation.[26]

Several lines later, the first page of the *Wake* (re)introduces the reader to the eponymous figure of Finnegan, the fall of whom, it would seem, is a story that is 'retaled' – that is, repeatedly retailed and retold – all throughout history:

> The fall (bababadalgharaghtakamminarronnkonnbronntonnerronntuonnt-hunntrovarrhounawnskawntoohoohoordenenthurnuk!) of a once wallstrait oldparr is retaled early in bed and later on life down through all christian minstrelsy. The great fall of the offwall entailed at such short notice the pftjschute of Finnegan, erse solid man, that the humptyhillhead of humself prumptly sends an unquiring one well to the west in quest of his tumpty-tumtoes: and their upturnpikepointandplace is at the knock out in the park where oranges have been laid to rust upon the green since devlinsfirst loved livvy. (003.15–24)

This passage, which underscores the importance of quotation through the idea of a tale that is forever retold ('retaled'), also introduces a number of important motifs in the text: first, it sets the scene of the fall in the Phoenix Park (a corruption of the Irish *Fionn Uisce*, meaning clear or white water) near Chapelizod in Dublin (Finnegan's toes seem to stick up near the Castleknock gate: 'the knock out in the park'); second, it opens an association between Finnegan and both fish and phoenixes ('parr' is a young salmon; 'Finnegan' includes a 'fin,' and Finn Mc-Cool [*Fionn mac Cumhaill* in Irish] is a legendary Irish hero who ate the salmon of knowledge); third, it suggests that the scene of Finnegan's 'pftjschute' (French, *chute* or fall) cannot be separated from the multiple languages that can be heard in Finnegan's scream as he falls: '(bababadalgharaghtakamminarronnkonnbronntonnerronntuonnt-hunntrovarrhounawnskawntoohoohoordenenthurnuk!).' Finnegan's scream is also the stuttering sound of thunder: it is the first of ten hundred-letter thunder-words found throughout the text. This one repeats the word for thunder in Irish, French, Japanese, Hindi, German, Greek, Danish, Swedish, Portuguese, Romanian, and Italian. As such, this thunder-word recalls the 'innumerable centres of culture' that provide the tissue of quotations that Barthes says constitutes a text. The initial stuttering ('bababa') of the multilingual thunder-word also recalls the story of the Tower of Babel from Genesis 11:1–9. After the flood, the story goes, the survivors left Mount Ararat and settled on a plain in the land of Shinar, where they set about building a tower whose top would reach Heaven; God was not terribly pleased by this, so he responded by giving each person working on the tower a different language. This act resulted in such confusion that the building of the tower stopped and its builders scattered across the earth. The *Wake* seems to adopt and adapt the story of the Tower of Babel: in the *Wake*an version, however, 'God' does not get to remain in Heaven; as Finnegan, he falls, and the odd 'language' that he screams in rumbles thunderously across the sky is heard as – and thus echoes in – the different languages of those on earth: us, the readers of *Finnegans Wake*.

The ripples generated by Finnegan's withdrawal from the text also produce the waves that drive the 'narrative' level of the text, which, at the end of Book I, episode 1 (I.1), begins to take on the character of an investigation into the circumstances surrounding his fall and disappearance. This investigation is conducted by the composite figure of the 'Mamalujo' (an odd amalgam of the four evangelists, *Ma*tthew, *Ma*rk, *Lu*ke, and *Jo*hn), who, at the end of I.1 try repeatedly to halt Finnegan's wake (024.16–25; 027.22–30) before appearing to give up: 'Repose you now! Finn no more!' (028.33–4). Unable to pin Finnegan down, they instead turn their attentions to an apparently less slippery figure: 'be that samesake sibsubstitute of a hooky salmon, there's already a big rody ram lad at random on the premises of his haunt of the hungred bordles' (028.35–029), 'Humme the Cheapner, Esc' (029.18–19). The four now try to dig back into Humme the Cheapner, Esc's past; however, the futility of their attempt starts to become obvious in I.2, where they are no longer looking into Humme the Cheapner, Esc's past, but into the question 'concerning the genesis of Harold or Humphrey Chimpden's occupational agnomen' (030.02–03). Humme has apparently become someone called Humphrey or Harold who got the surname 'Earwicker' due to his occupation of catching earwigs in a flowerpot (031.1–11). The difficulty of pinning down Humphrey's or Harold's first name seems to explain why the Mamalujo now begin to focus on the 'sigla H.C.E.' (032.14), which is short for the 'christlikeness of the big cleanminded giant H. C. Earwicker' (033.29–30). Just when it seems that they have 'solved' the riddle of H.C.E.'s name, the Mamalujo come across a ballad that appears to be yet another 'retaling' of the circumstances surrounding Finnegan's fall and disappearance: 'The Ballad of Persse O'Reilly,' written by an individual named Hosty (044.24–047.29). However, the ballad, which not only changes H.C.E.'s name to Persse O'Reilly (which echoes *perce-oreille*, the French for earwig), once more links him to Finnegan insofar as it associates him with Humpty Dumpty and accuses him of both rape (047.01–02) and the solicitation of homosexual favours in the Phoenix Park (047.07–12), the scene of Finnegan's fall. The situation goes from bad to worse when I.2 finally gives way to the free-for-all rumour-mongering in I.3 and offers the reader three very different reconstructions of Finnegan's/H.C.E.'s/Persse's crime during the course of which the Phoenix Park shifts locations as it becomes the setting for a fight on a plain in Ireland. Things are further clouded when a *vox pop* is taken, and all and sundry offer their interpretations and opinions as to the circumstances surrounding the fall/crime. Book I, episode 4, which assumes the juridical structure of a trial presided over by the Mamalujo, can be read as a last-ditch attempt to arrive at the 'true truth' (096.27) of the situation regarding Finnegan's/H.C.E.'s/ Persse's crime, fall, and disappearance and indicates just how disruptive I.2's and I.3's rumours and speculation have been. Alas, the trial, forced to call forward what can only be described as the conflicting testimonies of less-than-reliable 'witnesses,' becomes bogged down in a whole host of 'unfacts' (057.16). The judges are finally forced to admit their inability to arrive at the 'true truth' of Finnegan's/H.C.E.'s/ Persse's crime, fall, and disappearance and decide that the best bet is to wait for the letter from his wife, A.L.P., or Anna Livia Plurabelle, which promises to tell the truth about her husband.

In I.5, the reader is given a first glimpse of the letter from 'Annah the Allmaziful, the Everliving, the Bringer of Plurabilities' (104.01–02). A.L.P's letter also blends her with the hen – since it promises to tell the 'cock's trootabout' (113.12) Finnegan/H.C.E./Persse – that both writes and uncovers the letter as she scratches about on a midden heap. It would seem, then, that reading A.L.P.'s/the hen's letter is critical for coming to grips with what happened to Finnegan/H.C.E./Persse. However, the reader's perspective is limited: he or she needs 'the loan of a lens to see as much as the hen saw' (112.01–02). To overcome this impairment, the text simply advises the reader to follow her lead: 'Lead kindly fowl!' (112.09). Reading the letter can thus be said to be a species of taking the auspices – from the Latin *avis specere*, or the observation of birds – insofar as the *Wake* advises the reader to follow the actions of a bird. Taking the auspices also highlights what I would consider to be the most important scholarly source Joyce drew upon while composing *Finnegans Wake*: Giambattista Vico's astonishing eighteenth-century analysis of the cyclical nature of history, *The New Science*.[27] According to Vico, who was chair of rhetoric at the University of Naples when he wrote *The New*

Science, taking the auspices inaugurated human history because it first allowed men to divine – from *divinari*, to foretell – what the gods had in store for them (*NS* 8). However, it should be noted here that even though the hen can be said to be the writer of a letter that is to be deciphered by following her movements, Vico's *The New Science* also suggests that she should not be taken as its 'author' – that is, as the final guarantee of its true meaning or content – in any simple sense. This is because Vico conceived *The New Science* as a sort of proto-Barthesian scholarly text where the author is displaced by a 'reader' who is also a kind of 'writer': 'he who meditates this Science narrates to himself this ideal eternal history so far as he makes it for himself' (*NS* 349). It is thus Vico's *The New Science* that first 'infects' the *Wake* with not only radical textuality but also scholarly discourse, thereby opening it up to the staggering amount of theoretical readings it has been subjected to since the 1960s.

Academic discourse is also foregrounded in the course of I.5's exhaustive scholarly analysis of the hen's letter's salient features – its style, orthography, peculiar penmanship, techniques, and so on. Of the letter's many unusual features, perhaps the ones that stick out the most are the 'four crosskisses' (111.17–18) that the hen/A.L.P. uses to sign the letter. These four crosskisses later morph into a series of strange 'perforations' that puncture the letter's text:

> the fourleaved shamrock or quadrifoil jab was more recurrent wherever the script was clear and the term terse and that these two were the self-same spots naturally selected for her perforations by Dame Partlet on her dungheap . . . (124.20–4)

The shape of these 'quadrifoil perforations,' which have been inflicted on the text by its writer in the guise of 'Dame Partlet' from Chaucer's *The Nun's Priest's Tale*, we are told by the textual scholar connects them to 'all those red raddled obeli cayennepeppercast over the text, calling unnecessary attention to errors, omissions, repetitions and misalignments' (120.14–16). The chain of crosskisses, perforations, and obeli – '✝' – combines to suggest that the author of the letter damages and contaminates the text as she writes it. In other words, there can be no such thing as an 'uncorrupted' or 'pristine' text precisely because the writer – who is, as I suggested above, always already a kind of reader – is also the very force that corrupts the text in producing it. And, if there cannot be an uncorrupted version of the letter, then the document that was supposed to finally put the uncertainty surrounding

Finnegan's/H.C.E.'s/Persse's crime, fall, and disappearance to bed cannot deliver. This also suggests that there is no way of recovering an author-itative, godlike, father figure who would guarantee the stable and truthful interpretation of the past. All that is left behind is a corrupted, shifting, multilingual text that simultaneously promises 'truth' and ceaselessly frustrates any attempt to recover it.

The obeli that mar/mark the hen's letter also connect it to the Irish ninth-century illuminated gospel manuscript the Book of Kells, where, on the recto of folio 219, red obeli run down the middle of the page between the lines, and others around the margins, calling attention to a scribal error in the manuscript. The placement of these obeli in the Book of Kells also makes it possible to think of the hen's/A.L.P.'s letter as a text where the 'margins' mingle with the text's 'centre,' the place where the letter's lines of text cross to produce its 'cardinal points':

> One cannot help noticing that rather more than half of the lines run north-south in the Nemzes and Bukarahast directions while the others go west-east in search from Maliziies with Bulgarad for, tiny tot though it looks when schtschupnistling alongside other incunabula, it has its cardinal points for all that. (114.02–07)

All of this criss-crossing points to the letter's peculiarly kinetic textuality: if the letter is made up of criss-crossing lines of text, then it becomes possible to see how the letter's obeli-crosskisses 'mimic' the larger structure of its text. In other words, the letter's textuality makes it possible to see the '(w)hole' of its text in its 'parts' – and vice versa: that is, the †/Xs of the obelus, kiss, or perforations, each of which is only one small part of the letter, double for the entire letter itself, which seems to be composed of larger crosses. In this criss-crossing, the text is also radically de-centred: its margins, mistakes, and contaminants ceaselessly cross over in(to) its 'centre,' while its centre is endlessly expelled to its 'margins.' All of this suggests that not only does the text of the hen's letter displace the author, it also teaches the reader to read both kinetically and 'hologrammatically,' in the sense that the 'whole' of the criss-crossed letter can be read in its 'parts.' And if part can stand for the whole in the letter, then it is perhaps not surprising to learn that A.L.P.'s/the hen's 'polyhedron of scripture' (107.08) can be said to stand for the whole text of *Finnegans Wake*. This would explain why I.5's description of the language of the letter is perfectly applicable to the text of the *Wake* as a whole:

For if the lingo gasped between kicksheets, however basically English, were to be preached from the mouths of wickerchurchwardens and metaphysicians in the row and advokaatoes, allvoyous, demivoyelles, languoaths, lesbiels, dentelles, gutterhowls and furtz, where would their practice be or where the human race itself were the Pythagorean sesquipedalia of the panepistemion, however apically Volapucky, grunted and gromwelled, ichabod, habakuk, opanoff, uggamyg, hapaxle, gomenon, ppppfff, over country stiles, behind slated dwellinghouses, down blind lanes, or, when all fruit fails, under some sacking left on a coarse cart? (116.25–35)

The remainder of *Finnegans Wake* can be read as a tracing of the trajectory of the letter as it makes its way to the hands of the waiting judges in I.4: 'Letter, carried of Shaun, son of Hek, written of Shem, brother of Shaun, uttered for Alp, mother of Shem, for Hek, father of Shaun. Initialled. Gee. Gone' (420.17–19). Given that the letter needs all these other figures in order to be delivered, following the letter's journey also makes it possible to see it – and thus the text of *Finnegans Wake* 'itself' – as a social text that displaces and reinscribes the author in an anarchic carnival of textuality that draws together scholarly discourse – through, for example, its obsession with citation, its treatment of Vico's *The New Science,* and its staging of the scholarly analysis of the letter's text in I.5 – and Barthes's conception of text as a multicultural social space composed of a tissue of quotations. *Finnegans Wake* is, in other words, a peculiar social academic text.

'Night lessons': Scenes of Sexual/Textual Perversity

However, even in a text with the kind of citational, kinetic, playful, and fragmented textual surface described in the previous section, Book II, episode 2 – also frequently known as the 'Night lessons' episode – of *Finnegans Wake* stands out as typographically unusual. The pages of 'Night lessons' consist, for the most part, of a central column of text; framing this central column on three sides are marginal columns of text and footnotes that incessantly comment on it. The footnotes serve to make the pages in this episode look like that of a higher-level academic book, and the tone of the comments on one side of the page appears to be scholarly, sounding not unlike the type of marginal notes that might be made by a learned reader. By contrast, the tone of the commentary on the other side of the page and in the footnotes treats the central column of text in a much less deferential manner while 'editorializing' frequently on it. Nor is the text of II.2 simply content to evoke and mock the look and tone of higher-level academic texts and discourse; the central column of text also echoes texts emblematic of the most basic levels of training and learning, as Joyce notes in a letter from July 1939 to his friend Frank Budgen: the technique of 'Night lessons' is 'a reproduction of a schoolboy's (and schoolgirl's) old classbook complete with marginalia by the twins, who change sides at half time, footnotes by the girl (who doesn't), a Euclid diagram, funny drawings, etc.'[28] The Euclid diagram appears on page 293 – adorned with Anna Livia Plurabelle's initals, 'ALP' – while the 'funny drawings' appear on pages 299 and 308 (see fig. 6.1). The complex typographical layout of this chapter – which stands as testament to the labour and skill of the typesetters who actually designed and set the text of the *Wake* – thus both evokes and mocks the printed page of all levels of academic or scholarly discourse; and, as I will argue, it stages the disruption of a central academic authority by unleashing an editorializing 'marginality' that interrupts, reshapes, and reinscribes scholarly text.

It is II.2's concern for the margins of the page that also serves to connect the *Wake*'s textuality with the history of the book, and the scholarly book in particular: between 1525 and 1675, printed marginalia – that is, printed sidenotes and not just handwritten scribbles – appeared in about half of the books produced in English.[29] This common practice had fallen out of favour by the early eighteenth century because readers began associating the marginalia with scholarly labour, seeing them as intrusive and unsightly distractions from the supposed elegance of the main text; the marginalia were eventually relegated to the bottom of the page and became footnotes.[30] Thus, by offering its reader an episode where the centre column of text is enveloped by both marginal insertions and footnotes that editorialize on it, 'Night lessons' can be said to stage, in a remarkably allegorical and condensed fashion, the kinetic play of margins, foot, and centre that makes up the history of not simply the printed page as such, but more particularly the *academic* page; at the same time, II.2 is also a sort of scholarly séance, where the unquiet spectres of scholarly labour and book publication are summoned and allowed to possess the page once more, where their traces may be reread.

Although such early marginal insertions were, as Slights notes, keyed to authorship – and thus served to coerce the reader by making sure she or he was following the twists and turns of a text's argument correctly – the long-running debate about the problems posed by inserting such annotations into Scripture[31] indicates that there was, at the same time, a considerable anxiety about the potential for these

Xenophon.	Delays are Dangerous. Vitavite! Gobble Anne: tea's set, see's eneugh! Mox soonly will be in a split second per the chancellory of his exticker.	
Pantocracy.	Aun	MAWMAW, LUK, YOUR BEEEFTAY'S FIZZIN OVER!
Bimutualism.	Do	
Interchangeabil-ity. Naturality.	Tri	
	Car	
Superfetation.	Cush[1]	
Stabimobilism.	Shay	
Periodicity.	Shockt	
Consummation.	Ockt	
Interpenetrative-ness. Predicam-ent. Balance of the factual by the theoric Boox and Coox, Amallaga-mated.	Ni	
	Geg[2]	
	Their feed begins.	KAKAO-POETIC LIPPUDENIES OF THE UNGUMP-TIOUS.

NIGHTLETTER

With our best youlldied greedings to Pep and Memmy and the old folkers below and beyant, wishing them all very merry Incarnations in this land of the livvey and plenty of preprosperousness through their coming new yonks

from
jake, jack and little sousoucie
(the babes that mean too)

[1] Kish is for anticheirst, and the free of my hand to him!

[2] And gags for skool and crossbuns and whopes he'll enjoyimsolff over our drawings on the line!

308

Figure 6.1: *Finnegans Wake*, p. 299

marginalia to threaten the (divine) authority of the (sacred) text by opening it up to readings that would pervert the author's – God's – meaning. The potential of the margins to 'pervert' (divine) authority is both foregrounded and radicalized in the 'Night lessons' episode, where it becomes entangled with a certain sexual perversity. At one point in the episode, the twins – Dolph (Shem) and Kevin (Shaun) – knuckle down to their homework by using a Euclidean diagram to 'construct ann aquilittoral dryankle Probe loom' (286.19–20) – that is, to construct an equilateral triangle problem. During the exercise, one of the twins, Dolph/Shem, sees an opportunity to turn the diagram into a picture of their mother's – A.L.P.'s – vagina. When Kevin/Shaun finally sees his mother's triangle of pubic hair – 'Biddy's hair. Biddy's hair, mine lubber!' (305.19–20; 'Biddy' is yet another of A.L.P.'s many names) – he is both delighted with and annoyed at his brother. The twins, in other words, literally 'pervert' the academic information they are supposed to be faithfully reproducing; thus, the 'Night lessons' episode's scene of scholarship underscores how the transmission of text and meaning is subject to an essentially playful – and explosively perverse – contaminating dissemination that cannot help but threaten and disrupt all sorts of stemma – familial, textual, and semantic – even as it continues them. It should also be noted that, as frequently happens in Joyce, 'form' in this scene mimics 'content,' collapsing the distinction between the two: the culmination of sexual perversity in a perversion of text is played out in an episode where, again and again, the meaning of the central stream of authoritative text is disruptively enveloped by a perverse scholarly 'critical apparatus' – Dolph and Kevin's marginalia – that incessantly 'editorializes' on the text it is supposed to be reproducing in a manner that does not simply defer to its authority.

The power of a page's margins – this time it will be a footnote, the place of academic labour – to displace and reinscribe the authority and meaning of the 'main' or central text it accompanies also plays itself out in II.2's citation of the following sentence:

Aujourd'hui comme aux temps de Pline et de Columelle la jacinthe se plaît dans les Gaules, la pervenche en Illyrie, la marguerite sur les ruines de Numance[1] et pendant qu'autour d'elles les villes ont changé de maîtres et de noms, que plusieurs sont entrées dans le néant, que les civilisations se sont choquées et brisées, leurs paisables générations ont traversé les âges et sont arrivées jusqu'à nous, fraîches et riantes comme aux jours des batailles.[2] (281.04–13)[32]

This sentence, a virtually intact (in itself something quite unusual for the *Wake* as a whole) citation from Edgar Quinet's *Introduction à la philosophie de l'histoire de l'humanité* (*Œuvres Complètes*, vol. 2, 367) – yet another of the *Wake*'s scholarly sources – is adorned with the following footnote from Issy: 'Translout that gaswind into turfish, Teague, that's a good bog and you, Thady, poliss it off, there's nateswipe, on to your blottom pulper' (281.F2). Issy's footnote is, like Dolph and Kevin's marginalia, also explosively perverse; it transforms the beauty of Quinet's French prose into something approximating loutish flatulence and shit: the sentence has become 'gaswind' that has to be 'translouted' into 'turfish.' Issy's invocation of turf here also makes more sense if it is read in conjunction with the scene in II.3 where a Russian general is seen by an Irish sniper (named, appropriately enough, Butt) defecating and using a 'sob of tunf' – a sod of turf – 'to wollpimsolff' – to wipe himself – (353.16–17). Butt, outraged at 'that instullt to Igorladns!' (353.18–19) – Ireland is commonly, if not always affectionately, referred to as 'the Oul' Sod (of Turf)' – promptly shoots the general (353.21). The association of writing, turf, and shit thus explains why Issy says that the translation of the 'gaswind' of the Quinet sentence needs to be wiped off with 'blottom pulper,' a combination of blotting paper and toilet paper.[33]

However, Issy's footnote does not only transform Quinet's sentence into flatulence and shit; it also links it to the *Wake*'s more general association of excrement and urine with the writer and his or her text. Perhaps the clearest example of this association can be found in I.7's description of Shem the penman by his brother Shaun the postman. According to Shaun, Shem, who has since been revealed as a (co)writer/(co)transcriber of the letter discussed in the previous section, is 'sham' (170.24), who sits in his house, named the 'Haunted Inkbottle' (182.31) in 'condign satisfaction' (172.29), surrounded by the scribbled down snippets of other people's overheard conversations – the 'delicate tippits' (172.32) of 'every crumb of trektalk' (172.30). If Shem is 'covetous of his neighbour's word' (172.30), it is because it constitutes the raw material he uses to produce his 'chambermade music' (184.04) – that is, music made in a chamber pot. And if the text Shem produces seems 'quite puzzonal to the wrottel' – that is, personal to the writer – it is only because the words of others that make it up have passed through his body and are written in a 'stinksome inkenstink' (183.06–07).

The *Wake*'s scatalogical conception of art also carries over into Shaun's account of the fear Shem experiences when he hears thunder.

On hearing the terrifying call of the thundering God – the 'fulminant firman' (185.27) in whose thunder one can hear an echo of Finnegan's screams as he falls – Shem literally shits and pisses out a text in response: 'when the call comes, he shall produce nichthemerically from his unheavenly body a no uncertain quantity of obscene matter not protected by copriright in the United Stars of Ourania' (185.28–31).[34] And, by turning the call of the thunder-god into a shitty text that is littered with, among other things, 'once current puns' and 'quashed quotatoes' (183.22), Shem perverts the word of God by rewriting it in the shit-stained words of others. When all of this is taken together, it would seem that what the writer produces – text – is indissociable from both theft and contamination: that is, Shem, like the hen/A.L.P, is always already a source of contamination and theft insofar as he steals, warps, and perverts the divine words of the falling God and the everyday words of other people. Indeed, Shem's inauthentic doubling-distortion of the words of others is what seems to underlie his brother's irritation with his art: for Shaun, Shem's writing is nothing more than an unoriginal sham, a low form of 'bardic memory' (172.28). Shaun's annoyance at his brother simmers throughout the text until it reaches something of a rolling boil in III.1, when he angrily denounces the letter that he has been tasked to deliver:

> Every dimmed letter in it is a copy and not a few of the silbils and wholly words I can show you in my Kingdom of Heaven. The lowquacity of him! With his threestar monothong! Thaw! The last word in stolentelling! And what's more rightdown lowbrown schisthematic robblemint! (424.17–36)

Shaun's outburst here makes it fairly clear that as interesting as the letter is – and it is truly fascinating – its value does not lie in its ability to help the reader come to the final truth about the whereabouts of Finnegan/H.C.E./Persse and the circumstances surrounding his fall/crime/disappearance. Its value lies, rather, in how it holds out the possibility of reading a text for something other than God's/the father's/the author's/another's pristine truth.

Given all this, it is perhaps not surprising to see a different footnote of Issy's in II.2 literally halt – 'A halt for hearsake.[1]' – the flow of the main stream of text. Issy's footnote, in other words, literally intervenes in the authority of the central column of text, interrupts and diverts it, effectively taking over the page and leading the reader to wonder

and the face in the treebark feigns afear. This
is rainstones ringing. Strangely cult for this
ceasing of the yore. But Erigureen is ever.
Pot price pon patrilinear plop, if the osseletion
of the onkring gives omen nome? Since alls
war that end war let sports be leisure and
bring and buy fair. Ah ah athclete, blest your
bally bathfeet! Towntoquest, fortorest, the
hour that hies is hurley. A halt for hearsake.[1]

MODES COA-
LESCING
PROLIFER-
ATE HOMO-
GENUINE
HOMOGEN-
EITY.

[1] Come, smooth of my slate, to the beat of my blosh! With all these gelded
ewes jilting about and the thrills and ills of laylock blossoms three's so much
more plants than chants for cecilies that I was thinking fairly killing times of
putting an end to myself and my malody, when I remembered all your pupil-
teacher's erringnesses in perfection class. You sh'undn't write you can't if you
w'udn't pass for undevelopmented. This is the propper way to say that, Sr. If
it's me chews to swallow all you saidn't you can eat my words for it as sure as
there's a key in my kiss. Quick erit faciofacey. When we will conjugate together toloseher tomaster tomiss while morrow fans amare hour, verbe de vie
and verve to vie, with love ay loved have I on my back spine and does for
ever. Your are me severe? Then rue. My intended, Jr, who I'm throne away
on, (here he inst, my lifstack, a newfolly likon) when I slip through my pettigo
I'll get my decree and take seidens when I'm not ploughed first by some
Rolando the Lasso, and flaunt on the flimsyfilmsies for to grig my collage
juniorees who, though they flush fuchsia, are they octette and viginity in my
shade but always my figurants. They may be yea of my year but they're nary
nay of my day. Wait till spring has sprung in spickness and prigs beg in to pry
they'll be plentyprime of housepets to pimp and pamper my. Impending marriage. Nature tells everybody about but I learned all the runes of the gamest
game ever from my old nourse Asa. A most adventuring trot is her and she
vicking well knowed them all heartswise and fourwords. How Olive d'Oyly
and Winnie Carr, bejupers, they reized the dressing of a salandmon and how a
peeper coster and a salt sailor med a mustied poet atwaimen. It most have
bean Mad Mullans planted him. Bina de Bisse and Trestrine von Terrefin.
Sago sound, rite go round, kill kackle, kook kettle and (remember all should
I forget to) bolt the thor. Auden. Wasn't it just divining that dog of a dag
in Skokholme as I sat astrid uppum their Drewitt's altar, as cooledas as cul-
cumbre, slapping my straights till the sloping ruins, postillion, postallion, a
swinge a swank, with you offering me clouts of illscents and them horners
stagstruck on the leasward! Don't be of red, you blanching mench! This
isabella I'm on knows the ruelles of the rut and she don't fear andy mandy. So
sing loud, sweet cheeriot, like anegreon in heaven! The good fother with the
twingling in his eye will always have cakes in his pocket to bethroat us with
for our allmichael good. Amum. Amum. And Amum again. For tough troth
is stronger than fortuitous fiction and it's the surplice money, oh my young
friend and ah me sweet creature, what buys the bed while wits borrows the
clothes.

279

Figure 6.2: *Finnegans Wake*, p. 279

to what extent Issy may have switched places with the central text for the remainder of the chapter (279.F1; see fig. 6.2). Yet another displacement of the main stream of the text by a footnote occurs later in 'Night lessons' when another of Issy's footnotes seems to counsel the reader to 'Wipe your glosses with what you know' (304.F3). This time, however, the footnote does not *literally* disrupt the central stream of the text; nevertheless, by counselling the reader to gloss the text with what he or she knows, Issy's footnote radically shifts the power dynamics of authority in *Finnegans Wake*, thereby enacting a Barthesian displacement of the author by the reader. That Issy performs this shift through an act that is indissociable from *editor*-ializing is important; through her editorializing, Issy explicitly (re)articulates the place of the footnote with the place of the reader reading and the editor. Her editorial intervention radically transforms the text and how it can be read. And, since she speaks from a footnote – the marginal place of scholarly labour – Issy can thus be seen as a sort of academic editor who has the power to change texts: what is an editor, if not a peculiarly powerful reader who literally gets to change the texts she or he reads? And, if such an academic 'editor-reader' has the power to change texts, then she or he must also be something of an academic 'editor-writer.' It would seem, given all this, that the *Wake* invites its reader to see the footnote as a curiously social part of the page where editor, reader, and scholarly labour criss-cross and engage each other over and again. Further, since Issy's 'scholarly' footnote echoes Vico's *The New Science* – where, as I suggested above, the 'reader' is always already a kind of 'writer' – it is a doubly good place to hear the laboured moans of the *Wake*'s unquiet scholarly spectres. Read in this way, the text of II.2 can thus be said to be a kinetic literary allegory of the editorial interventions and framing that make up a scholarly text; and it is this literary staging of scholarly discourse which suggests that the distinction that separates 'literary' text from 'scholarly' text may not be as secure as one might have imagined.

Similarly unquiet scholarly spectres can also be seen hovering in the margins of the text during the scene – already discussed above – of the twins' sexual/textual perversion; and, when these ghosts invade the text, they once again herald a literal displacement of the authority of the central column of text by its margins. This displacement, which occurs just after Kevin admits to his brother, Dolph, that he is having problems constructing 'ann aquilittoral dryankle Probe loom' (286.19–20), takes the form of a long parenthesis that focuses on Dolph's early childhood (287.18) and appears to have been written by his brother Kevin. This parenthesis, which covers pages 287–92, takes over the page, thus becoming a sort of 'internal margin' – if such a thing can be said to exist – wherein the marginalia disappear – but not the footnotes. This internal margin also includes a piece of Latin that invokes two of the *Wake*'s primary scholarly sources, Giambattista Vico and Giordano Bruno:

> – *venite, preteriti,*[3] *sine mora dumque de entibus nascituris decentius in lingua romana mortuorum parva chartula liviana ostenditur, sedentes in letitiae super ollas carnium, spectantes immo situm lutetiae unde auspiciis secundis tantae consurgent humanae stirpes, antiquissimam flaminum amborium Jordani et Jambaptistae mentibus revolvamus sapientiam: totum tute fluvii modo mundo fluere, eadem quae ex aggere fututa fuere iterum inter alveum fore futura, quodlibet sese ipsum per aliudpiam agnoscere contrarium, omnem demun amnen ripis rivalibus amplecti*[4] – (287.19–28)
>
> (Come without delay, ye men of old, while a small piece of second grade imperial papyrus, concerning those to be born later, is exhibited with more propriety in the Roman tongue of the dead. Let us, seated joyfully on fleshpots and beholding in fact the site of Paris whence such great human progeny is to arise, turn over in our minds that most ancient wisdom of both the priests Giordano and Giambattista: the fact that the whole of the river flows safely, with a clear stream and that those things which were to have been on the bank would later be in the bed; finally, that everything recognizes itself through something opposite and that the stream is embraced by rival banks)[35]

This Latin clearly suggests that what the reader witnesses here is the explicit displacement of the central, 'authoritative' column of text by its ghostly, perverse, scholarly margins – 'those things which were to have been on the banks' are now to be found 'in the bed': the scholarly margins thus appear to be possessing the centre, displacing it and supplementing it. And, by highlighting those unsettling quasi-democratic, quasi-anarchic zones of textual play and unsightly scholarly labour that cannot be owned or dominated by a centralized voice of academic authority precisely because that 'authority' is utterly dependent on the work of/in those margins, the 'literary' text of the *Wake* stages the complex social dynamics of the 'scholarly' page in a way that erases any hard-and-fast distinction between 'scholarly' and 'literary' text.

If the *Wake* can be said to make the scholarly page of text more literary, it also insistently links the text and textuality that emerges to the complex social dynamics of the academic text: for it is there, in the margins of the page, that editors, readers, sources, and writers criss-cross and engage each other ceaselessly. These margins can also be said to be oriented towards a future, 'virtual' textuality that exceeds the printed page in that it need not be bound by a traditional or classical under-standing of the book, the page, or even the difference between schol-arly or literary texts: it is not by accident that the *Wake*'s textuality has long invited comparisons to hypertext.[36] In this (hyper)textual future, however, it would not be a matter of simply multiplying authors, or reducing/elevating any or all of the agents or forces that are at work in and on texts to the status of author; on the contrary, as I have tried to suggest, 'Night lessons' shows that it is the very concept of academic authorship itself that is necessarily rearticulated by the act of an editor-reader reading-writing a text, an act that exceeds the author and lib-erates an alternative and challenging understanding of how texts are made, performed, and changed.

NOTES

1 *Finnegans Wake* (London: Faber and Faber, 1939).
2 *Portrait of the Artist as a Young Man* (London: Penguin, 2000).
3 *Ulysses* (New York: Vintage, 2000).
4 Richard Ellmann, *James Joyce* (Oxford: Oxford University Press, 1982), 521.
5 For a playful discussion of one of these moments in the process of pub-lishing *Ulysses*, see Sebastian Knowles's *The Dublin Helix: The Life of Language in Joyce's* Ulysses (Gainsville: University Press of Florida, 2001). Establishing 'error-free' versions of Joyce's texts has been something of a holy grail for some time. Would-be editors have had not only to contend with the James Joyce Estate but also Joyce's composition habits. As men-tioned above, Joyce continually tweaked his texts as they passed through the various stages in the publishing process, inserting many notes and additions into everything from typescripts to galley proofs. This way of working meant that 'errors' made their way into the final texts. Accord-ing to Jack Dalton's 'The Text of *Ulysses*' (in *New Light on Joyce from the Dublin Symposium*, ed. Fritz Senn [Bloomington: Indiana University Press, 1972]), the first edition of *Ulysses* published contained about two thou-sand errors and is considered by some to be the cleanest. Hans Walter Gabler's 1984 edition of *Ulysses*, which attempted to correct these errors by going back to Joyce's manuscripts, typescripts, proofs, etc., became an object of controversy, which, to say the least, descended into a very

personal and acrimonious debate. The most vocal critic of Gabler's edition was John Kidd, who suggested that Gabler's edition had made some two thousand changes to Joyce's final intentions (see Kidd's 'The Scandal of Ulysses,' *New York Review of Books*, 30 June 1988, 32–9, and his *An Inquiry into 'Ulysses': The Corrected Text* [New York: Bibliographical Society of America, 1988]). The debate surrounding *Ulysses* made clear that there has never been a 'pristine' 'error-free' version of *Ulysses*: Joyce's text and error are inextricable from each other. One can thus easily imagine how these problems become exponentially multiplied when it comes to a far more complex text like the *Wake*, where every single word on the page looks as though it contains multiple errors. The *Wake* also poses some interesting problems for people like me who endeavour to write on its text: quotations for the *Wake* cause havoc for the spelling and grammar checkers in word-processing programs. These checkers spend so much time pointing out errors that the only way to work in peace is to shut them off or build a custom dictionary. The problem, of course, is that either course of action makes it very difficult to catch typographical errors in what you are writing, which can then – and this is endlessly frustrating – find their way into print and be blown up into something else. So, in addition to causing sleepless nights, working with Joyce demands a reappraisal of the ontology of the error.

6 See Ellmann, *James Joyce*, 649. For more on the Joyce–Beckett friendship, see Barbara Reich Gluck, *Beckett and Joyce: Friendship and Fiction* (Lewisburg: Bucknell University Press, 1979).

7 Roland Barthes, 'The Death of the Author,' in Barthes, *Image, Music, Text*, trans. Stephen Heath (London: Fontana, 1977), 142–8.

8 *The Morphology of the Folktale*, trans. Laurence Scott (Austin: University of Texas Press, 1968).

9 *Structural Anthropology*, trans. Claire Jacobson (New York: Basic Books, 1963).

10 *Course in General Linguistics*, ed. Charles Bally and Albert Sechehaye, trans. Roy Harris (La Salle, IL: Open Court, 1983).

11 For Barthes's discussion of the diminishing of the distance between reading and writing, see 'From Work to Text' in *Image, Music, Text*, 162. For Barthes's fullest examination of the writer-as-reader and 'writerly texts,' see his *S/Z*, trans. Richard Miller (New York: Hill and Wang, 1974).

12 At the same time, however, the notions of the reader, the text, and writing can also be understood to exceed the scientific ambitions of structuralism insofar as it can be said to move beyond a desire to quantify texts. Barthes's approach has, of course, resonances with many other strands

of literary theory that pay attention to the reader's role in (re)creating the meaning of a literary work. In the 1920s and 1930s, scholars such as I.A. Richards and Louise Rosenblatt devoted attention to how readers responded to texts. In the 1960s and 1970s the American and German schools of reader-response criticism, exemplified by the work of Norman Holland, Stanley Fish, Wolfgang Iser, and Hans-Robert Jauss among others, began to pay systematic attention to how readers read. New Criticism, as championed by William K. Wimsatt and Monroe Beardsley in the 1950s, argued strongly against any discussion of an author's intention, or intended meaning. However, although it can be said to share, to a certain extent, reader-oriented criticism's dislocation of the author, New Criticism also tended to discount the reader's role in (re)creating text. See, for example, W.K. Wimsatt and Monroe Beardsley, *The Verbal Icon: Studies in the Meaning of Poetry* (Lexington: University of Kentucky Press, 1954).

13 Michel Foucault, 'What Is an Author?' trans. Josué Harari, in *The Foucault Reader*, ed. Paul Rabinow (New York: Pantheon, 1984), 101–20.

14 One might wonder if Foucault's essay does not sometimes oversimplify both Barthes's and Derrida's positions, even though he avoids mentioning their names. As I suggested above, Barthes does not say that the author simply never existed; rather, he argues that the author is 'dead' insofar as she or he is no longer the figure we can look to as the final guarantor of a text's meaning. Instead, Barthes suggests that we turn towards the writer or scriptor and writerly texts. Indeed, Foucault explicitly accepts the author's disappearance when he states, 'we must locate the space left empty by the author's disappearance, follow the distribution of gaps and breaches, and watch for the openings that this disappearance uncovers' (105). In other words, that which emerges in the wake of the death of the author remains, precisely, to be seen.

15 See, for example, Derrida's discussion of Nietzsche and Heidegger in *Of Grammatology*, trans. Gayatri Chakravorty Spivak (Baltimore: Johns Hopkins University Press, 1976), 19–20.

16 Peter Shillingsburg, 'An Inquiry into the Social Status of Texts and Modes of Textual Criticism,' *Studies in Bibliography* 42 (1989): 62–3.

17 D.C. Greetham, 'Society and Culture in the Text,' in Greetham, *Theories of the Text* (New York: Oxford University Press, 1999), 403.

18 Catherine Bell and Val Napoleon, 'Introduction, Methodology, and Thematic Overview,' in *First Nations Cultural Heritage and Law: Case Studies, Voices, and Perspectives*, ed. Bell and Napoleon (Vancouver: UBC Press, 2008), 12.

19 Ibid., 16.

20 See http://www.gnu.org.

21 See http://www.opensource.org.

22 Allan J. Ryan, *Trickster Shift: Humour and Irony in Contemporary Native Art* (Vancouver and Toronto: UBC Press, 1999). Blakeley also notes that 'some artists were culturally opposed to the whole notion of written contracts' (159, this volume).

23 It is interesting to note that there is something of a restless 'indigenity' already at work in Joyce's collection of short stories, *Dubliners* (London: Penguin Classics, 2000). In the story 'An Encounter,' the narrator plays the part of a 'reluctant Indian,' which nevertheless enables him to open 'doors of escape' (11) from his dreary existence as a young Dubliner chafing under the twin yokes of stifling Catholicism and British colonialism.

24 The reading of *Finnegans Wake* that follows in this section draws on aspects of my discussion of the *Wake* in chap. 5 of my *Joyce: A Guide for the Perplexed* (London: Continuum, 2009). For an extensive discussion of the reading techniques needed to read *Ulysses*, see chaps. 2–4 of the same text. For a discussion of how the imagination functions as a citational force in *Finnegans Wake*, see my *Imagining Joyce and Derrida: Between* Finnegans Wake *and* Glas (Toronto: University of Toronto Press, 2007).

25 See *Annotations to* Finnegans Wake (Baltimore: Johns Hopkins University Press, 1991), 3.

26 See, for example, Ann M. Johns, *Text, Role, and Context: Developing Academic Literacies* (Cambridge: Cambridge University Press, 1997), 63.

27 Giambattista Vico, *The New Science*, trans. Thomas Goddard Bergin and Harold Max Fisch (Ithaca: Cornell University Press, 1968).

28 *Letters of James Joyce, Volume 1*, ed. Stuart Gilbert (London: Faber and Faber, 1957), 405–6.

29 William W.E. Slights, 'Back to the Future – Littorally: Annotating the Historical Page,' in *The Future of the Page*, ed. Peter Stoicheff and Andrew Taylor (Toronto: University of Toronto Press, 2004), 71.

30 Slights, 'Back to the Future,' 77.

31 Slights, 'Back to the Future,' 77. See also Deborah Kuller Shuger, *The Renaissance Bible: Scholarship, Sacrifice and Subjectivity* (Berkeley: University of California Press, 1994.

32 The original sentence and translation read as follows: '*Aujourd'hui comme aux temps de Pline et de Columelle la jacinthe se plaît dans les Gaules, la pervenche en Illyrie, la marguerite sur les ruines de Numance; et pendant qu'autour d'elles Les villes ont changé de maître et de nom, que plusieurs sont rentrées dans le néant, que les civilisations se sont choquées et brisées, leurs paisibles générations ont traversé les âges et se sont succédés [sic] l'une á l'autre jusqu'à nous,*

fraîches et riantes comme aux jours des batailles [Today, as in the time of Pliny and Columella, the hyacinth disports in Wales, the periwinkle in Illyria, the daisy on the ruins of Numantia; and while around them the cities have changed masters and names, while some have ceased to exist, while the civilizations have collided with one another and smashed, their peaceful generations have passed through the ages and have come up to us, fresh and laughing as on the days of battles].' See McHugh, *Annotations,* 281.

33 The association of text and shit in Joyce can also be found in episode 4 of *Ulysses* when Mr Bloom uses a page of the magazine he has been reading in the outhouse to wipe his bum.

34 This is widely regarded to be a reference to Joyce's *Ulysses,* which, because it was not yet protected by copyright in the United States, was pirated by Samuel Roth, who was drawn to it by its sexual content.

35 McHugh, *Annotations,* 287.

36 See http://hjs.ff.cuni.cz/archives/v1/framed/hypeproj.html for a list of Joycean hypertext projects that have come and gone. For an active (at the time of writing) hypertextual version of the *Wake,* see http://finwake .com/. For a *Finnegans Wake* Wiki, see http://www.finnegansweb.com/. For a sophisticated search engine, see http://www.fweet.org/.

PART THREE

The Page

7 Merely Conventional Signs: The Editor and the Illustrated Scholarly Book

CAMILLA BLAKELEY

'What is the use of a book,' thought Alice, 'without pictures or conversations?'
> – Lewis Carroll, *Alice's Adventures in Wonderland*, 1865

'What do you do?'
'I'm an accountant. I always say don't work for your money; make your money work for you. What do you do?'
'I edit scholarly books.'
'I see I'll have to watch my grammar around you!'
> – Conversation held with a party bore, Toronto, 1988

The smallest of party small talk deals exclusively in the realm of cliché, and the cliché about editors goes deep. We correct grammar and spelling. We dot the i's and cross the t's. And, of course, our medium is text. But editors deal in more than one form of communication; the text speaks but so do the images, the interplay of text and image, and the physical properties of the book. The editor does not create or select these elements, but she or he had better be able to conceptualize how they fit together and to assess how successfully they do so if they are to serve successfully as a coherent architecture, or map, for the reader.[1]

The editor of an illustrated book has three roles: she must fully understand how its textual and visual components balance one another to form an integrated whole; she must keep in play and maintain order among the intellectual, physical, and institutional factors involved in its production; and she must facilitate constructive relationships between those involved in bringing the project to completion. This chapter explores these strands in the process of producing an illustrated scholarly work. How do such projects challenge the way an editor thinks about the physical aspects of a book? How do they change the timing and structure of the process? What additional skills must the editor develop? How does the inclusion of illustrations affect the editor's relationship with the author and with the designer, and the mediation of the two? As well, I examine the potential need for an editor to manage additional institutional relationships. A university press will often seek a publishing partner to produce an illustrated book, collaborating with an institution such as a museum or an art gallery. What issues arise for the editor as a result?

The clearest way to illustrate these roles is by looking at a particular book and a particular process. The one I have in mind has enough pictures and conversations to have pleased Alice very much.

The Book

The Trickster Shift: Humour and Irony in Contemporary Native Art, by Allan J. Ryan, was published by the University of British Columbia Press (UBC Press) in 1999. The designer was George Vaitkunas, and I was both copyeditor and production editor. The book was co-published by the University of Washington Press, which functioned purely in a buy-in capacity: it bought a guaranteed number of copies in exchange for a joint imprint on the title page and shared logo space on the spine. There was a single version of the final product, designed for the Canadian and American markets simultaneously.

The Trickster Shift is an unusual book. It explores the effect and power of the Trickster figure in contemporary Native art. Woven intricately through Native cultural sensibility, the Trickster, often embodied as Coyote, expresses a wry, ironic humour. To capture that sense of play and shape-shifting influence, author Allan Ryan wanted the presentation of text and image to be as playful and seemingly unstable as his subject. Through his narrative he intersperses other viewpoints: anecdotes, poems, quotations, and interviews with Native artists, their voices and his switching back and forth. This is accomplished with a shift in typography, the main narrative being set in Utopia serif and the other voices in Thesis sans. (I rather like the way the names of the typefaces seem to reverse the roles of these two narrative forms; whose thesis is this piece of scholarship?) More extensive narratives – short stories, longer interviews, and artists' statements – are set on coloured pages.[2] Throughout, a rolling tally of footnotes serves as a counterpoint to the main narrative, adding a layer of meta-commentary:

Quotations and notes are used extensively to disburse the narrative voices and reflect the intertextual nature of the discourse. Neither quotation nor note should be considered a secondary or subordinate text. At various points in the conversation, other voices intersect with the principal narrative . . . Non sequitur, song, poem, prose, and personal anecdote enrich and enliven the discourse. In some instances notes take the form of extended annotation and include illustrations. In this they constitute a kind of hypertext or hyper-media, forms of non-sequential writing and visualizing that until recently were primarily associated with literary studies and computer science. More important, the text honours and participates to some degree in a non-linear process of representation shared by many of the artists interviewed.[3]

Thus, the page has to deal with at least three textual layers at once: the 'authoritative' voice of the scholar; the 'subversive' voice of the artist; and the contemplative, mediating voice of the note apparatus, another tune in the round (fig. 7.1). And that is only the text. The illustrations, of course, are key to the way the book communicates. There are 160, both colour and black and white, over 320 pages. To support the sense of the work unfolding as one long, seamless, twisting narrative, Jack Kerouac style, we decided to number the images in a single sequence rather than breaking them down by chapter.

Once published, the book won an award in the scholarly illustrated category of the Association of American University Presses book awards, an Alcuin Society design citation in the non-fiction illustrated category, and an American Book Award for literature – not for art or anthropology. The idea of scholarly text as literature is rare, at least in this period. That the book received recognition not for elucidating its discipline but for its style is a testament to its effort to blur the boundaries between text and image and to embody the trickster play that is its subject.

Allan Ryan, the book's author, has this to say about its narrative process:

I imagined the primary narrative in several ways: as an odyssey – like John Dunbar in *Dances with Wolves* – embarking on a journey of discovery, starting out, and meeting people along the way who taught him new things on a progressively deeper level.

As a play, with the images as stage sets and the interviews as primary dialogue with me providing connecting dialogue, and voices in the footnotes speaking from the wings, or the front seats, adding to the story. In this, they break down the actor/audience division.

As a novel with every paragraph connected in some way to the next one, with a definite story arc and denouement . . .

I also wrote it like a long song, crafting one paragraph before moving on to the next. There was no rough draft.

As an argument, like a lawyer, presenting more and more examples to build a case and in the footnotes continually referring back to earlier examples to strengthen my case.

And . . . I imagined it as a vital or vibrant trickster discourse or conversation – among, about, and as trickster, that would capture a multi-vocal conversation at a particular point in time and history – some of the artists are no longer living – and invite readers to become informed participants in the ongoing conversation. And that is happening.

After publication, I imagined it akin to a sacred medicine bundle, more than the sum of its parts, containing in the words and images of the artists a power to heal or at least begin to treat cultural and cross-cultural ignorance.[4]

That's an ambitious agenda for a scholarly work, and various dangers are evident: no rough draft; footnotes referring back to other notes; example piling on example; a conversation. This might be a recipe for ill-disciplined rambling. And the images: cartoons; photographs of installations and demonstrations; paintings; outdoor sculpture; collage; a wooden toilet; a Mohawk woman dressed as Elvis; painted stoneware; a shadowbox. All these complex intentions and elements necessitated following the first rule of scholarly illustrated book production: know what you're dealing with.

The Assessment

On receiving such a project, the editor's first task is to assess what is in hand, what is missing, and what might be extraneous. Has the author submitted what's expected? I'm assuming here that the author has been given at least basic guidance long before about technical considerations such as resolution, mode, tonal range, and file format for photographs, and requirements in terms of vector, bitmap, outline fonts, and greyscale for non-photographic illustration. For a sadly large number of projects, great efforts have been made to get images that are ultimately unusable, but that is outside the scope of my discussion here.

It is an especially critical act, as it is only in reading the strategically foregrounded passages that the terrible and tragic historical ironies are revealed. None is more forceful or poignant than the Wounded Knee component, which incorporates the final page from the final chapter of Dee Brown's haunting book (1972, 418).[26] The visible text reads:

dead Indians were left lying where they had fallen. (After the blizzard, when a burial party returned to Wounded Knee, they found the bodies, including Big Foot's, frozen into grotesque shapes.)

The wagonloads of wounded Sioux (four men and forty-seven women and children) reached Pine Ridge after dark. Because all available barracks were filled with soldiers, they were left lying in the open wagons in the bitter cold while an inept Army officer searched for shelter. Finally the Episcopal mission was opened, the benches taken out, and hay scattered over the rough flooring.

It was the fourth day after Christmas in the Year of Our Lord 1890. When the first torn and bleeding bodies were carried into the candlelit church, those who were conscious could see Christmas greenery hanging from the open rafters. Across the chancel front above the pulpit was strung a crudely lettered banner: PEACE ON EARTH, GOOD WILL TO MEN.

In conversation art historian Ruth Phillips said of Poitras, 'I think he's the blackest humorist of them all. To me, his work is dark to the point of depression, but for that reason it's among the strongest of all. I think he's important to your study.'[27] Whether Poitras is the blackest or the bleakest of humorists is debatable, given the work by some of the other artists in this chapter. He does, however, bring to this study and to the practice of aesthetic trickery a degree of conceptual sophistication that has few rivals.

The same juxtaposition of faith professed and faith practised that imbues the Poitras and Brown Wounded Knee 'collaboration' with so much ironic intensity is evident as well in Carl Beam's sharply titled *Calvary to Cavalry* (Figure 99), from his

98
Edward Poitras
Small Matters, detail, 1988-9
nails, wire, paper, Instasign,
75 × 176 × 5 cm

26 The slaughter of an estimated 300 Sioux, more than half of them women and chil-
    dren, at Wounded Knee Creek, South Dakota, on 29 December 1890, brought a
    bloody end to a half-century war waged by the American government against
    Indians for possession of the American West. In 1973 Indian activists inspired by
    the courage of their ancestors occupied the same site for seventy-one days in an
    armed stand-off with federal agents. Ironically, a century after the 1890 massacre
    the macabre photograph of Minneconjou chief Big Foot lying frozen in the snow –
    the ultimate Indian victim – is arguably as much a symbol of cultural survival and
    tribal tenacity as any studio portrait of Sitting Bull or Geronimo. See the discus-
    sion of Jim Logan's paintings *Unreasonable History* (Figure 140, p. 255) and *The
    Death of Big Foot* in Ryan (1994a). See also Hill (1989, 34).

27 J. Jerome Zolten says that creators of black humour try to 'transcend the pain and
    absurdity of reality ... by deliberately plumbing the tragic for comic possibilities.
    The goal is to subvert pain by undermining the seriousness of the subject ... The
    black humorist tries to undercut seriousness by painting over it with the comic.
    The implication is that the external will in some way alter the internal. Since
    laughing is a sign that "everything is alright," then laughing in the face of tragedy
    must mean that the healing process has begun' (1988, 135).

Figure 7.1: Typical page of text (191) from *The Trickster Shift* (courtesy UBC Press)

At the outset, the physical art manuscript must be accounted for: numbered very gently on the back with pencil; transparencies placed in separate labelled envelopes; digital images stored as separate files with recognizable names. If one does not exist, a comprehensive list of these original resources must be drawn up, giving each image an identifying number (which will almost certainly change); indicating whether it is available as a scan, print, transparency, or in multiple forms, and who owns the media; keeping a tally of costs; and noting institutional conditions attached to physical and intellectual reproduction (table 7.1). This list, or log, is a crucial tool to develop from the beginning. Constantly updated, it is the traffic control centre for the illustrated book and the editor's responsibility.

From the original art manuscript, too, a full reference set of photocopies must be made: the editor's working copy for the duration of the project. As an editor, the sooner I'm parted from the original art and know that it is with the designer, the more comfortable I am. All caption text must be physically separated from the images as well. A caption placed within a figure is categorized in the wrong place, as image rather than text. Or as the editorial mantra goes, a caption is 'the explanatory material that appears outside . . . an illustration.'[5] By separating all such text from image and collating it into a new file, the editor makes a rudimentary start at a textual element that may not exist at the start of the project: the caption file.

Of course, the initial sorting process applies to the text as well in terms of ensuring that all the elements are present and accounted for, files can be opened, the most recent drafts have been submitted. With respect to the illustrated book, however, an additional filter is employed, as the editor checks the connections between text and images. Are the images referred to directly in the text or only tangentially? Are they referred to by a number or by name? Has the author provided directions for positioning them? Are they to be placed throughout the narrative or grouped in a gallery, or is that undetermined?

Essentially, then, the editor's first task is to take apart the submitted materials in order to identify them, sort them, and manipulate them throughout the process so that, much like taking apart a musical instrument or a piece of machinery for maintenance, the cleaned and perfected pieces can eventually be assembled into a final working whole. Although such operations are physical and organizational, they have an intellectual component. In the course of this preparatory work, the editor gains a sense of the proportion of text to image. Are the images

Table 7.1
Categories in an art log

Figure no. (bold = new no.)	Title / description	Format	Ordered (Yes/ No)	Received / location	Cost of reproduction	Cost of permission	Institution	Notes / Credit and reproduction requirements
60	Annunciation	Colour transparency	Y	In house	$xxx	$xxx	Yukon Arts Centre Gallery	Photo: Joanne Jackson Johnson
								No crop/bleed
61	Jesus Was Not a Whiteman	Colour transparency	Y	In-house	$xxx	$xxx	Yukon Arts Centre Gallery	Photo: Joanne Jackson Johnson
								No crop/bleed
62	Bingo Dauber Fetish, Indian Brand Series, Part II	Photograph	Y	In-house	$xxx	$xxx	American Indian Contemporary Arts	Peter B. Jones
63	Soupbone and Skawndawg	Print for scanning (Line art)	n/a	In-house	$xxx	$xxx	n/a	Courtesy of the artist
64	What becomes a Legend most?	Colour transparency	N	MCAC	$xxx	$xxx	McMichael Canadian Art Collection	Photo: Larry Ostrom, Christie Lake Studios

clustered too thickly within the supporting text in places – making life difficult for both the designer and the reader – and are there long stretches of unillustrated text? Do chapters end consistently with text or with image? Does the work appear at least in broad terms to illustrate concepts in a balanced way? A book on architecture with twenty images of Georgian houses and two of Victorian Gothic may need to be rethought.

Armed with an assessment of the physical book submission and an initial sense of the needs and issues involved, the editor must start a conversation with the author and the designer.

The Meeting

Editing a scholarly work can be a solitary endeavour. Most copyeditors never meet the authors and may not even have much email contact with them. The design process might either be non-existent – the press decides to use a standard template – or be worked out wholly separately from the editorial process. This can work for a purely textual book and possibly for a book that contains a mere nod towards illustration. (The press will allow a dozen photographs and the author has provided twenty options. The editor whittles it down to sixteen on the basis of relevant content, and provides those to the designer, who culls the remaining four on the basis of quality. No meeting required, but image here is being treated rather cursorily and it could be debated whose interest that serves.) This modular work process does not suit a book that depends on visual media as a crucial channel of communication.

Once the editor has completed the round of classification just described with respect to the physical submission, *and the designer has had an opportunity to review the materials thus organized,* it's time for a meeting. There is no substitute for having the author, designer, and editor in the same room at this stage, or at the very least, at the ends of a conference call and with the same reference materials in front of them.[6] This is the time and place to establish purpose, expectations, and procedures. As George Vaitkunas notes, 'The design process for *Trickster Shift* was most enjoyable since I was able to meet with the author and editor at the earliest stages of the publishing project.' In other words, early communication makes the job not only easier but more pleasurable. This is significant. In scholarly publishing, you don't get the opportunity to 'make your money work for you,' as my party acquaintance put it; much of its value as a profession lies in the merit of the work itself.

Above I described the narrative intention of *The Trickster Shift*. It was at this first meeting that Allan Ryan expounded on his motivations; what had appeared at first as a rather overwhelmingly annotated discourse with some potentially messy bits of additional text was an admirably conceived project, but we needed to address several issues. The longer interviews had been provided in an appendix, which to my mind meant they were far less likely to be read, and certainly not to be read as part of the primary story. In keeping with the spirit of a narrative simultaneously multiple and continuous, like strands in a rope, the footnotes had been numbered from 1 to 225 sequentially across chapters, but this was more appealing as a concept than in practice, especially combined with the great quantity of cross-referencing. I was concerned that the reader would become exhausted.

As well, as Vaitkunas points out, 'The author had previously assembled a layout of an earlier version of the manuscript as part of a thesis presentation and, therefore, had some definite ideas about how the text/commentary relationship should be designed using parallel vertical columns, placing commentary to the side of the main text.'

While most of the artwork had been obtained, much of the permissions correspondence was still outstanding and as a consequence, it was not yet possible either to confirm the final set of images or to know what restrictions would be placed on their reproduction. We also looked closely at the balance of text and image and worked through potential difficulties.

We agreed that such a complex work had an overriding need for editorial and design simplicity; that is, in whatever ways were possible, we needed to make the mode of communication transparent. Captions should be streamlined to contain only the following details: artist, work, date, medium, dimensions. Credit information was to be removed and placed at the back. (This would mean a certain amount of chasing and cajoling of art institutions on my part to convince them to waive the requirement of placing the credit on the same page as the image. In the end, there was just one lonely holdout.) Footnotes were to renumber quietly at the beginning of each chapter, but images would number in a single sequence. To give the designer maximum flexibility, I was to request from the art sources bleeds if necessary, but not necessarily bleeds. I would also ask about minor cropping and use of details. Naturally, most art institutions and artists would refuse, and very few bleeds

Table 7.2
Production schedule, with colour

	Projected	Colour work	
Manuscript transmitted	1-Apr-12		
Manuscript cleaned up	15-Apr-12		
Manuscript to copyeditor	16-Apr-12		
Manuscript from copyeditor	9-May-12		
Manuscript to author	19-May-12		
Manuscript from author	11-Jun-12		
Manuscript to typesetter	2-Jul-12		
1st proof from typesetter	30-Jul-12		
1st proof to auth/proof/index	2-Aug-12	7-Aug-12	Colour placement and size approved
1st proof from auth/proof/index	30-Aug-12	14-Aug-12	Colour to printer for scanning
1st proof to typesetter	13-Sep-12	8-Sep-12	Colour scans ready
2nd proof from typesetter	27-Sep-12	11-Sep-12	Colour corrections to printer
2nd proof to typesetter	9-Oct-12	25-Sep-12	Final colour scans ready
3rd proof from typesetter	16-Oct-12	5-Oct-12	Corrected colour placed on disk
Files to printer	24-Oct-12		
Books in	3-Mar-13		

or crops or details can be found in *The Trickster Shift*. The handful it does contain, however, provide punctuation and emphasis. Miraculously, we were permitted to place one image over a full spread. The designer was to find a clean and clear typographical means to show the alternation of speakers/writers. I was to break the appendix of interviews into units, and suggest logical placement through the narrative – to find conceptual ways to bring these voices into the story – but to avoid the chorus becoming a cacophony, we also needed a design solution that would permit them to be read fully separately from the main narrative. This was another aspect of hypertext, as Ryan labelled it, at a time when readers were not as familiar with the concept as they are now.

As well as working through the conceptual approach and its practical implications, the three of us dealt with some of the nuts and bolts. I put forward a schedule (table 7.2). In addition to the usual timetabling exigencies, a heavily illustrated book using colour imposes another cycle in the production process if the scanning is being done by a third party, in this case, the printer. The schedule must therefore be drawn up in close consultation with the designer, who is the person most affected. We also covered the outstanding permissions issues. Some artists were culturally opposed to the whole notion of written contracts, and this added a layer of complexity. We needed clear permission and clear conditions of reproduction for all the artwork as soon as possible. Ryan had personal relationships with many of the artists so he would tackle contacting them, and I would tackle asking the institutions for exemptions to credit restrictions. As the publisher's representative, I was responsible for tracking all the administrative issues and keeping them up to date, a task that applied throughout the life of the project. Vaitkunas would make a thorough technical assessment of the artwork received to date and all new pieces as they arrived, to ensure that they were suitable for reproduction.

With the issues identified, the route laid out, and at least most of the pieces in hand, the editorial work could begin.

The Edit

All the expected skills and sensitivities an editor marshals for every project apply as much to the illustrated work as to any other. Of course, the text must be subjected to the same stylistic scrutiny. The concept of play, almost of call and response, was a little dazzling in *The Trickster Shift*, and the text needed to be quietened down somewhat. The reader was occasionally sent madly off in all directions, with references to earlier pages in the text and notes where they were not necessarily the most obvious way to deal with a point. I removed some of the cross-referencing and suggested merging notes from time to time or moving a note to the text and making it part of the main discourse.

These were primarily structural concerns. In addition, the standard strictures of house style applied. 'I know you had to rearrange a few things to conform to a UBC Press stylistic format,' said Ryan.[7] This process does not differ fundamentally from the copyediting associated with the purely textual scholarly work, but a broader range of tasks exists because the illustrated work has additional textual elements and considerations. The index for an illustrated book, for example, is more complex to edit than for a work without images because specific forms of reference are conventional. Captions, credits, and callouts add to the list of editable elements.

In terms of line-by-line stylistic editing, however, my work was light. Ryan was a song writer before he became an academic, and that background was evident. Typical academic authors are not first and foremost writers so much as subject matter experts, and their interest in language as art can vary widely. Some craft their narratives meticulously; others are less engaged with form and more likely to rely on the editor's judgment. Ryan's style was unusually concerned with imagery and rhythm, and he was deeply conscious of his own mode of expression. When I asked him about the experience of being edited, he noted, 'Sometimes editors will make a word change that disrupts the rhythm, forcing me to ask them to restore it to the original version.'[8] Clearly, the editorial task in this particular work had an aural dimension to match its conceptual and visual challenges.

Various editorial tasks are essential with respect to illustrations, and the editor's remit is exactly the same as it is for text: clarity, consistency, correctness. How will the text refer to the image? Will it mention each one specifically, and is a callout, or catch, positioned immediately after the first such mention? Will it call the image by a number? a name? a position? 'The figure opposite/above/below' might work in some contexts, but with such a variety of directions for the gaze already present in *The Trickster Shift*, that seemed unwise. How will the images be numbered, if at all? The 1.1, 1.2, 1.3, 2.1, 2.2 of the typical academic text was perhaps a little stiff, and as I mentioned, we decided on a single, fluid sequence, but that of course would all have to be reworked if an image was omitted or added. At what point would the final number sequence be imposed and in how many places would it need to be changed? *The Trickster Shift* did not have a plate section, but for books that do, the editor must be concerned with fitting the number of images to the plate section. The publisher can afford eight / sixteen / thirty-two glossy pages; an image deserves a full page / should not be more than a half page / is central to the discussion but aesthetically a misfit. What about maps or graphs? Will they number with the photographs or separately? What would be most intuitive, most unobtrusive, for the reader? The editor helps to make the jigsaw pieces fit, not all by herself, but certainly she plays a pivotal role as the gatekeeper of the content. Some of these considerations must seem to border on the mundane, but they're crucial. In the service of the transparency we sought for the reader in *The Trickster Shift*, such considerations had to be determined and implemented – and unnoticed. How interesting that the machinery of the illustrated book, even more than that of the purely textual work, must ultimately be invisible. It must get out of the way of the reader.

As well as ensuring consistency of reference with respect to the illustrations themselves, the editor must treat captions with the same scrutiny. The content, style, length, inclusion or exclusion of credit, and typographical format are all worthy of discussion with the designer. Does he want each element on a separate line with a hard return? Does he want small caps marked? How? Will credit information be run up the side of the image, separately from the main caption, and if so what is the most efficient way to prepare the file?

The editorial attention that an illustrated work requires is thus a mix of the conceptual (Is the structure functioning well and is it transparent for the reader?); the stylistic (Is the language nuanced and powerful?); the conventional (Are standard style choices applied consistently?); and the technical (Are the files prepared and marked up appropriately?).

The Relationships

Producing an illustrated book, it is evident, involves several types of engagement beyond the fundamental one between author and reader: between text and image on the page, between editor and designer, between publisher and art institution, to name only some. The editor is at the nexus of these associations and must appreciate the nuances involved. Editors can be found in all fields of book publishing, for example, who believe that the designer's job – a bit tacked on to the end of the process – is to carry out the intentions of the author and the editor. The normative hierarchy implied in this approach is debatable for any successful project but especially so for the illustrated book, for which collaborative and communicative relationships between author and editor, author and designer, and editor and designer are essential.

The Designer and the Editor

How do designers and editors help one another? One way has to do with the logic of the content. As Richard Hendel notes, 'The designer cannot properly address a text until an editor has understood and clearly dealt with the *physical* aspects of the content: how chapters and chapter titles are arranged, how subheads are dealt with, kinds of extract, etc.'

(175, this volume). This is what Vaitkunas refers to as 'the formidable task of organizing all the raw content.' He concurs with Hendel:

> I rely on the editor for a number of things, including a summary of the key themes of the manuscript as well as indication of any parts of the manuscript that require special attention, provision of rough manuscript and sample images for preliminary design purposes . . . and well-marked final manuscript.[9]

These tasks are clearly helpful to the designer, and especially so when dealing with a complex illustrated book, but is the editor primarily an administrator? I think that in the most successful projects, the relationship is multifaceted.

As a collaboration, the editorial–design exchange can be a source of collegial incentive. I find that any designer whose work and process I admire will prompt me to monitor my own professionalism. One designer, for example, routinely asks me to copy fit on book jackets. My instinct the first time this occurred was that the text should have primacy – but why? A jacket, after all, is primarily a visual instrument. And after getting over my presumption that the words should get pride of place, I realized that the design principle of less-is-more applied equally to editorial concerns, especially when dealing with the concentrated impact of a jacket. My copy got better as a result, and the designer now gets the space he needs to make a jacket work. No one is going to read the back of a book if it is crammed with tiny text.

When I asked Vaitkunas about collegiality, he responded, 'I rely on the editor for motivation. When I see that the editor is going the extra mile in preparing material professionally and in a timely way, I am inspired to reciprocate.' There is of course a difference between one role supporting another and two roles offering mutual support. As Vaitkunas noted, the roles of editor and designer

> inform and influence one another through the considerable dialogue that usually occurs from the outset of a project. Further, many of the decisions made by the editor regarding the final manuscript, such as the hierarchy and length of headings, the length of a title, or details of punctuation, have an impact on the look of a book. Likewise, the look of a book conveys ideas and meanings, thereby adding content of a secondary variety.[10]

Form and content really do inform one another in an exchange that cannot be separated into constituent parts.

As a resource, a good designer will contribute invaluable visual information to a project. The designer who informs himself closely about the subject matter of a project earns my respect quickly. It's not just about good-looking pictures. I have, for example, worked repeatedly on military history titles with a particular designer because he knows far more about the discipline than I do. He knows the difference between a First and a Second World War German army helmet, a distinction that escaped the cover designer of one recently published trade book. He knows that one flag flying above another at the stern of a ship signifies victory for the possessor of the uppermost flag. That might seem arcane, but it was key to a highly effective cover design for one project on naval history (fig. 7.2). It is especially important for the scholarly book to be visually accurate as well as textually accurate, and the designer may have visual knowledge that the editor doesn't, or even the author doesn't.

As a mediator, the editor can filter and smooth the designer–author relationship. In thinking about the triad of designer, author, and editor, I asked Vaitkunas whether it helped or hindered to have his relationship with the author mediated by an editor. He responded:

> While I usually enjoy direct contact with authors and value their feedback, there are times when it can become difficult. Scholarly books are often the culmination of years or even decades of toil and their authors can have strong views and preconceptions regarding design. In these cases I am most appreciative of the editor's diplomatic capabilities.[11]

With respect to *The Trickster Shift*, as noted, Ryan had already worked out a potential text layout. With a background in graphic design, he had some clear ideas about how he wanted the book to look. Vaitkunas

> found a different solution which presented the main text above the commentary with the latter shifted along a horizontal axis. This made both texts more inviting to read and reinforced the notion of 'shifting' central to the author's thinking about humour in Native art. The horizontal shifting was also applied to other typographic elements, including the title page and epigraphs. At first the author wasn't so sure about the solution but, *after some explanation and support from the editor,* quickly came around to appreciating it.[12]

In other words, the editor can be the designer's advocate, and this works far better than being the designer's 'boss.'

Figure 7.2: Cover design for *Frigates and Foremasts* (courtesy UBC Press)

As an evaluator, the editor can help to assess the visual content, both technically and conceptually. While an experienced scholarly editor knows that a table or a graph requires as much editing as a narrative – often more – most of us have no training in how to look at a photograph. We need to learn from the designers we work with. I now won't waste a designer's time by passing along an image that's one-inch square with evidently insufficient resolution or a copy of a newspaper print that will moiré badly. These are rudimentary technical assessments, but useful. Further, I will detect the unsuitability of an 8 × 10″ print showing one key person in a large group, none of whom will be large enough to identify when the image is placed in a 6 × 9″ book. By listening to designers, I've learned to notice whether the background of an image is distracting or the foreground is cluttered with extraneous detail. At the same time, I must let the designer do his job. An editor doesn't have to, and shouldn't, take on alone the job of paring twenty images down to three or four. I can provide the designer with the options and explain how many are needed (and why). Conceptually, what is the primary purpose of the image? A photo section will encourage the reader to focus on the images and enjoy them for their own sake – not necessarily a good idea if they are poor and used only to convey essential visual information tied closely to the text. Scattering images throughout the text, conversely, emphasizes their role of textual support.

These are editorial decisions, but they are *visual* editorial decisions. It is essential to understand that a designer is an editor, too. He can assess what role the images are capable of playing. I need to inform him, and I need to get out of the way.[13]

The Author and the Editor

> I very much appreciated your integrity and sympathy/empathy from the beginning, and your desire to make my voice as articulate as possible. *I felt we had a necessary trust from the start.*[14]

Here, Allan Ryan pinpoints the heart of the author–editor relationship: the necessary trust. The editor must function as trusted advocate for the author of the illustrated work as well as advocate for the designer. If the wheels are in motion as they should be, these functions are not in conflict, but misunderstandings are still possible. A photograph may have impact and presence, but it may not serve the author's purpose. I learned this lesson when working on a book about the business of couture fashion. The author, who was a curator of fashion and textiles, brought to the project a trove of professionally shot photographs of all sorts of gorgeous haute couture dresses and an open mind about how they were to be handled. It was a rare moment of freedom for the designer. We were permitted cross-overs of full-colour images spread from one page to another. We were allowed details. The designer did an initial layout, and among others, one lush image of a dress detail seemed worthy of a full page; the close-up of the fabric alone deserved the space. The author took one look at the proposed layout and said no. The close-up of the arm and side torso of the dress, she explained, served one purpose: it was a prime example of pit rot.[15] No one in the fashion business would want a full page on the consequences of sweating. Perhaps I couldn't have foreseen that one, but it was my job as editor to understand the import of each image as closely as I understood the text. If I had informed myself, and thus the designer, more fully, I could have anticipated that misunderstanding, and the art log I monitored would have had a note about the appropriate and inappropriate use of the image in this case.

What if the work is illustrated but the author is not a 'visual thinker,' to use a phrase of Ryan's? 'Not all writers who include illustrations are visual thinkers. Some academics, for example, may have no interest in how the book looks, their primary focus being on the text/history/analysis – that is, the ideas that reference the illustrations.'[16] Such cases are the visual equivalent of those in which the academic functions as subject matter expert rather than writer per se, and the editor becomes more closely involved with the text as a result. In such cases, I will work closely with an author to understand what she or he sees as the point of each image and discuss whether that point is truly communicated to me, the lay reader, by the image in question. I will ask the author to categorize the images into must have / nice to have / don't have to have, and discuss the rationale. Very often the content imperatives, when considered closely, will weed out the most unsuitable images early on. The designer's assessment will further weed out the aesthetically poor ones.

When I asked Ryan what skills he thought essential for the editor of an illustrated scholarly work, he interpreted the question as having a textual focus. He was less interested in the editor's ability with respect to the principles of visual assessment and organization that I've identified above and more interested in the implications for the editor of a text whose *subject* is the image:

What I do think you need to edit an illustrated book is an aesthetic sensibility (as opposed to a purely visual sensibility), a facility for using metaphor and poetic language, to represent a range of human emotions . . . The editor should have command of language that can reflect, if need be, the nuances of the artist's thoughts and reflections on practice, or those of the author – especially if the editor needs to suggest alternate wording or sentence structure. So it is command of literary/visual/emotional language that is needed, as opposed to objective/scientific/informational language. The objective dispassionate approach has not gone totally out of fashion, but the purported objectivity of such writing is now regularly questioned. It is best to have a full linguistic palette in hand.[17]

I found this a fascinating premise: that the editor must approach the illustrated work differently first and foremost because of its language. Certainly this is another editorial dimension of the fine art publication, in which content and form are even more closely meshed than in other illustrated works.

I also asked Ryan about the nature of the author–designer–editor nexus from his point of view. Was it collaborative? Did he feel included and respected? Was there any sense of one aspect dominating another? Again, he pinpointed what I think is key to the issue:

I guess whether the project is a three-way collaboration or a designer–editor collaboration depends on how assertive the author is about what the book should look like, or how involved he/she wants to be in the process. Or how much input the press allows (or tolerates). *It is in their best interest to have a happy author.*[18]

I agree. It is always in a press's interest to have a happy author, while keeping the needs and realities of the project at the forefront. It is also always part of the editor's role to ensure that this is so. With an illustrated work, it's just more complex.

The Institution and the Editor

What about the interests of the press? I asked Peter Milroy, former director of UBC Press, what he sees as the role of the illustrated book in terms of the mandate of a scholarly press and the nature of the editorial task. His assessment was very mixed:

While I have a number of colleagues who would strongly differ with me on this, over the last decade I have concluded that illustrated books are not necessarily an appropriate enterprise for scholarly publishers ... Illustrated works can certainly make a substantial contribution to the lists of university publishers. Some illustrated books – particularly in the fields of fine arts scholarship – make a direct scholarly contribution to the study of visual works. But other works that provide a visual element to intellectual work that is primarily about ideas are of a more questionable nature.[19]

Can illustration actually detract from scholarly merit? Yes, if it is treated as window dressing. Milroy approaches from an institutional perspective the point that Ryan raises about academics who are not 'visual thinkers.' If the non-visual thinker creates a visual work, how strong can its intellectual value be? I'm not convinced the question must be answered with a rule, although I agree that it must be asked. A university press must justify its publications on the basis of their intellectual worth, whether measured by words alone or by words and pictures together. The same rigour of assessment must be applied, and illustration should serve an intellectual purpose as well as an aesthetic one. The academic author who is not primarily a visual thinker may need more editorial and design support to ensure that the illustrated work has value, but that does not mean the inclusion of illustrations is unwarranted.

Scholarly merit is a key issue for the institution, and scholarly independence is related to it. Milroy identifies a significant potential problem in this respect:

While sharing some characteristics with trade books, the kinds of illustrated books that are usually published by university presses have relatively small markets and thus lack economies of scale that make them viable. Thus they need very large subventions. As a result of their tremendous financial needs they are principally the product of institutional agendas and are entirely dependent on the financial commitment of institutions. Thus the independence of the project is in many ways prescribed by the sponsor.[20]

Producing an extensively illustrated scholarly work is expensive. The small or medium-sized press must seek out publishing partners such as other presses or museums and galleries, or sponsors such as art foundations. And the interests of a museum or a gallery do not always coincide with those of a university press; scholarship may need to be downplayed in the quest for a broader audience. As an example, Milroy noted, 'the level of referencing that is expected of a scholarly book can be an impediment and some kind of middle ground has to be established. A scholarly publisher with a broad publishing agenda . . . is in a unique position to find this balance.' More particularly, the editor may need to suggest ways to prune the documentation, make the language less 'academic' and more accessible, and minimize the scholarly apparatus by working closely with the designer to ensure that it is structurally and visually unobtrusive.

I asked Milroy what he saw as the role of the editor in bringing an illustrated scholarly work to fruition. Did she or he need any exceptional skills or qualities from the perspective of a press? He identified two aspects of the job beyond the specifically editorial: the ability to control costs, and the ability to mediate among the parties involved. The role of editor-as-diplomat is especially vital to the multi-institutional work:

> Certainly the skills of a production editor working on such a project are more demanding than those required for other types of projects. The complexities and costs entailed in every aspect of the production are key, and the editor must play an intermediary and interpretive role between the designer, the typesetter, any junior or freelance editorial staff involved and the author – and frequently the institution that is supporting the project. Such projects demand very tight scheduling and cost control and leave little room for error.[21]

The Trickster Shift had a relatively simple institutional context: the secondary press, the University of Washington, placed very few demands on the producing press, the University of British Columbia, other than requiring a shared imprint. But one aspect of the project did involve negotiation. The original subtitle was *Humour and Irony in Contemporary Canadian Native Art*. Washington did not want to include the word 'Canadian,' on the rationale that American outlets would be more likely to stock the book without such a designation. That marketing decision was negotiated between the two press directors and the author, but for other projects, the need to navigate the institutional maze can affect the editor more directly.

Two examples illustrate the point, one successful, the other not. Both projects were initiated by museums, and both had sought publishing partnerships with a university press. I acted as copy and production editor in both. For one, the publication was to accompany an exhibition and had been written by the two curators. One had an academic background and her writing was conventionally scholarly. The other came from the community that was the subject of the exhibition and had extensive contacts there. His writing style was conversational and featured interviews and anecdotes. These two aspects of the subject worked when the text was presented in short, self-contained units in an exhibition setting, but it did not function as narrative. The manuscript was a disparate collection of text pieces in support of imagery. This was the opposite of illustration-as-window-dressing. It was essentially text-as-window-dressing. Fortunately, the museum had decided that the press would have full control of production. The museum reserved cover approval for itself, but it did not provide any of the editorial or design expertise. The press was able to put together a project management team that it knew and trusted, and to produce the work in an uncompromised way. We evaluated the needs of the project and the way to meet them, and the museum gave us free rein. Editorially, the example makes the point that the sum of the illustrated scholarly work must be greater than its parts: text and image must form a seamless whole. Institutionally, it makes the point that complex illustrated projects need focused management: business collaboration is one thing, production/creative collaboration another.

The other example is another museum–press partnership. In this case, however, the museum had a publication department of its own. The decision was made to use the editorial resources of the scholarly press and the design resources of the museum. The result was a project management team with very different working styles and assumptions. Despite best efforts, communication was poor. The project had many challenges inherent, and competing ideas about the needs of the work so hampered progress that it was eventually shelved. That failure, while unusual, highlights that heavily illustrated scholarly works are complex, difficult to produce, and ultimately stand or fall on the ability to bring a wide range of interested parties together: authors, editors, designers, artists, curators, administrators, scholars. And those parties, crucially, must understand and respect one another's roles.

As readers we still believe that our culture, our civilization, lies 'as in magic preservation in the pages of books.'[22] The material aspects of the book remain central to the editor's work, and piloting the illustrated scholarly book on its passage to publication is perhaps the most fulfilling editorial task I can conceive of.

I know of more than one editor and more than one designer who will, on at last receiving from the printer the object, the thing itself, immediately smell it. That new book smell. The visceral pleasure of the object has not disappeared from our lives as readers, and the successful academic editor – grammarian, stylist, administrator, intellectual, diplomat, (sometimes) martinet – understands that good books engage us not only by what they say or how the words express it but by how they smell and feel and look.

NOTES

1 I had originally called this chapter, rather prosaically, 'Greater Than the Sum of Its Parts,' but while it's undeniable that the textual, graphic, and typographic elements of an illustrated work combine to form a greater whole in terms of meaning and emotive effect, this doesn't capture their equally important function of providing direction through the reading process, whether transparently or overtly. We need the physical conventions and signposts of the reading experience to be intelligently handled. Or as the voyaging characters in *The Hunting of the Snark* more succinctly debate, 'What's the good of Mercator's North Poles and Equators / Tropics, Zones, and Meridian Lines? / So the Bellman would cry: and the crew would reply; / "They are merely conventional signs!"' (Lewis Carroll, *The Hunting of the Snark*, II. st. 3).

2 The use of typographic play and distinctive page treatment in the service of meta-textual commentary is of course nothing new in non-scholarly publications. Laurence Sterne's *The Life and Opinions of Tristram Shandy, Gentleman* (1759–67) comes to mind, with its all-black page of mourning, blank page for the reader to insert her own drawing, dashes of varying length, and deliberately skipped pagination (not to mention the generous, though uncredited, incorporation of other voices – Robert Burton, Francis Bacon, and Rabelais, among others). It seems entirely fitting that Martin Rowson's contemporary reworking should have taken the form of a graphic novel (Woodstock and New York: The Overlook Press, 1996). Children's literature has innumerable examples of textual play, notable among them the concrete poem in Lewis Carroll's *Alice's Adventures in Wonderland* (1865) that forms not only the typographic tail of the mouse but also a tale within the tale, another voice in the text. More recently, Nick Bantock's *The Griffin and Sabine Trilogy* (Vancouver: Raincoast Books, 1991–93) revived the epistolary novel to great effect with removable letters and postcards, taking the classic

multi-vocal genre to another level of visual expression. Steven Hall's *The Raw Shark Texts* (Toronto: HarperCollins, 2007) turns some fifty pages into a typographic flipbook, in which type forms the figure of a shark slowly approaching through the ocean of the white page. Less a work of distinctly separate narratives, it nonetheless uses such visual techniques to represent ideas come to life, or perhaps multiple versions of the self. Examples abound, but we are more used to seeing visual forms of textual multiplicity in literature designed primarily to entertain. Playful scholarship is rarer.

3 Allan J. Ryan, *Trickster Shift: Humour and Irony in Contemporary Native Art* (Vancouver and Toronto: UBC Press, 1999), xiii.

4 Allan J. Ryan, personal communication, 18 February 2009.

5 *The Chicago Manual of Style: The Essential Guide for Writers, Editors, and Publishers*, 16th ed. (Chicago: University of Chicago Press, 2010), 3.21.

6 Sadly, meetings in person have become less and less possible with the outsourcing of editing and design services, so I recognize here that the meeting is very likely to be virtual.

7 Allan J. Ryan, personal communication, 23 July 2009.

8 Ibid., 23 July 2009.

9 George Vaitkunas, personal communication, 1 July 2009.

10 Ibid.

11 Ibid.

12 Ibid., emphasis added.

13 Let's compare this ideal for a moment to another project, about which I must maintain a certain diplomatic reticence. There was no professional editor for this particular scholarly publication, the authoring institution having determined that a collection of archival documents didn't need one. After all, the original text spoke for itself. These documents were a fascinating part of Canadian history, correspondence over the course of the last century that revealed the evolution of a political world view. At the outset, there was no thought that illustration was necessary. After some persuasive efforts, the commissioned designer managed to win the day on the idea that readers would gain from *seeing* some of the subjects under discussion as well as reading about them. Imagery could punctuate the text, creating breathing spaces that would provide historical flavour and context. The project was rightly expanded to a full-blown illustrated scholarly work, but no budget was allocated for mediation between text provider and designer: no editorial, organizational authority separate from the (institutional) author. The result was a dismaying lack of structure and a process that took three times longer than originally estimated. The authoring institution made unguided decisions about organization,

flow, coherence, and selection and placement of illustrations; the designer was forced to assume the tasks of a text editor and had no advocate for the design role. When one piece is missing from that essential triangular relationship – author, editor, designer – both process and product can be compromised.

14 Allan J. Ryan, personal communication, 23 July 2009.

15 Alexandra Palmer, personal communication, June 2001.

16 Allan J. Ryan, personal communication, 23 July 2009.

17 Ibid.

18 Ibid., 23 July 2009, emphasis added.

19 Peter Milroy, personal communication, 24 July 2009. Milroy is right to note that his opinion here is contentious. It may also be more relevant to the Canadian context than the American one, in which the mandate of many state presses, in particular, includes regional work that often benefits from illustration. Books on the flora, fauna, or geography of a region, for example, will necessarily involve a fairly complex illustrative component. UBC Press itself has historically had a similar mandate in its institutional relationship with the Royal British Columbia Museum, which has authored works of natural and regional history requiring extensive illustration.

20 Ibid.

21 Ibid.

22 Thomas Carlyle, 'The Hero as Man of Letters,' in Carlyle, *On Heroes, Hero Worship and the Heroic in History,* six lectures (New York: J. Wiley, 1859).

8 Let's Ask the Designers! Book Design, Technology, and the Editor–Designer Collaboration

Part 1: On Book Design

RICHARD HENDEL

Book design has conventionally been called the invisible art because when it is done well, the design should not be obvious. In a once famous essay on book design, Beatrice Warde wrote that the design for books should be as transparent as a crystal goblet should be for wine. What Warde meant was that the design of the vessel should not call more attention to itself than to its contents – the contents being more important than the form.

Warde was not alone in her attitude that book design should differ from other kinds of graphic design. More than other graphic designers, those who design books need to be aware of conventions regarding how people read and how books are manufactured.

There are, of course, situations where conventional ideas about book design and readability can or should be violated, but in general most books are intended to be read as books have been read since the time of Gutenberg. Assuming that readability is the primary goal of book design, designers need to know how to use typefaces that are appropriate in design and arrangement.

The conventional 'rules' of typography are allegedly based on what is best for the reader and suggest what a good text page should look like. These 'rules' state that an ideal page should have a top margin smaller than the bottom margin, and that the gutter margins should be smaller than the front margins (so that facing pages appear to be a unit). The length of line of text should be about sixty-five characters because a longer line of type causes visual problems – the eye has to pause too many times within the line, making movement from one line of type to the next difficult. These guidelines should not be slavishly followed, but neither should they be ignored.

The reason that books come in a range of more or less standard formats is based on the relationship of paper sizes and press sizes. Varying the size of a book by as little as one-eighth of an inch may add a significant cost, as could using artwork that bleeds off the page. Books are more often upright rectangles because book paper is manufactured to specification assuming an upright rectangle will be the format. The fiber from which paper is made creates a grain, and paper should fold with the grain.

At the beginning of a project, designers must have a clear idea of what they are working with. The designer cannot properly address a text until an editor has understood and clearly dealt with the *physical* aspects of the content: how chapters and chapter titles are arranged, how subheads are dealt with, kinds of extract, and the like.

There are two editorial issues that affect design: form and content. The more an editor has clarified the form of the manuscript, the better the designer is able to transform it typographically. Book designers need to be able to understand the structure of the entire manuscript before they can begin the design. Too often designers are given only a small portion of what purports to be a representative sample of the manuscript; sometimes the sample is edited but frequently not. The designer is asked to build the design on the sample without knowing how often certain elements such as subheads and extracts really occur. What may seem representative to an editor often isn't, as frequently a sample represents the few anomalies in the text rather than the general style of the content. Working from an unedited manuscript, or before the title has been finally decided, can be dangerous. I was once asked to design a book about Ernest Hemingway with the title *Papa,* and, with such a short title, I used very large type on the title page and carried the oversize type as a device for the chapter openings. When the title later became *Picturing Hemingway,* a complete redesign was necessary.

An example of how editing affects design can be seen in the maps of the London and New York subway systems. John Beck, who devised the now iconic plan of the London Underground, had a far easier visual problem to solve because the system itself is so clearly edited. The New York subway system, by contrast, is far more complex in its structure, and so the challenge to explain it visually is a genuine dilemma, and a map as good as Beck's has never been possible.

Ideally, then, before the design can begin, the manuscript should be edited. The English typographer John Ryder wrote about the need for 'visual editing.' He believed that editors were concerned only with correcting spelling and grammar but were uncritical about how it all might look. Ryder felt that editors should be more critical about how something in the manuscript will eventually appear in the printed book – the need to edit visually *before* the design process even begins.

Whether or not it is the fault of inexperienced editors or recalcitrant authors, designers are often presented with nagging editorial problems. Seemingly simple yet obvious difficult situations are often lurking at the very opening of a chapter: one chapter will have an epigraph and the others none, or only one chapter will have a subtitle, subhead, or extract at the opening, or one chapter will have a one-word title while the rest have many words, or the very first word in a chapter will begin with quotation marks. Each of those situations creates its own visual problem. Of course, the editor or author can often make a case for each of these scenarios, and certainly they are not always avoidable, but just as often they probably are. The same is true of chapter titles that are obviously quotations and technically, it could be argued, require the use of quotation marks in the display type used for the chapter title. However, using quotation marks in display type (especially American-style double quotation marks) seems not only redundant but ugly and assumes the reader hasn't the sense to sort out the fact that the titles are meant as quotes.

It is very useful for the designer to have a transmittal sheet from the editor, one that indicates a list of acronyms and abbreviations, the longest and shortest subtitles, and other anomalies in the text. This isn't just because designers are too lazy to find these themselves; these elements are far easier for the editor to identify while the manuscript is being edited. The list of acronyms and abbreviations gives the designer the option of not treating these as full caps, as they almost always look better set as small caps (even when beginning a sentence).

Running heads are meant as an indication of a chapter's content and need not be a literal reiteration of the entire chapter title (and subtitle). Far too often running heads can be much too long and awkward. It would be better to shorten them to keep them from seeming to be a line of disconnected text.

I am always surprised when designers tell me editors require them to set CIP data exactly as the paragraph comes from the Library of Congress. CIP text is exactly that, a paragraph that should be best set following the style of the design established to relate to the rest of the copyright page information.

Tables are more problematic than almost any other part of the text. How a table is structured should first of all acknowledge how it might fit on the upright rectangle of a book page. The wording of column heads and stubs needs to be considered carefully to see how the information can be compressed or abbreviated, and a table that resists compression to fit on one page needs to be evaluated to see if it might be possible to avoid having to turn it or run it across a spread.

For good design to exist, there also needs to be some compromise between editor and designer. Editorially banning hyphenation at certain places (such as at the overleaf, at the end of a paragraph, or after the first two letters of a word) can often create something even more egregious.

While designers and editors would most likely agree that it is a good idea not to allow widows (the short of end of a paragraph starting a page), prohibiting orphans (the beginning of a new paragraph) at the foot of the page is one of those situations where design specifications and editorial restrictions can quickly become a problem. Assuming the designer may allow for a page to run a line short, while insisting that facing pages align, the typesetter is left with a situation where someplace in the text a line (or more) must be gained or lost, often at the expense of increasing or decreasing word spacing – sometimes dramatically.

Equally important as editing, before the design can begin, are certain production considerations: the book's size, the expected number of pages, how the manuscript will be supplied to the designer, who will do the typesetting, who will be the printer. American book production has a certain range of standard formats. The designer needs to know what the publisher's intentions are as to format and number of pages. Most of the time the publisher will have done an evaluation of the manuscript, estimating the average number of characters (i.e., letters and spaces) required to produce the number of pages to make the book financially viable. Editors and authors always seem to measure the text in words rather than characters, but words are too imprecise a measure because of their obvious variation in length. One publisher I know requires 3,600 characters per page (in a six-by-nine-inch format); at the same time many serious designers find anything above 2,800 characters intolerable.

Since the advent of the Macintosh and electronic editing, more designers than ever before now set their own type. Publishers seem to feel that it is more economical to keep much of the composition of their books in-house rather than send work to an outside typesetter.

Though this may be true for straightforward, uncomplicated text, professional typesetters are often far better at setting tabular material, foreign-language type, and other special content. Even more so, though, a high-quality typesetter will take special care with fonts, making slight adjustments that are seemingly imperceptible but make a qualitative improvement to the way the page looks. When all the costs of dealing with an outside type shop are measured against all the costs of setting the job in-house, for me, the modest increase is worth the expense.

If the designer is not setting the type for a job, knowing who will be the typesetter is important for a number of reasons. Of primary importance is knowing what fonts the typesetter has. Digitized fonts are relatively inexpensive compared to the cost of metal type, but even so, a typesetter is likely to be reluctant to buy a font that might be used for one job and never again, to say nothing of the investment of time it takes to adjust a font.

Some typesetters are especially adept when setting ragged right text, poetry, foreign language, or tabular material. Personally, I design differently for different typesetters – rarely asking for an unusual (if appropriate) font or a complicated setting when I don't know anything about the typesetter.

The ideal situation for any designer, then, is to have an edited manuscript, a transmittal sheet from the editor, definite instructions from the production department as to format and desired length, and knowledge of who will be typesetting the book.

Designers generally first decide which typeface or faces to use for the text and the headings. Most experienced designers have a few favorites, faces they know well. In the days before computers there were many fewer choices, and, as the same fonts were used on many jobs, designers became very familiar with the workings of a few typefaces. Having the experience of using a typeface in so many situations, a designer would get to know what sizes and leading seemed right. Now, with new typefaces available every few days, there is always the temptation to try them all.

What determines the choice of font may be no more complicated than that a particular font is the designer's favorite at the time. However, the choice might be based on a far more complicated or arcane reason. The subject matter of the text may suggest something (e.g., the American Civil War and the use of nineteenth-century fonts), or it could be influenced by the way the author writes or by the content (e.g., choosing a font with well-designed numerals in a book where numbers are critical). The choice might be dictated by illustrations in the text (e.g., choosing a typeface that relates visually to the art) or by the need to have a lot of type on the page. Complications increase when the designer chooses to use a different typeface for the headings than that used for the text.

Some typefaces that seem just right for text look awkward or anemic in larger display sizes, so it should not be assumed that headings can just be set in a larger size or bolder version of the text face. In designs that are meant to allude to some specific time or event, it is useful for the designer to know enough typographic history to choose a typeface that is appropriate to the time, but also visually appropriate to the text face. These relationships can be very subtle.

After the choice of the font or fonts, the designer needs to decide the *mise en page* – how the page will be laid out. Should the design be essentially centred or asymmetrical? Should the text be set justified or ragged right? Should the margins be traditional or novel? Because the format of the book (i.e., the trim size) and desired characters per page are often already established, the designer has to work within these limitations. Balancing the need for good readability with practical production requirements, the designer has to consider everything from the size of the type to the measure (length of the line of type), the leading (space between lines), and the margins.

There are two schools of book design: one strives for a timeless or neutral design, and the other prefers a design that is more allusive to the subject matter or is intended to reflect a contemporary aesthetic. Timeless design cannot be purely that because fashion in the use of certain typefaces changes. Allusive or 'contemporary' design is a more problematic situation because in striving for a certain amount of novelty, designers may too easily compromise readability. There are books where showing off is a good thing, but the designer has to select those with care.

An English editor, critical of what he thought was the over-design of our books, said that American book design was notable for designers' restless urge to find a new place for the folio. While it is true that book design can be overdone, there are places where a designer can take some liberties with conventions. One of these can be the design of front matter, for example. There used to be a theory that there should be a direct relationship between the design for chapter openings and the design for pages such as the contents, list of illustrations, preface, and so on. But front and back matter pages are often different in style and content from the main text, and designers now feel a bit more free to treat them differently. Differently, that is, within the general style of the rest of the book, so that the style of the headings used for the front and back matter may be the same typeface as that used for chapter titles, but smaller and possibly in a different place on the page. These should have some definite relationship to each other.

In most scholarly texts there is usually a collection of other problems to be solved. Levels of subheads within text must be clearly distinguished from the text and from each other. An experienced editor will know that to ask for more than four levels of subhead is probably unwise as most readers will be unlikely to keep the differences straight. Of course it is possible to design more levels than four, but unless the book is being designed in outline style, this is the kind of structural problem that is best resolved editorially.

There are many kinds of extracts: prose, verse, dialogue. And there can be numbered lists, unnumbered lists, lettered lists, and bullet lists. This is one of the reasons it is always useful for the designer to have the *complete* and *edited* manuscript to work from given that the content, size, and frequency of extracts and lists may vary greatly.

Neophyte designers tend to make too much of extracts. Extract text needs only to be distinguished from the main text by a subtle shift in the design. The old convention of setting it in a smaller size troubles me because readers must readjust to a very different rhythm on the page. One useful way of treating extract is simply to set it the same size and style as the main text, but indenting the quoted text the same as a paragraph indent, with a half line space above and below. Long extract text might be set ragged right if it runs over more than a page, as an entire page of indented, justified text would be indistinguishable from main text.

The design for the contents page is especially important for a complicated book with levels of subheads in the text. Recently it seems that editors have preferred to eliminate listing subheads within chapters, retaining only the main chapter title and subtitle. My preference is to keep the subheads, as I think they give a potential reader a useful outline of the book's contents as well as allowing for a more challenging design problem.

The half title, title page, and copyright page are special cases. Perhaps almost too much time is lavished on these pages, which few readers pay much attention to. But it is precisely these pages that reveal how much the designer has thought about the design of the book.

As the half title generally comes directly before the title page and often directly before the first chapter, it needs to have some visual connection to them both.

The title page can be the most elaborate design within the book. Still, it need not be so overdone as to seem more exuberant than the book jacket. But without the jacket, the title page becomes the visual identity for the book. All too often, the design for the title page can appear to have little relationship with the rest of the book or seem ill-considered. The fonts chosen for the title page should probably be the same as (or very similar to) those used for the rest of the book.

The copyright page is all too often the most ignored part of a book, both by readers and by editors. There is no reason it need be treated with such indifference, but many times final text for that page is not even shown to the designer (especially in the case of a freelance designer). The page often ends up with the equivalent of no design. This is one of the most problematic pages to design because of the endless amount of required text to be accommodated. Some publishers have decided to move much of the copy (such as the CIP data) to the back of the book. There are few enough readers who care about the material on the copyright page. However, if one wants to know if a book has been well designed, it is only necessary to look at that page. Yet as designers may not even see the page in its final form, they cannot be held responsible for a poorly designed or typeset page (even one on which their design credit may appear).

Dedication pages are equally a problem because there is so little type to deal with. Dedications are important to the author, so it is always a challenge finding the right size and location for those few words. The design should not be so elaborate that it relates to nothing else in the book, but at the same time it can be more decorative than other elements.

The style for each aspect of the back matter (appendices, endnotes, bibliography, and index) needs to be evaluated especially carefully, for these elements should be related to each other visually when possible. If endnotes are relatively brief, perhaps they might look better set in two columns. If they are discursive, it might be better to set them with the note numbers hanging outside the text so a reader can find the note number more easily.

The migration of footnotes to endnotes was meant to save time and money, but in a book where notes are more than references, they would be far better as footnotes.

Increasingly authors seem to insist on supplying photographs and prepared artwork for their books, and increasingly this material creates problems. Authors and editors are all too often unaware of practical production issues such the resolution of scans for reproduction or printing problems with charts, graphs, and maps. In an ideal world the designer would evaluate every piece of art for quality and content *before* the manuscript is edited. It has always been a mystery to me why editors cannot see as clearly as I that a photograph is out of focus or does not show clearly what an author thinks it does.

Historic photographs are special problems, and there are times when the only image of something important can be extremely poor. In that case there isn't much to be done if it must be used. Given enough lead time, though, a designer can often improve the image using computer software like PhotoShop. What is too often beyond help is the scan that is too small and too low in resolution. Artificially increasing the resolution will not help. Where historical photographs are used, designers should be aware of the implications of altering their content.

Maps, charts, and graphs are, unfortunately, often prepared before the text is designed. They rarely relate visually in any way to the text design and often do not fit the page. I personally feel that maps, charts, and graphs should be considered part of the text design and that they should be controlled (and paid for) by the publisher in the same way the publisher is financially responsible for the typesetting. It has never seemed unreasonable to me to have the publisher assume this expense or at least to charge such costs against the author's royalties. At least by so doing, the publisher and author would have to address the need for each of these visual additions to the text.

Authors may spend many years writing their book, and they often have in mind the way they think books (especially their book) should look. Designers, of course, cannot know what the author's ideal book looks like. They try to create the design based on the kind of criteria I have listed above.

For their part, publishers, to save time and money, often resort to using a standardized template for the design of many of their books. This is unfortunate because no two books fit totally comfortably in the same design. Certainly, it is not necessary for every book to be designed from scratch. Most designers keep a basic design in their heads (if not on their computers), and they can adapt that model more freely than if they had to work with a formal template.

Much of what I have said relates to the design for relatively straight-forward text. There are, of course, many other kinds of books that require special editorial and design considerations (e.g., reference books, guide books, art books, plays). For books of poetry, the designer often needs to be aware of special problems throughout the text. And finally, with the advent of the e-book, designers will inevitably face a new range of issues to be addressed. How books will appear on electronic devices will create their own challenge for designers. Sigrid Albert addresses many of these considerations in the second part of this chapter. When the designer and the author disagree about a design, it is up to the publisher to decide who wins. Perhaps it is heretical for a designer to acknowledge that the tilt should always be toward the author (assuming what is wanted makes sense for the publisher). Designers need not be so territorial; there will always be another book to design. But, for an author, that book may be the only one.

8 Part 2: Changing Technology and the Editor–Designer Collaboration

SIGRID ALBERT

Any current analysis of the collaboration between academic book editors and book designers cannot ignore the fact that the world of academic publishing is changing dramatically: the complete book production process is being converted from analog to digital. The conversion process started with early digital typesetters in the 1970s, progressed through the desktop publishing revolution[1] of the 1980s and early 1990s, and entered the online realm with its hypertext markup possibilities around 2000. This transition has brought on-demand printing, online content distribution, searchable book databases, and increasingly sophisticated digital readers into the picture, and continues to progress towards separation of content and design. This means that much like in database-driven websites, book content is increasingly being stored in databases and tagged with content-related markup – such as chapter titles, subtitles, subheads, extracts – by the editor, while the visual design is controlled by a separate style markup – such as margin widths, font, font size, font weight, colour, or line height – delivered by the designer. In its ideal manifestation, this separation allows rapid switches between design templates for visually optimized delivery of content to a wide variety of digital or print media.

We will therefore take only a brief look at the traditional collaboration between editor and designer, then discuss how the rapid technological changes in academic publishing are changing the nature of this collaboration, and finally make some predictions for future developments in the editor–designer relationship.

The Traditional Book: The Editor–Designer Collaboration

Editing and design are part of any traditional book production process. There are differences as well as parallels between the editing and the design process. Chronologically, most of the editing is completed first and design follows, but the editor's work continues at the design stage. There are three distinct parts to the process from the perspective of editor–designer collaboration: organization, unification, and the resulting book object (fig. 8.1).

As reviewed in the opening chapters of this volume, there are several types of editors involved in the making of a book: the acquisitions (or sponsoring) editor, among other responsibilities, develops lists in particular fields and subject areas, shaping the press's identity, and therefore is invested in the way the books are branded and marketed; the managing editor and production editor are in some presses the same person while in others they assume different roles, which can be summarized in general terms as overseeing the manuscript formatting, copyediting, design and typesetting, proofreading, and printing. As we saw in chapters 3 and 4, managing editors often hire freelance copyeditors; similarly, in many university presses, the book or cover design is hired out to a professional freelancer. In these cases, the freelance designer usually works with the managing editor or production editor. The managing/production editor assigned to a manuscript will meet formally with other members of the in-house staff (e.g., acquisitions editor, senior editor or department head, marketing director, etc.) to review the book production and marketing goals, and is subsequently in a position to implement a plan best suited to the needs of the particular manuscript and eventual book, based on the input provided by the members and the group as a whole. In this chapter, I refer mostly to this in-house editor, who has intimate knowledge of the manuscript organization, formatting, and physical requirements.

Part 1: Organization and Structure – Design Stage

In addition to editing for style and content, the editors have done the work of dividing the book into elements such as prologue, sections, chapters, chapter titles, chapter subtitles, headlines, subheads, extracts, poetry, dialogue, epilogue, appendixes, footnotes, or endnotes in the manuscript. Parameters such as page count, number of colours, and book size are decided and provided to the designer in advance.

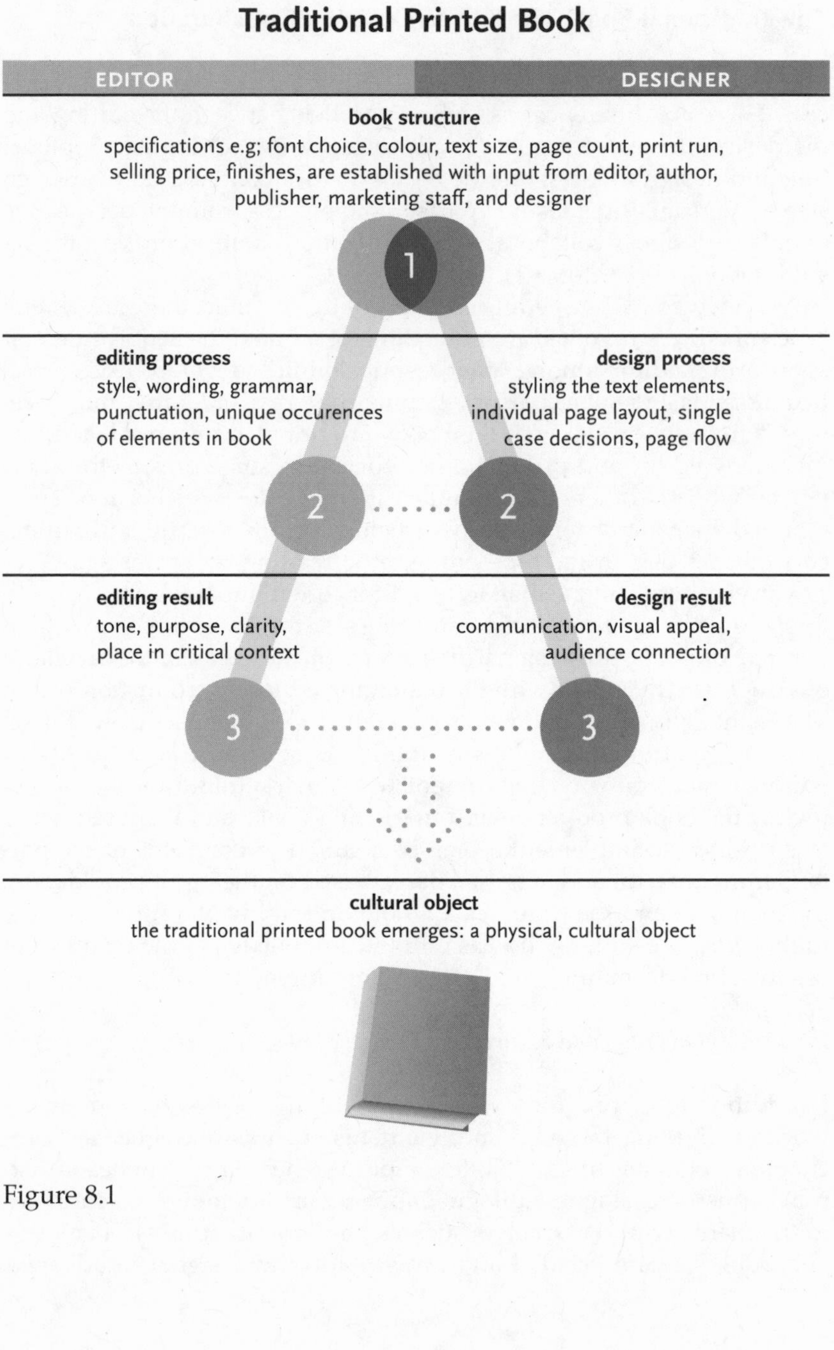

Traditional Printed Book

EDITOR	DESIGNER

book structure
specifications e.g; font choice, colour, text size, page count, print run,
selling price, finishes, are established with input from editor, author,
publisher, marketing staff, and designer

1

editing process
style, wording, grammar,
punctuation, unique occurences
of elements in book

design process
styling the text elements,
individual page layout, single
case decisions, page flow

2   **2**

editing result
tone, purpose, clarity,
place in critical context

design result
communication, visual appeal,
audience connection

3   **3**

cultural object
the traditional printed book emerges: a physical, cultural object

Figure 8.1

There are also many editorial concerns to communicate to the designer that move beyond the physical aspects of the book, for example, the intended audience (undergraduate students versus scholars in a particular field or in a range of disciplines versus, on occasion, the general reader), or specific content or context that could have implications for the design ([in]appropriate use of certain images or colours, need for diacritics or special characters, etc.). The style of the book's content will also determine the design approach; for example, content can be descriptive, linear, or interpretive, each of these necessitating a different approach to the illustrated book.

The designer gives visual shape to both the book's content and its hierarchy by creating a grid-based layout and selecting appropriate typography. Richard Hendel has discussed how to determine the most appropriate design for the structure as well as the content of the book.

The structural level of the book is also where most of the communication between the editor and the designer takes place, as the designer works from the editor's markup after having received the manuscript and instructions on the tone and feel of the book. The designer provides design mock-ups of all the book's hierarchical elements. Then the editor together with the author, the acquisitions editor, and the marketing team evaluates whether the design is appropriate to the book's intended style, content, and audience, and communicates any updated directive to the designer. (Marketing considerations may become more prevalent in a trade book, where the layout may approach an entertainment-oriented magazine style, photography may be art-directed to project a specific, consistent message and look, and the sequence of images and content may be arranged to achieve a certain effect and emotional impact on the viewer.) The physical book specifications, such as page count and book size, are sometimes revisited as a design emerges.

The language of communication between editor and designer is an important aspect of the collaboration; the managing editor, who represents the views of the press as expressed in the aforementioned meeting, guides the designer by using descriptive language rather than translating the instructions into design specifications. For example, an editor might say 'since this book does not have sections, and only four chapters, the chapter openings need to be emphasized.' It is then up to the designer to translate 'emphasis' into one of a wide range of typographic tools. For example, emphasis can be created by larger type, or bolder type, or by giving each chapter opening its own verso page, or printing the chapter opening page in a solid ink, or adding an image at

NANCY JANOVICEK

no place to go

SHELTER MOVEMENT

LOCAL HISTORIES OF THE BATTERED WOMEN'S

Figure 8.2: Cover design for *No Place to Go* by Nancy Janovicek. This cover for a book about the history of the battered women's shelter movement in Canada is an example of the interpretation of the following instructions to design 'a

the start of each chapter. An experienced editor will not suggest specific design solutions such as 'increase the font size of the chapter heading by two points and make it bold,' but rather will describe the desired effect. The designer then uses his or her experience to choose the optimal visual device to achieve that effect. From a designer's perspective, the language used by the editor to convey goals and style for the book, often called 'a briefing,' an expression derived from the advertising world, is therefore very important. The designer's skill in extracting a good briefing from the in-house editor by asking the right questions is also helpful in the collaborative process.

Not only are communication skills important, but so too is the ability of both the editor and the designer to identify at which stage of the process they are at any given time, and the ability to move that process along smoothly to deliver the best possible result within the given time, budget, and capabilities (fig. 8.2).

Part 2: Unification and Detail – Layout and Production Stage

Before the design process begins, the copyeditor passes through a unification stage while working on the text, to create a consistency in structure and language. Decisions made here in the larger service of the book are communicated to the designer. Examples of such decisions might be the preferred treatment of chapter epigraphs, or whether there will be

---

type cover . . . We're looking for a cover that is built around the main title (the letters) and is quite stylized. Could the main title be a central "image"? Colour scheme: 1970s–1980s colours could be used to indicated that this is a recent *history* of the women's shelter movement, not an assessment of current issues . . . What to avoid: Don't use a photo of women protesting or an image of a victim.' These instructions are probably more in-depth than is normally the case. They were interpreted by the designer to create a typographic cover in which the subtitle formed the 'L' in the word 'place' and thus appear squeezed into the title, symbolizing a tight spot, i.e., no place to go. The sombre brown and grey colour scheme further added to the feeling of being unwelcome. The lacy-looking graphics were created from a wallpaper pattern and employed to soften the overall effect of the cover design while referring to a recognizable element of a traditional concept of 'home.' (A colour thumbnail of this cover can be viewed on the UBC Press website: http://www.ubcpress. ubc.ca/search/title_book.asp? BookID=5269.)

footnotes or endnotes, or whether a font with unique characters has to be used in the case of quotes from a different language, or the minimum number of lines of text to appear on a chapter opening page, or a 'house style' of punctuation. The planning of the layout is, in this regard, a shared responsibility between the editor and the designer.

The designer (or the typesetter) applies the overall grid and look to all elements of the book. The detailed, unifying work is done here: a diagram may be adjusted, a widow avoided by increasing the size of a figure, a single instance of poetry or extract may need to be designed, several levels of headings may occur in a sequence, an awkwardly long or short chapter title may have been overlooked during the design stage or modified by a last-minute edit, necessitating global changes. Any queries about elements of the book are directed to the managing editor.

Whereas the managing editor or the copyeditor, in the previous stage, tagged for the typesetter textual elements that had to be considered in the design, a partial reversal takes place during the page proofs stage, when the design and the content are reviewed and aligned, and any text or illustrations 'straying' are reined in to fit the design parametres. During the layout stage, then, the editor continues to communicate with the designer to help keep the book's layout consistent with the design and to edit text for visual fit, for example in the case of widows or orphans, or to make descriptive text appear closer to a crucial illustration. The pagination of the scholarly book should be final before the indexing begins; repagination is cumbersome and should be avoided.

Part 3: The Result – A Cultural Object

When the book is finished, the remaining interaction between the managing editor and designer is at best an informal post-mortem, but the book is part of both their life's work in a more lasting way than any advertising campaign would be in a designer/client relationship in a commercial setting. The traditional printed book as a highly crafted cultural object, whether in a humble, low-budget or a luxurious, highly produced format, is the goal of the editor and designer. At the highest level of the book production process, the editor has shaped a piece of history, and the designer has shaped a piece of art. Ideally, the goal is to create a beautiful self-contained three-dimensional object with a unique appearance, personality, and value. The book is entered in library catalogues and assigned a year of publication. It thus provides a snapshot of academic discourse as well as of the state of book design at a certain point in time that gives it its place in history and culture. Any flaws in content, layout, or printing are preserved, become part of the book's historical perspective, and may be revised in a future edition, incurring new editing, design/typesetting, and printing expenses. (See also John Young's chapter in this volume on reprints.) The success of the book as a collaborative product between publisher, author, editor, and designer becomes evident over time, and can be measured by the amount of critical acclaim, impact on academic discourse, frequency of quotation, and sales to the intended (and unintended) audience.

The Modern Book: The Editor–Designer Relationship in Transition

Traditionally, the printer was the publisher, the editor, the designer, and the printer of the complete book. Publishing and editing became separate disciplines from printing around the eighteenth century. Design, typesetting, and printing became separate specialties only in the twentieth century. From there, changes started to accelerate, with digital typesetting machines allowing designers to do paste-up themselves, and then with desktop computers to start doing very complex layouts and sending complete layouts in the form of photo-mechanic transfer output to printers. Now designers send digital files to printers via online transfer, and printing is often digital, with no metal plates produced.

The so-called digital revolution in academic and commercial book publishing is affecting the editing and design process and the collaboration between editors and designers. In the United States, print-on-demand surpassed traditional book production for the first time in 2008.[2] Book manuscripts, proofs, artwork, fonts, specifications, and production schedules are increasingly housed in databases to improve efficiency of communication and access to up-to-date files at all times, which has the effect of reducing the amount of communication required between editor and designer (fig. 8.3).

Part 1: Organization and Structure – Design Stage

The manuscript still needs to be edited for style, content, and structure as before. However, the final production parameters such as page count, number of colours, and book size may exist in several iterations depending on the medium of delivery. A full-colour hardcover and softcover version of a book may still be produced for filing with libraries,

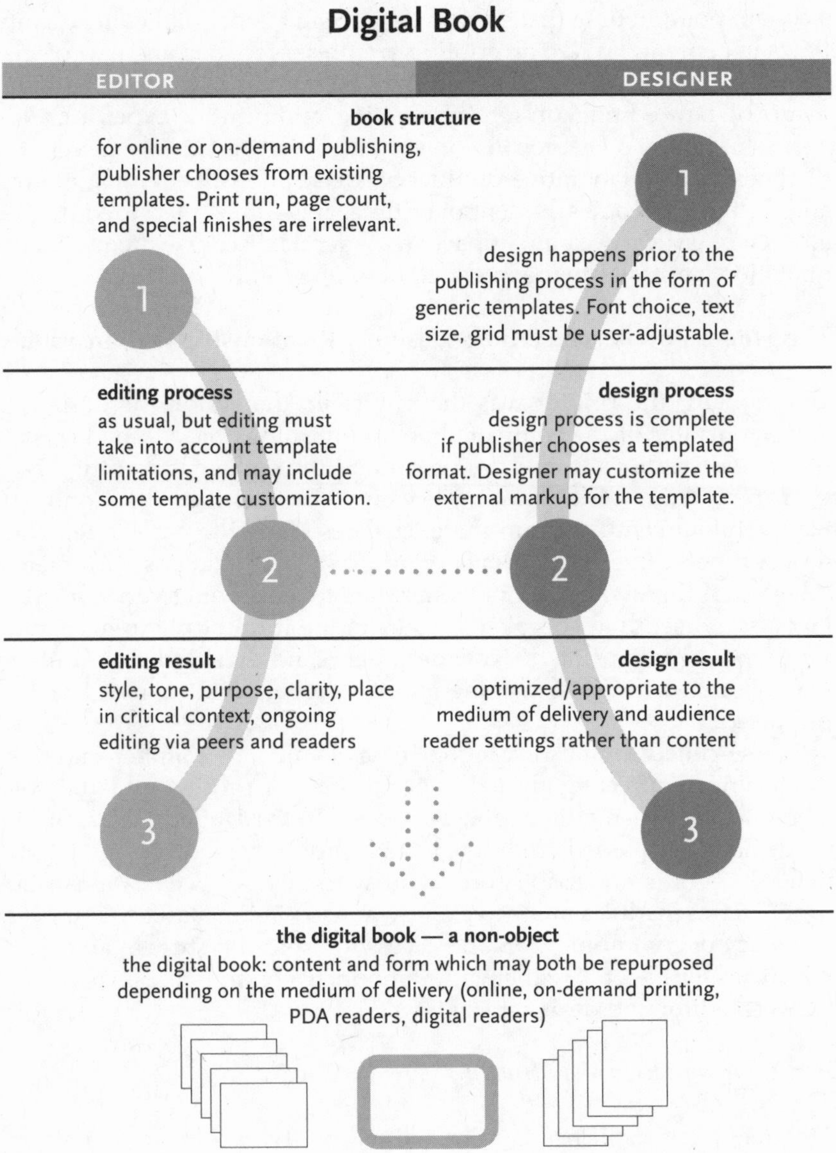

Digital Book

book structure

for online or on-demand publishing, publisher chooses from existing templates. Print run, page count, and special finishes are irrelevant.

1

design happens prior to the publishing process in the form of generic templates. Font choice, text size, grid must be user-adjustable.

1

editing process	**design process**
as usual, but editing must take into account template limitations, and may include some template customization.	design process is complete if publisher chooses a templated format. Designer may customize the external markup for the template.

2 ⋯⋯⋯ **2**

editing result	**design result**
style, tone, purpose, clarity, place in critical context, ongoing editing via peers and readers	optimized/appropriate to the medium of delivery and audience reader settings rather than content

3 **3**

the digital book — a non-object

the digital book: content and form which may both be repurposed depending on the medium of delivery (online, on-demand printing, PDA readers, digital readers)

Figure 8.3

but a black-and-white version may also be created for print-on-demand (POD) copies. The book design still has to reflect the structure and end goal of the book, but the POD version may have to be adjusted to fit the POD distributor's specifications, which differ from those of traditional printing presses. The designer may not be called in to adjust the book for POD; often a desktop publisher can adjust the book at lower cost for this purpose.

The ideal language of communication between the managing editor and the designer is not affected by these changes, but the vocabulary has to be expanded to include consideration of different delivery media. The designer may approach the book differently if she knows that it will have to be converted to a POD book. Also, a list of formats required by the editor for the digital book archival system is now a standard part of the design specifications. Book covers as well as interiors are converted by the designer into a variety of formats based on very specific digital instructions such as pixel count, resolution, file format, colour space, platform, and software version. These files are uploaded into specific compartments in the digital archive, where they can be retrieved for different purposes and by different parties, such as managing and production editors, marketing staff, e-book distributors, printers, or authors, as needed. A fluency in digital media, file transfer, and file formats is assumed to be a basic requirement of this process, and the language of desktop publishing, such as 'photoshopping, cloning, upsampling, resolution,' until recently used only by the designer, is becoming increasingly familiar to editors. In addition, with email communication, online file transfer and storage, 'uploading, downloading, file attachment, zipped archive, ftp'ing' are also part of the communication between editor and designer.

The book production process can now be measured by the files that have been completed and are uploaded in the digital archives. Storage of digital information and its management has become firmly entrenched in the book production process between editor and designer.

From the designer's point of view, the design process has not changed at its basic level of giving form to content. The design process, despite the technological advances, still requires a synthesis of information and a variety of visual choices to form an aesthetic unity. What has changed is the vast amount of information, fonts, images, and inspiration at the designer's fingertips, to the point where the difficulty is not in finding images but in choosing the most appropriate image. Also, visual sophistication of academic books has increased over the decades. With increasing online information on book design, book publishers' marketing departments and designers have been influenced by trends in the commercial design and publishing realm.

Where designers used to present a rough sketch, working on the computer has resulted in expectations of highly finished concepts on the part of clients, including editors. It is much easier than before the arrival of personal computers and typesetting software, of course, to produce highly finished layouts. But the specificity at such an early stage in the process can sometimes lead to a loss of experimentation and lack of visual interpretation, if the designer focuses on a specific solution too soon and spends all of his or her time in perfecting details rather than in developing the concept, in order to satisfy the client's expectation for a polished first sketch. In addition, the automation of typesetting has resulted in a loss of customization of justified text, font kerning, and sometimes a lack of expertise by designers in the elements of typographic style.

As mentioned above, the communication between editor and designer must include many references and technical terms from the digital realm. It is impossible to create a modern book without digital specifications and a variety of file formats.

Part 2: Unification and Detail – Layout and Production Stage

Increasingly, the typesetting of a book is no longer a part of the designer's job, as efficiencies are increased by having dedicated experts manipulate the text to the designer's specifications. There are two options: (a) the designer marks up the sample pages with style sheet instructions, and a typesetter formats the book according to those instructions, or (b) the managing or production editor selects a design template, which the typesetter uses, to flow the text into an existing digital format that is set up with so-called style sheets and 'house' preferences. Option (a) is still often used for heavily illustrated or trade-style books that benefit from a custom design and a unity between cover and interior, while option (b) is commonly used for books with few illustrations.

Because of these changes, there is less communication between editor and designer at the layout and production stage. There is some communication between editor and typesetter, of course. Sometimes the editor has to go back to the designer to clarify an issue in the typesetting specifications. As Camilla Blakeley also shows in her chapter on the illustrated book, the managing editor acts as the bridge between designer and publisher, designer and author, designer and typesetter, and often designer and printer as well.

In option (a), the designer will review typeset proofs of the book to check for visual consistency and point out any concerns to the editor. In option (b), the designer does not get involved in the typesetting at all, but will have designed only the book cover. This is becoming increasingly common due to budget and time constraints in the academic publishing world. Only a few books each year are designated to be custom designed, while the majority are typeset following existing templates. These templates have built in all elements of style that may occur within a book, so that the manuscript can be tagged with the editor's markup (currently done by either the managing/production editor or the copyeditor, depending on the press) in advance and then 'flowed' into the template, with the markup tags allowing the text to be converted into the correct visual style upon text import. Styles can also be changed globally if needed, to allow a minimal amount of customization for each book.

However, the initial template will have been designed by a professional designer, and would also take into account ease of POD distribution and general legibility and aesthetics. It is usually a clean, neutral-looking layout that is, like a newspaper template, versatile in order to accommodate a variety of content and style elements. The designer has created a design template without prior knowledge of specific content. The managing editor in essence has the final word on the look of this book, in that she, having shaped the remit with the acquisitions editor and marketing manager, designates the structure of the book, such as the number of heads and subheads.

Part 3: The Result – A Cultural Object for Rapid Distribution

The templated book will often still have a custom-designed cover, but the interior is no longer unique. The book is still a cultural object, but any changes and new editions can be created rapidly without any help from the designer, sometimes even without a typesetter. This is a sign of things to come, as the use of templates will only increase in the future with online content delivery. The purpose of the following section is to look into the future. Many editors and designers who started their careers in the traditional publishing years understandably lament the new developments, but the purpose here is not to look back with longing, but to describe a trend in the publishing field that is unlikely to be stopped, and to look for those areas where the collaboration of editor and designer might continue and evolve.

The Digital Book: Increasing Editor–Designer Separation?

Even in on-demand or online book publishing, both the textual and visual aspects of a book must still be addressed. How they are addressed may be affected by future shifts in technology, the capabilities and limitations of the medium of delivery, and audience or user needs, expectations and preferences. Since this very book is certain to become yet another flawed cultural object, the following prognosis may turn out to have been completely off the mark even in the near future, but it reflects the current state of flux in the world of publishing from the perspective of a book designer.

Part 1: Organization and Structure – Design Stage

Final production parameters will likely increasingly dictate the type and amount of editing and design to be done on a book. Some academic authors are even starting to see publishers, editors, and designers as unnecessary, and are publishing and delivering their own content online via Open Access.[3] However, for those books that do get produced via a publisher, managing and production editors will most likely be choosing from a wide array of book templates rather than just one or two in-house templates, as is currently the practice. Book templates for a wide variety of books will likely be available for purchase online, much like web templates already are. In the self-publishing field, this is already in place with the proliferation of self-publishing websites such as blurb.com or lulu.com.

Few books will be destined for printing as a large run, and only key books or books for older audiences will still be printed in the traditional hardcover or softcover formats. Most books will be made available for POD, or delivered online via PDF or other formats, to digital readers or smartphones. Considerations such as print run, page count, and special finishes will become immaterial, as the medium and the template will determine the number of pages, colours, and special touches. A smartphone book can only show about ten lines on the screen, meaning the traditional concept of a book is no longer applicable. Digital book formats are searchable, can be bookmarked or accessed via the Table of Contents, so that they do not even need page numbering anymore, making the folio as well as the verso/recto concept disappear. The disutility of traditional page numbering in the face of multiple e-book formats has led to the suggestion that, for purposes of citation, the older system of paragraph numbering, which is still used in the field of classics, be revived.[4] (See, for example, the use of this practice in the digital monographs published by Gutenberg-e: http://www.gutenberg-e.org.) Likewise, the selling price will be determined mostly by the medium and the importance of the book, not by its length.

Designers will create fewer custom designs and will find more work either designing versatile templates or customizing existing templates. They can only charge a small fee for each template usage but will be able to get royalties by licensing their templates multiple times. Investing in programming and software technology will increasingly make a difference to a designer's success as a template creator. Different templates might be available for art history books, scientific books, legal books, encyclopedic books, heavily illustrated books, or text-only books. A publisher might get a designer to customize a template for the publisher's use, but the initial template purchase cost would only be a small licence fee. Templates might be upgraded regularly by the designer to reflect software compatibility updates, and relicensed for a small fee.

Font choice, text size, and grid are still important but will be restrained by online default font availability and by the delivery medium. The publisher is more likely to choose from a variety of templates and styles to deliver the book more efficiently rather than contracting a designer for a custom book design. The publisher chooses a templated format for its flexibility of display in different media and for its accessibility to different audiences.

A large benefit of the flexibility of the external markup is that accessibility to books for the visually or hearing impaired will be much improved with customized content delivery. The content will be completely separated from design via external markup that is supplied as a separate digital file containing only code for each textual element, that is, the element name and its associated description of colour, size, and arrangement on the page.

A disadvantage of this lack of control on behalf of the designer and the managing editor as well as over the final delivery vehicle is that design and editing cannot easily be customized to the medium. This is a significant change, not just from a designer's but also from an editor's perspective. The unpredictability of the final medium of a book makes production decisions more difficult, since the book has to be planned as 'content' to be 'repurposed.' This changed approach will influence the traditional understanding of what a book is. Some editorial and typographic nuances will have to be sacrificed at the expense of the reader.

The book designer will therefore be increasingly designing book templates for an unknown content, or designing for content of a general nature. There is a possibility for collaboration with editors, however, as editors and designers may partner up to share their expertise and collaborate on templates. Likewise, the editor may call in the designer to customize a template for a specific purpose.

Those few books that receive the luxury and expense of a custom design and treatment will likely be tour-de-force examples of multimedia design, bringing in video or dynamic graphics instead of static illustrations if required, extensive cross-referencing via hyperlinks, and the ability to discuss the book's contents in a digital academic forum. Some publishers are already specializing in high-end digital books[5] called user experience books. While most of these books currently deal with the subject of User Experience design (UX design), the books are increasingly being created as UX products themselves.

Part 2: Unification and Detail – Layout and Production Stage

The managing editor and copyeditor will have to do more online work in terms of cross-checking, referencing, and connecting the book to its future and ongoing online 'life.' There are already indications that the editing of online books is changing, with collaborative communities being formed who use sophisticated Open Source software such as Drupal,[6] giving them access to a wide range of 'modules' that help with different functions of the editorial process. The copyeditor will have to find new ways of approaching book editing, much as the designer will have to rethink the traditional custom book design approach. The managing or production editor will have a greater responsibility in ensuring that the template functions correctly and that the book structure is preserved in the absence of a designer. The managing editor might be working only sporadically with a designer to check the layout. But in general, the layout stage will be heavily automated, and most of it will depend on clean editor's specifications and proper manuscript markup.

The designer will be focused on the creation of either book templates or customized, high-end multimedia books, or on the very rare printed book. The digital platform will to some degree standardize the appearance of books, much as Wordpress has done in the realm of websites, where one chooses from a variety of appropriate 'themes' or templates that then determine the look and feel of the book. But similar to websites, well-designed templates and well-designed custom books will always stand out and will draw in users. The user experience can be optimized and quantified to a certain point, but just as in colour theory, one never knows how the next person experiences a colour or a layout. People have too many visual and cultural differences to all prefer the same layout. A customized design finely tuned to the content it displays will continue to add value to a book, but it will become increasingly important to include user controls for setting font sizes, colours, and even layout options. Digital readers and smartphones can also be rotated from horizontal to vertical formats, and the markup has to allow for that flexibility.

Some may argue that designers will increasingly be considered just decorators and maybe even be superfluous because shape-giving can be automated and templated to such a high degree. Similarly, there are arguments that editors will become superfluous, because authors no longer have to go through the traditional publisher to post their book online. I would argue that editing and design are entering a new realm where craft, diligence, and excellence are going to be increasingly valuable. New standards for measuring a book's quality may have to be added, but the standards of written and visual communication will still apply. Acquiring editors will still be needed to identify authors working in a press's speciality field and to develop a recognizable image of the scholarship that the press publishes. Skilled copyeditors are still important for their expertise in cleaning up prose and improving raw text, and are not easily replaced by computerized style and spell checks. Designers will still be required in order to give a book a unique character, to add value with visual sophistication, to improve navigation and user experience, to customize, or to create professional templates for books. The coming changes are not to be feared, but they don't have to be mindlessly embraced either. Designers and editors need to think about where they can add value to the process and how they can continue to learn about their craft, and they need to become innovators.

Part 3: The Result – Online Delivery of Content and Design

Keeping track of ongoing edits to books will become a constant task, as an online book is never 'finished' in the same way a printed book is. The managing or production editor will likely be among a few authorized people to make ongoing edits to the book's content. Edits will be tracked online as well, and the book will become an ongoing collaborative process mainly between author and editor (and increasingly the reader, as authors may take into account readers' comments and modify the text), while the shape of it will continue to shift.

Conclusion

The future of book publishing is in great flux, and therefore uncertain. What is certain is that academic books have a place, and that professional editing and design both add value to the academic publishing process and to the result. With books increasingly distributed online, both editing and design changes may have to be ongoing as a book evolves, rather than resulting in a printed product. This change in final product will certainly change the nature of the collaboration between editor and designer, and it already has. The collaboration and the communication will reflect the technology used in the production of the book. The best vehicle for content delivery will also be chosen to serve the book's purpose and will become part of the new tools of the editor and the designer.

NOTES

1 Cognitive scientist and online communications researcher Stevan Harnad describes four revolutions in the means of production of knowledge: the invention of language; the invention of writing; the invention of movable type (the printing press); and the invention of digital publishing. Harnad 'Post-Gutenberg Galaxy: The Fourth Revolution in the Means of Production of Knowledge,' *Public-Access Computer Systems Review* 2, no. 1 (1991): 39–53 (also reprinted in *PACS Annual Review*, vol. 2, 1992; and in R.D. Mason, ed., *Computer Conferencing: The Last Word* [Beach Holme, 1992]).

2 See Jim Milliot, 'Number of On-demand Titles Topped Traditional Books in 2008,' *Publishers Weekly*, 19 May 2009, http://www.publishersweekly.com/pw/by-topic/industry-news/bookselling/article/9038-number-of-on-demand-titles-topped-traditional-books-in-2008-c2-a0-.html.

3 For an overview of the mission and membership of Open Access Scholarly Publishing Association, see http://www.oaspa.org/ or the European book initiative, Open Access Publishing in European Networks, at http://www.oapen.org/. *Editor's note*: Open Access is a system devised to offer free access to journal publications. It has been proposed for scholarly book publishing despite the fact that its implementation potentially requires a major overhaul of the financial and traditional distribution models. For a discussion of the challenges and opportunities that forms of 'open access' present to university presses, see Sanford Thatcher, 'The Challenge of Open Access for University Presses,' http://alpsp.publisher.ingentaconnect.com/content/alpsp/lp/2007/00000020/00000003/art00002.

4 Thanks to the anonymous reviewer for bringing this to my attention.

5 http://www.rosenfeldmedia.com/ and http://www.uxmatters.com/mt/archives/2008/05/rosenfeld-media-ux-publishing-startup-an-interview-with-lou-rosenfeld-and-liz-danzico.php.

6 http://drupal.org/node/69912.

9 Iconic Pages in Robert Antoni's Fictions: A Speculative Edition

JOHN K. YOUNG

> Day and night now you chiseling (clichépoverty you starvingartisan)
> $olo vi$$ioning ma$terial produc$ioning$ fa you $upermarket$ quick
> conumpioning$! Elliotsmith now you standback, dubois is you amaze:
> you done create de very fossil of you predescenters imagination!
> – Robert Antoni, *Divina Trace* (210)

The Summer 1989 issue of *The Paris Review* included a story, 'A Piece of Pommerac' by Odillo Antoni, that was published because it literally caught the eye of the journal's famed editor. In the middle of twelve Joycean pages, narrated by the monkey-god Hanuman from the Ramayana epic, appears an aluminum mirror page that 'was the first thing that interested George Plimpton when he saw it,' according to Antoni.[1] Two years later the British publisher Quartet issued the full novel, *Divina Trace*, from which the *Paris Review* excerpt was drawn, with a U.S. edition from Overlook, a division of Viking.[2] While Overlook's hardcover included the mirror page only on the verso side because of financial constraints, the Overlook paperback edition in 1992 inserted mirrors on both sides. Antoni's second novel, *Blessed Is the Fruit*, published in 1997 by Faber in the U.K. and by Henry Holt in the U.S., features another iconic page in a central location: a sheet of transparent plastic that appears in the middle of the novel's second (of three) sections. While Antoni had originally hoped for a sheet of glass instead, this would have caused obvious problems with a sustainable binding.

I chart this brief publishing history to begin raising the conceptual issues attendant on a hypothetical future edition of Antoni's first two novels. While the publication of trade editions with mirror and plastic pages itself represented a minor publishing miracle, their potential academic reproduction in the future would recast these commercial tensions while highlighting the editorial and even ontological issues such material artefacts raise, either in print editions or – especially – in digital versions. Given the critical and scholarly attention Antoni has received so far, such editions are at least not entirely hypothetical, and, as I hope to argue, the larger issues they raise speak to the editing and interpretation of contemporary Caribbean literature more broadly. A Trinidadian who was educated in the United States and who now lives in Portugal, Antoni has employed these kinds of textual devices to compel his readers literally to see themselves reflected in and through his books' pages, representing contemporary Caribbean culture and its audiences as enmeshed in a web of cultural, racial, historical, and narrative associations that produce not linear or hierarchical structures but simply 'one big callaloo' (*Divina* 365).

The major editorial obstacle for a future Antoni edition would be finding ways to reproduce these particular instantiations of what Peter L. Shillingsburg calls the ' "eventness" of texts, the clues to the cultural contexts that informed the writing and reading of the works when they were fresh.'[3] Editorial representations of that 'eventness' would be especially complicated in this case, as Antoni's iconic pages would resist both physical reproduction – his original publishers were barely persuaded to include these costly devices in such commercially inaccessible novels, and neither book has been widely reprinted – and even digital versions (how might one see *through* two sides of a computer screen, for example?). Thus the editorial and epistemological issues that Matthew G. Kirschenbaum and others have diagnosed in the shift to image-based humanities computing become especially problematic when applied to an (imagined) electronic edition of *Divina Trace* and *Blessed Is the Fruit*. Indeed, Antoni's first two novels, seen in this light, not only remark on their own commodification through manufactured pages that deny consumers' usual forgetfulness regarding commodity labour, but also anticipate their own editorial obsolescence, generating a complicated self-reflexiveness both in their original publication and in the (im)possibility of their eventual editorial reconstruction. This essay thus works across the disciplines of textual and postcolonial scholarship, in addition to its investigation of commercial and academic editing, concluding that if the act of publishing and reading a postcolonial novel is fraught with Ranajit Guha's sense of always being 'not at home'[4] within empire or its ruins, so too is the act of producing and reproducing such books.

As a quick index of how these texts have thwarted their own mechanical reproducibility so far, consider the two archival forms in which 'A Piece of Pommerac' is available, beyond bound copies of its original serial publication: on microform, the mirror pages lose all of their reflexiveness, appearing now simply as two black sheets. And the online edition of the journal, issued through the Humanities International Complete database, omits Antoni's story altogether from its copy of this issue, apparently surrendering completely from the task of (re)producing this page.[5] While both of these responses seem obviously and even painfully inadequate from an editorial standpoint, they also speak to the deeper ontological issue that the mirror pages represent in any edition: as each reader will necessarily see a different image reflected by those pages (even the same reader at different points in time would create this effect), the mirror pages literalize the theoretical maxim that no two copies of a work are truly identical (and therefore cannot be copied). Before delving into these thorny questions more thoroughly, I begin with a brief overview of Antoni's career so far, focusing especially on the publication history for his first two novels in their first hardcover and first paperback editions.

'If my life were only a story': Antoni's Early Career

Born in the United States in 1958, Antoni grew up largely in the Bahamas but also 'draws upon two hundred years of family history in Trinidad and Tobago,' as his website states.[6] Antoni completed his PhD from the University of Iowa in 1990 and spent ten years on the English faculty at the University of Miami (1992–2001) before largely leaving the academic world. In addition to *Divina Trace* and *Blessed Is the Fruit*, his publications so far include the story collection *My Grandmother's Erotic Folktales* (2000), which has sold more copies in Finnish translation alone than either of his first two books sold in the U.K. and U.S. combined;[7] and *Carnival* (2005), which revises Hemingway's *The Sun Also Rises* in a Caribbean context and was shortlisted for the 2006 Commonwealth Writers Prize. Perhaps not coincidentally, given their greater commercial success, neither of these more recent books features the kind of materially iconic page around which Antoni's first two books (literally) revolve. All of Antoni's works are set on the fictional island of Corpus Christi and explore, among many other themes, the vexed questions of Caribbean cultural identity, especially as these relate to competing feelings of familiarity or foreignness within various cultural contexts. As he explains in an interview with his fellow Trinidadian novelist Lawrence Scott, 'I'm a stranger wherever I go, but I can also feel at home . . . It's a contemporary phenomenon, I think, particularly for many West Indians, as the society is so displaced.'[8] As I outline in further detail below, this theme of postcolonial displacement appears in Antoni's creolized language, in his characters' mixed-race identities, and in the material forms of his first two novels, particularly as the mirror pages in *Divina Trace* compel its readers both to inhabit a (potentially) othered perspective and to reexamine their own images and identities in the midst of this jumbled cultural narrative.

Divina Trace distributes its narrative among five speakers, all members of the central character's family, who generate competing medical and cultural explanations for the birth of an anencephalic fetus, which most of them call a 'frog baby,' and debate the biography and canonization of Magdelena Divina, an apparently human incarnation of a Divina statue. The five competing perspectives speak through the protagonist, Johnny Domingo, who simultaneously seeks to (re)order his own versions of the past. The book's first and third sections thus have five chapters, with the order of speakers reversed from the first section to the third. The middle section, which is here collectively titled 'A Piece of Pommerac,' contains three chapters, the first and third 'spoken' by a statue of La Divina Pastora, the Black Virgin, and the second narrated by Hanuman, the monkey-god of the Ramayana epic.

In addition to the mirror page(s), *Divina Trace* includes two other instances of what George Bornstein and Theresa Tinkle[9] have called an 'iconic page': reproductions of medical photographs and surrounding text taken from Sir Eardley Holland's *British Obstetric and Gynaecological Practice*, an (actual) book owned by Johnny Domingo's father, which depict an anencephalic fetus. These pages mark the beginning and end of the narrative, as the first appears almost one hundred pages into the book and the second occurs approximately one hundred pages from the end.[10] While the original hardcover edition included a negative offset image of the photograph for its second appearance, the U.S. paperback reverts to a 'regular' image, which accidentally mirrors the page's first occurrence and thus no longer reverses the narrative's direction as in the hardcover. According to Antoni, Quartet, his British publisher, forgot to offset that page in their original plates for the book, but caught the mistake in time for the printer to cut out the page manually in each copy and sew in a new one.[11] When Overlook issued the paperback, they had previously bought Quartet's original sheets, but this time did not catch the error prior to publication.

The mirror page(s) represent the approximate center of *Divina Trace*, pages 203–4 of 426 and about in the middle of the seventh chapter of thirteen. Just as Hanuman retells the story of the Ramayana in the disparate versions of that epic, here he recasts the events of Antoni's novel as themselves a Caribbean version of the Ramayana. Hanuman speaks in his own monkey language, concluding the paragraph before the mirror page: 'Ayes close now you page-searching, by touch, again by smell, you simian fossil potto, simian primate missinglink:' (202). The colon is a key bit of punctuation, as it directs the reader toward the mirror and thus incorporates that page directly into the narrative. Once the linguistic narrative resumes, Hanuman continues addressing the reader as well as himself: 'SEEING IN DE PAGE you own monkeyface ee-eeing, quick out you dreamsleep walcott!' (205).[12] The mirror page(s) rather brilliantly translate this complicated structure of speaker, character, author, and reader into a single visual and bibliographical device, literally projecting the reader's self-image into the novel as he or she turns the page. The mirror's effect, as one critic concludes, is therefore to create 'a startling objectification of the nonverbal core of consciousness and a means by which the reader must literally "inform" the story with his own "mirror-form."'[13]

Antoni divides his second novel's chapters into the same 5–3–5 structure, but this time the fourth and fifth chapters from the third section begin the book, the third chapter from the third section divides the first and second sections, and the first and second chapters from the third section end the book: the table of contents thus proceeds: 4 5 / 1 2 3 4 5 / 3 / 1 2 3 4 5 / 1 2. (Antoni labels each section a chaplet, for the part of a rosary comprising five decades. The rosary's text also provides the book's title.) Each chapter contains ten subsections. There are two main speakers, each comprising one half of the narrative: Lilla Grandsol, a mixed-race woman who is marked culturally as white, and Vel Bootman, Lilla's black servant; while Lilla's narrative primarily proceeds in reverse chronological order, explaining retrospectively her current situation, Velma's begins in her childhood and follows sequentially from there to the present moment at which the novel begins and ends.[14] As Antoni explains in introducing a 1993 excerpt from the novel published in *Conjunctions*, he envisioned the narrative's structure as: 'L (V) L L/V: V/L V V(L).'[15] Where *Divina Trace* narrates and renarrates its central episode from five perspectives (or six, counting Johnny Domingo himself),

Blessed Is the Fruit restricts itself to the two women's response to Vel's pregnancy and their eventual decision to care for the child together, despite the class and racial barriers that have come between them.[16]

The middle chapter, entitled 'Sleep' and written in italicized verse, merges Lilla's and Vel's perspectives through a series of couplets that retell the events of the novel so far (Lilla's story) and 'pre-tell' the second half of the book (Vel's story). Each couplet contains one line from Lilla's point of view and the other from Vel's. The ostensible consciousness governing this chapter belongs to Bolom, Vel's baby.[17] The transparent pages – the textual pages on either side are 204 and 207, so the plastic sheet is implicitly paginated as 205 and 206 – lie in the middle of the middle chapter, dividing the fifth and sixth subsections at the point where the top line of each couplet shifts from Lilla's perspective and language to Vel's. By turning the transparent pages, the reader literally sees each half of the book mirrored in the other (the plastic sheet reflects the page as it is lifted) and also sees through each half of the book, bringing them together visually and physically. This merger enacts the narrative's conflation of the class and racial divisions that initially separate Lilla and Vel, but which eventually reveal themselves to be grounded in illusory categories, as Lilla is marked as white in social and cultural terms but is of mixed racial heritage, while Vel's baby will be marked as black despite its own mixed race (Bolom's father is Lilla's own father).

In addition to the more complicated editorial and ontological questions posed by the mirror and transparent pages, a future edition of Antoni's early novels would also have to contend with the more usual vagaries of publication, which have combined authorial with non-authorial intentions. These include the new cover art for the first paperback edition of *Divina Trace*, which was not authorized by Antoni as the hardcover's jacket design had been. The paperback cover depicts a different Caribbean statue, according to Antoni a Cuban Black Virgin and not La Divina Pastora, the image it is presumably supposed to represent.[18] The distinguishing feature of this saint is a set of facial scratches, a mark Antoni incorporates into a passage revised for paperback publication (the italicized portion is new): 'make theyself a fortune with she fat football face on the cover and *the two scratches overlooking she right cheek from the time Sr Baloum try to dig out she eye'* (265).[19]

The paperback does, however, include the mirror on both sides of that page in contrast to the first edition, but like the *Paris Review* text. 'I had to fight for it in every conceivable way,' Antoni said of the mirror page at Overlook, 'because it runs up the price of the book substantially.'[20] Price was also a factor with the transparent page for *Blessed*, which Antoni imagined as 'the idea that the reader shatters this pane of glass or page of glass in the act of reading.'[21] Antoni's conception of the page was thus originally that it would literally be a glass page, but this plan was impossible because the weight of the glass would have destroyed the book's binding. Even with a plastic page instead, the binding could apparently not have remained intact. Allen Peacock, Antoni's editor at Henry Holt, explained that 'we weren't able to find a book manufacturer who could guarantee that the book wouldn't have fallen apart. The result would have been that we would be left holding the bag.'[22] The solution Holt finally reached with its printers was for the page, now designed to be slightly smaller than the rest of the book, to stand alone, with the plastic sheet inserted by hand into all 6,000 copies of the novel. Consequently, Antoni's readers can remove this page if they like, either taking it out of the book or replacing it elsewhere. In either case, the reader reconstitutes the novel's material condition, and in so doing reverses the page's original manual insertion. In this way the transparent plastic page recalls the original marbled pages in *Tristram Shandy*, which appeared in different versions in each published volume.[23] Antoni's transparent page should be the same in each copy of the novel, but the process of manual insertion almost guarantees that some copies will have been sold with the plastic sheet in a different location. Because this page is implicitly paginated, a reader could reconstruct its proper place, but again this process and reinsertion would individualize the reading experience in a new way.[24]

A future edition of *Divina Trace*, then, whether approached along intentionalist, materialist, or fluid-text lines,[25] would present some fairly straightforward editorial issues: accounting for revisions between periodical and book publication as well as post-publication variants, and representing editorially the shifts between a single- and double-sided mirror page. Even if not actually reproduced in both versions, this last change could at least be handled in a footnote or other apparatus. Antoni's drafts and manuscripts, should they become available, would add to this textual history; one might imagine, for example, that Antoni added the following phrase to the Hanuman chapter after learning of its acceptance for *Paris Review*: 'Allday at you writingdesk, lefthandinyoupans, who ga publish dis monksense? garillaorgy! *Francoisi Review?*' ('Pommerac,' 173). Beyond these variants and versions, however, both the mirror and plastic pages represent more complex editorial and

ontological problems, arising from and extending beyond their postcolonial Caribbean contexts, to which I turn next.

'A hundred different *living* versions': Editing Iconic Eventness

As is usually the case in such matters, the practical problems of how to
reproduce Antoni's mirror and/or plastic pages are themselves theoretical, as a particular method of editorial reproduction necessarily entails a corresponding theoretical orientation towards editing and finally
towards textuality itself. On one level the simplest option would be a
new print edition of *Divina Trace* and *Blessed Is the Fruit*, which in the
case of the first novel would include either a one-sided mirror page
only (in a McGannian preference for the first published edition) or a
double-sided mirror page (in an intentionalist preference for the 'corrected' paperback, or even a materialist preference for the *Paris Review*
text), or some combination of both pages (in a fluid-text preference for
the entirety of a text's production history). Similarly, a scholarly print
edition of *Blessed Is the Fruit* could include a plastic page along the lines
of those already produced for the commercial hardcover and paperback versions. This solution, of course, would likely run up against the
obvious issue of cost: in an environment in which university presses
aim for books with an optimal length of two hundred pages and with
few illustrations, especially colour, it is difficult to imagine an editorial board approving these kinds of material features, especially for an
author who so far has hardly achieved anything like canonical status.

If we turn to the (arguably) likelier case of a future digital edition,
the editorial issues are at once simpler and more complex. On the one
hand, the likelihood of mechanical error would presumably decrease
substantially, thus reducing the chances of an inadvertent single-sided
mirror, or a negative offset for a medical photograph being accidentally
omitted, or the plastic page being inserted at the wrong spot in the book.
(Similarly, my own hardcover edition of *Blessed Is the Fruit* includes
no title on the spine, an apparent postmodern statement of displaced
identity that turned out to be a production error.) On the other hand,
how would a digital edition actually produce either of these iconic effects? Current means of electronic reading that use e-ink technology,
such as Amazon's Kindle, could not easily reproduce either a mirror or
transparent page. Alternative technologies might include holographic,
3-D, or virtual retinal displays, with VRD probably the best option
among these future scenarios. Originally developed at the University of

Washington's Human Interface Technology Lab in the early 1990s, VRD 'projects a modulated beam of light (from an electronic source) directly onto the retina of the eye, producing a rasterized image. The viewer has the illusion of seeing the source image as if he/she stands two feet away in front of a 14-inch monitor. In reality, the image is on the retina of its eye and not on a screen.'[26] While its primary applications so far have been in the military and medical fields, this technology could conceivably project a mirror or transparent page within the scanned image of other book pages, though such editorial applications are obviously far afield (exactly how far I am not qualified to judge).

In any case, whether in a new print edition or online or projected virtually onto a reader's retinas, future versions of *Divina Trace* and *Blessed Is the Fruit* would necessarily lose some of what Shillingsburg calls the 'eventness' of texts, for, as he observes of editing Victorian fiction, the original moment of a text's production, distribution, and reception is always irrecoverable historically, at least beyond a certain point. (Similarly, the original digital or other inscription would itself acquire its own historical situatedness, what Kirschenbaum has called the 'singularity of the digital present.')[27] By 'eventness' Shillingsburg refers materially to texts' 'origins . . . their original dates, original publishers, original typefaces, and original page arrangements and weights.'[28] While a responsible edition of Antoni's novels would certainly include reproductions of such original pages in some form, and would direct readers to the historical contexts of these texts' production, the nature of these iconic pages themselves – their textual condition, in Jerome McGann's terms[29] – would render *any* reproduction of their eventness impossible, including even those generated by multiple copies of the original editions. This is because every copy of these novels – at least those actually read – creates its own unique text as it incorporates the reader's physical experience of the text, especially by seeing one's reflection(s) in the mirror page(s) but also by handling the transparent page in relation to the surrounding pages. This claim may seem to make too much of a striking textual feature that is, after all, only a couple of pages within narratives that surpass four hundred and three hundred pages respectively, and my intention is not to erect a philosophical mountain from a textual molehill. Nevertheless, my contention is that if we take the mirror page in particular as a full-fledged element of the text, there is in the end no way to read it except as an impossibly Borgesian copy of itself, that is, as a text designed for reproducibility but which in the actual experience of reading becomes inherently resistant to reproduction.

The mirror pages raise theoretical questions about textuality as well as philosophical questions about aesthetics, but I will turn first to matters of editorial theory, hoping to expand from there to the ontology of these pages as literary objects – or, rather, as textual events. At the editorial level, the experience of reading and hypothetically editing the mirror pages recalls the basic distinction between 'work' as a collective term for a series of texts, and 'text' as a particular instantiation of the work, when that entity itself has no single material manifestation. In outlining the various implications of this distinction, Shillingsburg moves from the category of potential version, 'the abstract incipient ideas about the work as it grows in the consciousness of the author,' to the developing version, which will result in 'physical outcomes' such as drafts or notes, and finally to the essayed version (or more likely essayed versions), which 'has physical embodiment in a text, [but] it is not the physical text.'[30] This split between a particular 'physical embodiment' and the essayed version as a representation of the work occurs for Shillingsburg because of a fundamental distinction between the work as a conceptual entity and its various material forms:

> The material text – whether it is the author's or the publisher's, whether it represents version 1 or n, whether it is accurate or corrupt – is a necessary representation without which the work cannot be experienced, but it is not identical with the work, for no *particular* copy of the work is needed for the work to be experienced.[31]

The work for Shillingsburg thus transcends any single document or collection of documents, even while it depends on these material forms for access by readers.

Approached in these terms, the work *Divina Trace* would comprise Antoni's notes and drafts, excerpts published separately from the novel, and copies of the book's first edition and subsequent reprints. As Shillingsburg suggests, a reader's experience of the work would depend on no particular copy. In this case, however, each particular copy of the hardcover, paperback, or *Paris Review* excerpt will literally create its own version by virtue of the unique face that will appear in the mirror page(s). Even the same reader returning to the same copy will encounter a new person reflected there, for as philosophers have argued since Hume, new selves continually appear across moments of time. This means that each individual copy of the work, when read, will create a unique textual variant in the material encounter between the reader's reflection(s) and the surrounding linguistic text. To a certain extent, Shillingsburg's account of textuality in its material and immaterial forms leaves room for such a possibility: individual variants can and have occurred in single copies, and, as noted above, the original process of producing marbled pages in *Tristram Shandy* resulted in individual pages within each copy, so that no original edition is precisely identical to any other. At the editorial level, we might still comfortably conclude that the work *Divina Trace* encompasses all the physical documents noted above, in addition to countless and ultimately irreproducible 'copies' of readers' faces reflected in the mirror pages. Each of these readers' reflections, within Shillingsburg's structure, would contribute to an evolving, organic conception of the work, even if capturing this collection of mirror images would remain impossible within any edition of the work. In this respect, any edition would necessarily only gesture towards this broader realm of readerly experience, manifesting on a single page the broader problem of recovering historical contexts for a contemporary edition.

When we turn to the philosophical implications of the mirror pages, though, the work/text view of *Divina Trace* grows more complicated, as the relationship between an individual copy of the work and the work as a conceptual entity begins to shift outside of a linear structure. As the famous example of Borges's Pierre Menard indicates, two texts that are identical linguistically may still be distinct ontologically. As Arthur C. Danto concludes, 'graphic congruities notwithstanding, these are deeply different works.'[32] Danto, of course, does not mean 'work' in the editorial sense, and indeed the bibliographical differences in the material texts produced by Cervantes and Menard would be plentiful and plain; an editor, in any case, would presumably perceive them as ontologically distinct, not as an original edition and a later reprint of the same work. What makes Cervantes's and Menard's texts 'deeply different' for Danto is their circumstances of production: 'It is not just that the books are written at different times by different authors of different nationalities and literary intentions: these facts are not external ones; they serve to characterize the work(s) and of course to individuate them for all their graphic indiscernibility.'[33] For as Borges's narrator explains, Menard's aim is not 'Being, somehow, Cervantes and arriving thereby at the Quixote,' but rather 'continuing to be Pierre Menard and coming to the Quixote *through the experiences of Pierre Menard.*'[34] This route to producing his excerpt from the *Quixote* makes Menard's text, Danto writes, 'an extremely original work, so original, indeed, that we would be hard pressed to find a predecessor for it in the entire history of literature.'[35]

If Menard's originality derives from his ability to produce a linguistically identical text that remains ontologically unique due to the different historical circumstances of its production, Antoni's originality derives from the mirror pages' ability to produce materially identical texts that remain ontologically unique due to the different individual circumstances of their reception. Along these lines, it is worth relating *Divina Trace* to Gérard Genette's distinction between immanence (for literature, the physical form[s] from which we read or 'perform' the work) and transcendence (the various ways in which a work transcends its immanence).[36] For Genette, as for Shillingsburg, a work of art is inaccessible except through its immanence, yet the work is never wholly reducible to any of the physical objects through which we access it. We might make this general statement about *Divina Trace* as we would with any other novel: the experience of reading this complex representation of Caribbean history and identity transcends the physical experience of turning the pages, processing the typefaces, and the like. Yet in this case, again, the physical form of the work itself is inherently and almost infinitely variable, as each reader finds his or her own face reflected on the page(s) lodged in between Hanuman's Wakean narrative. In this sense the mirror pages crystallize Joseph Grigely's insight that texts operate not as objects we encounter, but as events in which we participate, which makes their editorial representation all the more problematic. 'Because events are temporally discrete,' Grigely explains, 'they are finite in a useful way. Yet because events take place in space, they are in another sense infinite.'[37] Thus Grigely concludes of oral texts that are literally realized in their performance ('Homer reciting the Iliad or Johnny Rotten ranting at Wembley'): 'If such texts have a problem (some might call it an advantage), it is that they cannot be replicated; there is no going back to an event that, once gone, is gone forever.'[38]

Understood in these terms, the mirror page(s) in *Divina Trace* operate similarly as material objects that occasion textual events in the process of their performance by readers: each individual encounter with these mirrors cannot be reproduced, only described, and so *Divina Trace* – and, in similar yet perhaps less dramatic ways, *Blessed Is the Fruit* in its unique experience of the plastic pages – exists as a work that cannot, ultimately, be edited, except in such a way as to gesture towards the forever fluid circumstances of its reception. This fundamental resistance to reproduction, rooted as it is in the vexed history of the Caribbean and in the creolized present from which Antoni's fictions emerge, speaks finally to what Antonio Bénitez-Rojo calls 'a touch of real genius' in the mirror pages and their fecund blankness.[39]

'When the Book Read': Reflecting Creolization

The above discussion of the editorial and philosophical implications generated by Antoni's iconic pages has largely set aside their postmodern, postcolonial, Caribbean contexts, but of course these are a central feature of both novels – in their language, their narrative structures, their representations of individual and cultural history, and in their material features. In each of these respects, *Divina Trace* and *Blessed Is the Fruit* proceed from and represent a condition of creolization (in Bénitez-Rojo's terms) or Creoleness (in Walter D. Mignolo's), a hybrid epistemology that grows out of the contemporary Caribbean's vexed and inescapable relationship with its colonial histories. For Mignolo, Creoleness 'describes a territorial and geohistorical location' and 'offers another "methodology," thinking at the crossroads and in the borders of colonial history which, like French language for Creole, cannot be avoided but must be appropriated and then turned inside out, so to speak.'[40] While Mignolo describes an epistemological condition, Bénitez-Rojo identifies a state of cultural and historical flux: 'creolization is a term with which we attempt to explain the unstable states that a Caribbean cultural object presents over time. In other words, creolization is not merely a process (a word that implies forward movement), but a discontinuous series of recurrences, of happenings, whose sole law is change.'[41]

Antoni's novels respond to these conditions in their language, which both transcribes Creole words and rhythms and, as Lise Winer notes, invents Caribbean neologisms in the midst of an already unsettling linguistic experience for non-Caribbean readers, 'lulling readers into a false sense of stable insecurity.'[42] Overlook requested a glossary for *Divina Trace*, but Antoni 'insisted they didn't do that; half of the words are made up anyway.'[43] This interest in both hybrid languages and neologisms stems from Antoni's emphasis on 'the "slipperiness" of language, the places where language becomes inventive and ambiguous, and in crossing-over *between* languages.'[44] Thus the monkey language of the Hanuman chapter in *Divina Trace* emerges from a much broader creolized approach to language and combines with the jumbled order of the narrative and a self-conscious sense throughout that Caribbean culture is both *'whatever America wants you to be'* (303, original emphasis) and simultaneously 'one big callaloo with all of we boiling up swimming together inside, and nobody could know any longer who was who and what was what, much less care to make a difference' (365). In all of these ways *Divina Trace* is self-consciously (and, literally, self-reflexively) about the experience of its own reading, for readers both Caribbean and 'American,' 'white' and 'black.'

The mirror page(s) create a space for the book's multiple readers to intersect virtually, as we can at least imagine the different kinds of images and responses produced by these reflections. In this way *Divina Trace* collapses the two ethical dimensions often ascribed to fiction by such philosophers as Martha Nussbaum and Richard Rorty, yielding for Western readers both 'details about the kinds of suffering being endured by people to whom we had not previously attended' as well as a reflection that 'lets us redescribe ourselves.'[45] More importantly, the mirror epitomizes what Bénitez-Rojo terms 'the novel's double performance: in the mirror, the Western reader will see a joke or an irony or a mystery, but the Caribbean reader will see any one of his/her multiple masks.'[46]

This sense of the mirror's textual event as one that specifically expresses a state of creolization returns us to the deeply performative and ultimately uneditable condition of the text.

As creolized narratives, *Divina Trace* and *Blessed Is the Fruit* continually adopt doubled perspectives, relating the present moment to various and often unstable versions of island and family history while also positioning Caribbean cultural narratives in relation to colonialism, in both its European historical forms and its contemporary U.S. influences. The resulting mix of African, South Asian, Warrahoon, European, and other cultural backgrounds yields a fragmented mix of Caribbean magic realism and European modernist *Bildungsroman*, what Bénitez-Rojo terms 'a bifurcated novel, fractal, gaseous.' By brilliantly lodging an ostensibly material artefact in the midst of this 'chaotic performance,'[47] Antoni creates the image of a stable textual object, when its actual performance among the range of readers reflected in the structure and content of the narrative itself will inevitably dislodge the mirror pages from their apparent singularity, rendering them ontologically beyond the confines of a stable editorial object while marking Antoni's text and work as deeply expressive of a truly fluid, creolized textual event.

NOTES

1 Telephone interview with the author, 10 September 1997.

2 Antoni's first name shifts from Odillo (actually his father's middle name) to Robert (his given name) for *Divina Trace* and his subsequent publications: as he explained in an interview with the author (10 September 1997), 'Odillo' represented 'a stage I was going through' at the time of the *Paris Review* publication.

3 Peter L. Shillingsburg, *From Gutenberg to Google: Electronic Representations of Literary Texts* (Cambridge: Cambridge University Press, 2006), 139.

4 Ranajit Guha, 'Not at Home in Empire,' *Critical Inquiry* 23 (1997): 482–93.

5 Ironically, attempts to reproduce the (absence of the) mirror page in the *Paris Review* microfilm proved technically unfeasible for the present volume, doubling that lack in these pages.

6 http://Robertantoni.com, 20 October 2009.

7 Eric D. Smith, 'Pandering Caribbean Spice: The Strange Exoticism of Robert Antoni's *My Grandmother's Erotic Folktales*,' *Journal of Commonwealth Literature* 39 (2004): 22n1.

8 Lawrence Scott, 'Robert Antoni,' *Bomb* 91 (2005): 56.

9 George Bornstein and Theresa Tinkle, eds., *The Iconic Page in Manuscript, Print, and Digital Culture* (Ann Arbor: University of Michigan Press, 1998).

10 John C. Hawley, SJ, 'Robert Antoni's "Divina Trace" and the Womb of Place,' *ARIEL* 24 (1993): 93. Although Hawley cites the second photographic page 'exactly one hundred pages from the end of the story,' it occurs on page 301, and the narrative ends on page 426. As I discuss below, even more exact uses of pagination appear in Antoni's second novel.

11 Telephone interview with the author, 16 September 1997. Antoni reports that he first saw this photograph as a child, in his father's copy of Holland's textbook. Quartet's printers decided a photographic reproduction of the page would be too faint, given the book's age, and so proposed a drawing. Instead, Antoni made his own sculpture of the anencephalic fetus based on the textbook photo, and then worked with a photographer to produce an image matching the original. Finally, Quartet combined this photo with a page designed to replicate the textbook typeface (ibid.). The published page is thus a simulacrum, in Baudrillard's sense: a published copy of an image designed to reproduce a published copy of an 'original' image, the anencephalic fetus itself.

12 'Walcott' is a revision introduced after the *Paris Review* publication, where the line reads 'quick out your dreamsleep marmoset' (177); Antoni

explains that he wanted Derek Walcott's name 'to appear in one of the most visible pages of the book' (interview, 10 September 1997).

13 Richard F. Patteson, *Caribbean Passages: A Critical Perspective on New Fiction from the West Indies* (Boulder: Lynne Reinner, 1998), 164.

14 Lilla is spelled 'Lila' in a 1993 *Conjunctions* excerpt.

15 Antoni, 'From *Blessed Is the Fruit*,' *Conjunctions* 20 (1993): 150.

16 A concern for correspondences between numbers pervades the novel, beginning with the question, 'do we make these numbers for the world? or does the world make *us* for these numbers?' (6). The most striking numeric sequence occurs on page 366, the last page of the penultimate chapter. Vel, who has been living in virtual isolation with Lilla in her parents' house for five years, realizes that they have only thirty-three dollars left in what had been a seemingly endless supply of money. Thirty-three is a significant number on many levels: the book revolves around three central characters, Lilla, Vel, and Vel's baby, Bolom; both women are thirty-three years old at this point in the narrative; and there are thirty-three pages left in the book (and 366 – 33 = 333, an even more perfect number for these purposes).

17 In his introduction to an excerpt from *Blessed* in *Conjunctions*, Antoni explains, '*This dream, however, is really the fetus' dream – the fetus' dream of its figurative parents who are these two women. (This fictional device actually has a medical precedent: physicians report that they have identified REM movements in unborn infants, so fetuses do in fact dream)*' (151, original emphasis).

18 Interview, 16 September 1997.

19 The first edition reads 'she hand on she heart' in place of this phrase.

20 Interview, 10 September 1997.

21 Ibid.

22 Telephone interview with the author, 18 September 1997.

23 On Sterne's marbled pages, see D.F. McKenzie, *Bibliography and the Sociology of Texts* (Cambridge: Cambridge University Press, 1986), 27–8, and Peter de Voogd, who explains that the marbling process in the 1760s required each page to be crafted individually, so 'not only are there two different marbled pages in each volume, but . . . every volume is different from all other volumes too' ('Laurence Sterne, The Marbled Page, and "The Use of Accidents,"' *Word & Image* 1 [1985]: 284).

24 As McKenzie notes, most modern editions of *Tristram Shandy* at best print a photocopied image of the marbled pages from a particular edition, and in so doing 'they subvert Sterne's intention to embody an emblem of non-specific intention, of difference, of undetermined meaning, of the very instability of text from copy to copy' (*Bibliography and the Sociology of Texts*, 28). While Antoni did not design the transparent page in *Blessed Is*

the Fruit with similar intentions, its actual production makes possible their expression.

25 For a cogent overview of these theoretical approaches to editing, see John Bryant, *The Fluid Text: A Theory of Revision and Editing for Book and Screen* (Ann Arbor: University of Michigan Press, 2002), chaps. 1–3.

26 Michael V. Capps, 'Virtual Retinal Display Technology,' Naval Postgraduate School, Monterey, CA, 28 December 2009.

27 Matthew G. Kirschenbaum, *Mechanisms: New Media and the Forensic Imagination* (Cambridge: MIT Press, 2008), 23.

28 Shillingsburg, *Gutenberg*, 139.

29 Jerome J. McGann, *The Textual Condition* (Princeton: Princeton University Press, 1991).

30 Peter L. Shillingsburg, *Resisting Texts: Authority and Submission in Constructions of Meaning* (Ann Arbor: University of Michigan Press, 1997), 68–9.

31 Shillingsburg, *Resisting*, 92, original emphasis.

32 Arthur C. Danto, *The Transfiguration of the Commonplace: A Philosophy of Art* (Cambridge: Harvard University Press, 1981), 36.

33 Ibid., 35.

34 Jorge Luis Borges, 'Pierre Menard, Author of the *Quixote*,' in Borges, *Collected Fictions*, trans. Andrew Hurley (New York: Viking, 1998), 91, original emphasis.

35 Danto, *Transfiguration*, 37.

36 Gérard Genette, *The Work of Art: Immanence and Transcendence*, trans. G.M. Goshgarian (Ithaca: Cornell University Press, 1997).

37 Joseph Grigely, *Textualterity: Art, Theory, and Textual Criticism* (Ann Arbor: University of Michigan Press, 1995), 115.

38 Ibid., 115.

39 Antonio Bénitez-Rojo, 'Three Words toward Creolization,' in *Caribbean Creolization: Reflections on the Cultural Dynamics of Language*, eds. Kathleen M. Balutansky and Marie-Agnès Sorieau, trans. James Maraniss (Gainesville: University of Florida Press, 1998), 60.

40 Walter D. Mignolo, *Local Histories/Global Designs: Coloniality, Subaltern Knowledges, and Border Thinking* (Princeton: Princeton University Press, 2000), 243, 246.

41 Bénitez-Rojo, 'Three Words,' 55.

42 Lise Winer, 'Comprehension and Resonance: English Readers and English Creole Texts,' in *Creole Attitudes, Genesis, and Discourse*, eds. John R. Rickford and Suzanne Romaine (Amsterdam: Benjamins, 1999), 402.

43 Interview, 10 September 1997.

44 Antoni, quoted in Scott, 'Robert Antoni,' 57, original emphasis.

45 Richard Rorty, *Contingency, Irony, and Solidarity* (Cambridge: Cambridge University Press, 1989), xvi.

46 Bénitez-Rojo, 'Three Words,' 61. Combined with the language and narrative of the work as a whole, Bénitez-Rojo concludes that each reader projects in the mirror not just his/her face but also his/her ideology – every mirror is a text in which the observer reads him/herself. For some the reflected image will be that of the Creole; for others it will be a native of some country in the Caribbean; for others it will be the reflection of his/her own race. These reflections, invested with the political and social ideas of the observer, will never be coherent images, but rather distorted ones; they will be images in flux, or rather images in search of their own images. Therefore, the mirror of *Divina Trace* reflects the many faces of Caribbean readers, but in the end it reflects an identity in a state of creolization, a reflection that oscillates between history and myth; that is, a paradoxical mask launched into the distance by the explosion of the plantation (61). For other readings of the mirror pages, see also Rhonda Cobham, 'Of Boloms, Mirrors, and Monkeymen: What's Real and What's Not in Robert Antoni's *Divina Trace*,' in *Sisyphus and Eldorado: Magical and Other Realisms in Caribbean Literature*, ed. Timothy J. Reiss (Trenton: Africa World Press, 2002), 39; Raphael Dalleo, ' "Tink Is You Dawson Dis Yana?": Imitation and Creation in Robert Antoni's *Divina Trace*,' *ARIEL* 32 (2001): 36; Hawley, 'Robert Antoni's "Divina Trace" and the Womb of Place,' 93; and Eric D. Smith, 'Johnny Domingo's Epic Nightmare of History,' *ARIEL* 31 (2000): 170.

47 Bénitez-Rojo, 'Three Words,' 60.

PART FOUR

The Electronic Edition

10 Reading Material Bibliography and Digital Editions

YURI COWAN

The etymology of editing (from *edere*, 'to put forth') reveals that sharing and dissemination are essential elements of the editing process, and although scholarly editors have occasionally seemed more invested in establishing the hermetic perfection of their texts than in opening texts up to their readers, the impulse of the scholarly edition has always been outward. The audience for big expensive print editions of relatively obscure works of literature has long been limited to the libraries that could afford them or to the scholars who ferreted them out of dark corners to reveal their significance to other scholars (and ideally to their students in the humanities as well). But what sort of sea change does the social dynamic and scholarly milieu undergo when a new online audience of critics and students discovers an archive as detailed as the William Blake archive,[1] as diverse as Romantic Circles,[2] or as rich as the Networked Infrastructure for Nineteenth-Century Electronic Scholarship (NINES)?[3] And who exactly comprise that audience; and what kinds of texts most interest them; and how do they read and make sense of digital editions? These are big questions, and even fifteen years after 'The Rationale of Hypertext,' we don't really have all the answers; in fact, Peter Shillingsburg has observed that after almost twenty years of diligent digitizing we still do not even have a standard idea of how we want to do digital editing.[4]

Hitherto, scholarship on digital editions has not inquired very far into the kind of readers electronic editions are intended to attract. There is, however, an admirable open-mindedness about the kinds of criticism that a digital edition is capable of inspiring. In encouraging editors to think about the kind of reading assumed or forced by digital editions, I hope here to remind textual scholars that we still to a certain extent lack a sense of how digital editions are to be used, both by researchers and in the classroom, and to suggest ways in which the inclusiveness of digital editions and digital archives, combined with their illustrative capabilities and ready links to library holdings, may serve to introduce readers to the principles involved in the study of material texts. I also want to suggest that although the digital archive is a relatively new form, with its own sets of material constraints, we can learn from the experience of past organizations that engaged in similarly ambitious textual recovery and editing in the medium of print, and that an understanding of the challenges faced by the nineteenth-century Early English Text Society in collaborating on, editing, and disseminating newly rediscovered medieval and Early Modern texts might speak to the social dynamic of our own scholarly editing practices.

Material bibliography is an area of study that might seem at odds with digital formats, but it is in many ways at the heart of the digitization enterprise, as the electronic edition can convey a wide range of historical and contextual matter and is moreover capable of placing the raw material for textual and bibliographical analysis in visual form directly in the reader's control. The desire of librarians for new ways of conserving books and space goes back to the mid-twentieth-century microform projects, which comprised the first of many attempts since then to grapple with the problems of material storage and access, sacrificing some image quality as a result. In one sense, digitization might be similarly said to put another barrier between the reader and the physical book, but it is probably more accurate to say that readers now can see more examples of page design and typography than ever before. Digitization also allows access to historically under-represented works to an even greater extent than microforms and even libraries, for although the opening of the literature canon predates digital editions, it has particularly been furthered by the creation of digital archives of previously unavailable books.

Although the most idealistic rhetoric surrounding the creation of digital archives has concerned the democratizing effect of access to texts, the visual archive has also revealed the diversity of historical books with regard to design, and may have even more research potential than the searchable texts that have formed the focus of the digitizers' energies. Many of the most prominent sites are free, or at least free for most academics: from the sprawling Internet Archive[5] and Project Gutenberg[6] through archives like the still open but more professional Digital Scriptorium[7] and NINES, to sites like Chadwyck-Healey's Early

English Books Online (EEBO)[8] and Gale's Eighteenth-Century Collections Online (ECCO)[9] that are accessible only through a library or subscription. The best of these have rich collections of images. In EEBO, students in undergraduate Shakespeare courses have access to visual representations (however rough) of the diverse quarto playbooks of the early seventeenth century; the scarcity of primary documents for classroom use is no longer a reason to dismiss the necessity of a thorough historical understanding or to assume an ahistorical typographical immutability of literary texts. The usefulness and possible uses of digital texts for criticism do not need to be rehearsed here, although there is certainly room in current scholarship for an article that describes the social impact of digital editions and archives on the kinds of scholarship that are now being practised.

It is true that for the most part, as Peter Shillingsburg suggests in 'How Literary Works Exist,' 'students and critics' practising this kind of scholarship will continue to comprise the main readership for digital editions. It would be wrong to argue that this is a limited audience, though; books have always been limited in their readership, in one way or another; moreover, besides critics and students and the interested general public (who might be more numerous than we think, especially for celebrated doubly gifted writer/artists such as Blake and the Pre-Raphaelites), we should count bibliographers and editors among the readership for digital editions as well. A new generation of textual scholars is developing, encouraged by associations such as the Society for the History of Authorship, Reading, and Publishing (SHARP) and by the diverse possibilities and less prescriptive atmosphere of digital editing to try their hands at making editions. Because current scholarship is temperamentally inclined to resurrecting non-canonical texts, and therefore in many cases these editors are attempting works that exist in limited forms (even sometimes in single editions), their practice obviates the complex issues surrounding the synthesis of multiple versions of a canonical work into a single eclectic or perfect text – the enterprise that has traditionally been the Grail of textual scholarship. Indeed, influenced by the school of Jerome McGann and enabled by the copious storage capacities of the digital environment, digital editors are quite content to display as many versions as we can access and scan. This was certainly the case for me when I chose to edit William Morris's *Ordination of Knighthood* for the William Morris Online Edition;[10] the *Ordination* has only one manuscript and two printed versions, of which one was printed by Morris himself. Indeed, for many in the new generation of editors, we are not so much 'editing' as we are creating editions, and we are making archives rather than forming eclectic texts.

It is even possible that, as the hitherto carefully conserved print archive is injected into the more public digital sphere, as images of manuscripts, incunabula, and the fine press movement become commonplace and as typographical masterpieces and previously ephemeral works of popular culture and pulp are alike archived and shared, the rare book itself is being demystified. It is an intellectual environment in which any scholar, and any informed student, can now be an editor or curator. We are deeper inside these texts than we have ever been, and literary scholars count more editors among our numbers than ever; *nous sommes tous éditeurs*. This is partly a function of technology: the major research libraries have become more accessible with cheaper travel, and the conversion of texts into digital form is now a fairly straightforward process. But much of this new interest in textual recovery and editing has also to do with the rise of new disciplines. Cultural Studies' political shift of focus to non-canonical works was the earliest impetus for this spread of editorship, while the rise of the study of Book History and its associated interdisciplines has given rise to a broader awareness among historians and literary scholars of the sociology and socialization of texts, in the process making researchers more aware of the book as an artefact of past ways of seeing the world.

There exists a rough parallel to our historical moment in the early work of the Early English Text Society (EETS), founded in 1864. At midcentury, Frederick Furnivall began to exercise his tireless genius for social organizing on the creation of an ever-expanding catalogue of Old and Middle English texts, with the aim of introducing Victorian readers to their national medieval cultural heritage. Though the nationalistic tone of its editors is not mirrored in our own era of humanistic, inclusive canon extension, the EETS in its early years is exemplary of the social dynamic of scholarly editing, and may afford us some useful ways of thinking about the intersection of readership, editing, and material bibliography. In a way, the EETS and similar enterprises in the nineteenth century (such as Furnivall's Chaucer Society, the Ballad Society, and the Camden Society) represent in a print medium the kind of mushrooming interest in editing and textual recovery that the electronic medium has sparked. They, too, sought to fill in the gaps in the historical record, especially those to do with works that had been neglected by reason of déclassé associations with the domestic and the low; they, too, worked at a feverish pace to put as much material as possible before the public eye; and they, too, discovered surprising new resources of editorial expertise to fill the need.

The number of people interested in publishing medieval English literature at midcentury may or may not be surprising, given the Victorian taste for all things medieval, the Victorian curiosity about the everyday life of the past, and the tireless Victorian work ethic. What is certainly worthy of note is that a large number of the readers of medieval literature were the very scholars and amateurs who formed the audience for the works that the Society was producing. (It was, for example, a great coup when W.W. Skeat's edition of 'Peres the Ploughman's Crede' was put on the syllabus for a senior English class at the City of London School in 1867.)[11] The communication circuit was in many ways a circular one. Anthony Singleton remarks that 'curiously, while EETS found readers in short supply, editorial workers were comparatively abundant . . . Over sixty different people were identified as editors on the title pages of its publications, and the assistance of a significant number more was acknowledged within their various prefaces and introductions.'[12] The collaborative methodology of the Society is reflected, for instance, in the large volume entitled *English Gilds* (1870); when the editor, Toulmin Smith, died, his daughter Lucy Toulmin Smith took over the editorial duties, including in the apparatus a lengthy exchange between her father and Lujo Brentano debating the degree and quality of the guilds' radicalism. The social networks that informed the output of the Society are illustrated in the *Gilds* volume, with its two editors and major collaborator; similar social networks now drive the big online editorial projects. The executive council of NINES alone numbered twenty-seven scholars as of February 2010.

Just as the current interest in creating electronic texts has led to a great variety of kinds of editions in terms of the amount of detail included, and the quality and extent of textual emendation, so the early days of the EETS saw a diverse and prolific output from amateur and professional scholars alike. Several of the early editions of the society would eventually have to be re-edited, and some of the EETS's contributors and advisors recognized early on that the Society's inconsistent practices would lead to uneven results. Henry Bradshaw, librarian of Cambridge from 1867 to 1886 and one of the foremost textual scholars of the age, was in close contact with Furnivall while the latter was working on the EETS's publications. In a letter of August 1867, he reveals his uneasiness, writing to Furnivall that 'until some of you begin to *edit* books, there is no chance for any of us learning anything.'[13] But Furnivall never saw himself as an editor, and wilfully chose not to understand: in a letter to Bradshaw dated 8 February 1871 he modestly claims that 'you're the man to *edit* Chaucer, if only you will. I'm the man to print the texts.'[14] Bradshaw recognized that even if Furnivall was pretending simply to publish medieval manuscripts as he found them, it was impossible for him to avoid making decisions of an editorial nature. Even if print could faithfully mimic the textual peculiarities of a manuscript, there could be no mere reprinting of the manuscript. There were bound to be errors in copying, and there would always be editorial judgements imposed upon the text – precisely the sort of errors and actions that can be reversed if necessary over time in editions published digitally.

Furnivall and the Early English Text Society were aware from the start of the physical limitations imposed upon their project by the print medium. The EETS was able to adopt a number of idiosyncratic characters, such as the occasional crossed ascender for *h* in the Hengwrt manuscript of Chaucer, but other problems of textual fidelity remained, and there were many dissenting views about how the Society's texts should appear: David Matthews describes how, in 1869, Furnivall fortunately rejected as ahistorical suggestions that EETS books be printed in black-letter, like type facsimiles.[15] The producers of modern editions have the advantage over their Victorian counterparts not only of the availability of digital facsimiles, but of a comprehensive array of characters and fonts. This will be an important innovation; the exigencies of nineteenth-century page design had a lasting effect on the way we now imagine some of these medieval texts. The placement that we now find natural for the 'bob' in *Sir Gawain and the Green Knight*, for instance, stems from Richard Morris's 1864 edition of the poem: in the unique manuscript and in the 1839 Bannatyne Club edition, the bob is placed directly to the right of the line preceding the four-line 'wheel,' while editions after Morris have adopted his placement of the bob on a line of its own preceding the four-line wheel. It is hard to quantify the effect of such alterations on the reading experience, but such effects undoubtedly exist. Richard Morris's first great volume for the EETS, giving for the first time all the poems of the British Library manuscript Cotton Nero A.x., is now only a footnote to scholarship on the *Gawain* manuscript; the poems had eventually to be re-edited. But many of Morris's readings have been retained; and as the example of the bob in *Gawain* attests, Morris is a silent partner who needs to be acknowledged in all future editions as a major factor in the transformation of the text on its way down to us. His influence is considerable.

It is possible that modern digital editors are more like Furnivall than like Bradshaw or Morris; we are 'printing' (creating digital archives), rather than 'editing,' and our primary criterion is accessibility rather than a polished, responsible scholarly text (that crossed-ascender *h* would trip up most digital searchers). But we do have the advantage of being able to give the reader a more complete archive, and letting him or her decide which historical text is the most appropriate to the purpose, even if not all those texts are searchable (our other important criterion for digital editions). In the days before hypertext, Chaucer scholars had the Chaucer Society's *Six-Text Edition* (1868) of the *Canterbury Tales*, edited by Furnivall himself. Printed on often-brittle pulp paper, the edition offers parallel texts of six important manuscripts. Until the advent of electronic editing and the Canterbury Tales Project, there would be nowhere else to make six major manuscripts of *The Canterbury Tales* speak to each other in one place. The text (unlike certain of the more notorious publications of the EETS, especially the earlier ones) does keep relatively close to the originals. It is still not a completely faithful transcript, however, and the use of square brackets denotes an editorial willingness to intrude that is unacceptable in a work that was meant to be used in an authoritative way by still other editors without access to facsimiles of the originals. But the impossibility of facsimile reproduction on that scale meant that transcription was a necessary evil, and so editorial intervention and error, the idiosyncrasies of scribal culture, and the restrictions of available type meant that the *Six-Text Edition* would be an edition rather than an archive.

The Early English Text Society relied upon a network of scholars and amateurs whose reach exceeded their grasp, since the technology did not exist to create the kind of archive that would have been suited to Furnivall's eclectic, inclusive temperament. A letter from Bradshaw to Furnivall conjecturally dated December 1874 reveals Bradshaw's essential sympathy for Furnivall's difficulty: 'I am afraid bibliomania is a grievous thing, if one takes any special fancy. but [*sic*] I confess I like exhausting a matter if it is to be done.'[16] Even Bradshaw, as exacting an editor as the Victorian period would produce (so exacting, in fact, that he rarely finished his projects), recognized that the archive needed to be as complete as possible because editions would need to acknowledge other states of the same text and similar problems in other texts. What Jerome McGann calls the 'radial' reading experience offered by hypertext editions speaks to not only the establishment of texts and apparatus, but to the historical material state of texts as well. In *The*

Textual Condition, McGann describes radial reading as occurring when the book sends its reader to other books in order to make sense of what it says.[17] Radial reading is not only about becoming familiar with allusions and sources, but is as much a bibliographical practice as a critical one; in practising it, readers simultaneously fend off a prescriptive understanding of texts as super-historical entities and open themselves up to sympathy with alternative textual and bibliographical states. Likewise, the apparent bibliomania of the EETS's researchers was not only about book-fetishism, exploration, and completism; the impulse to recover and edit texts was an impulse to share and to connect them. The EETS's output thus relied upon its members' access to the institutions that held the books they were editing; without the British Museum reading room or the Oxford and especially Cambridge connections, the largely amateur EETS would have been on the outside looking in. An important lesson of the nineteenth-century Early English Text Society's exuberant project of textual recovery is that open access to both digital and print editions is essential to future textual scholarship.

The Early English Text Society is still going strong. Many of its works are now available in the Middle English Compendium,[18] but although on the surface one might imagine that the digital archive will be the EETS's solution to the problems of textual representation and access that Furnivall faced in those anarchic early days, there still exists some hesitancy about relying solely on digital editions. Peter Robinson writes that

> the EETS board has so far (to my knowledge) refrained from an absolute declaration that all future EETS editions will be prepared and published in digital form. And frankly, it would be irresponsible for the board, or any similar agency, to issue any such edict at present. Before any such declaration could be made by a major editorial group, we would need to satisfactorily address the two issues on which this article focusses: we would need to establish an overwhelming agreement within the community that digital editions are indeed the way to go; and we would need to have tools available so that any editor who had the skills to make a print edition could make a digital one instead.[19]

Robinson illustrates how far the EETS has come organizationally from its amateur roots, evoking an organization for which textual scholarship has become more rigorous and scientific, and less hasty. The new EETS has also long since abandoned any hyperbolic claim to a broad readership; medievalists alone are now its bread and butter, and its editors are all professionals. In spite of the fact that many of its works are now available in the Middle English Compendium, the debate within the EETS is thus also about the control of texts. I am not using 'control' in a pejorative sense here; I am not sure that it is authoritarian to want to establish and share the best text of any work, and neither am I willing to state unreservedly whether digital editions are, as Robinson says, 'the way to go.'

But the current Early English Text Society's misgivings about moving into a digital format certainly suggest that the question of the physical form of texts remains as much an issue in the twenty-first century as it was in the nineteenth.[20] Where the nineteenth-century EETS tried to represent scribal characters with special sorts and editorial emendations with italics and square brackets, the twenty-first-century editor can scan and reproduce the page of the original work, edit the text, and justify the emendations later if necessary by reference to the readily available facsimile. Grappling with the issue of completeness, John Lavagnino observes that 'today, it would often be more economical to reproduce an author's manuscript photographically rather than to set it in type, but this is almost never done *except* in publications intended for scholars; in microfilms and printed facsimiles of authors' manuscripts, all intended for study rather than reading.'[21] What Lavagnino says here about manuscripts probably applies to print editions, as well, and since he wrote those words (in 1996), photographic reproduction and scanning has become even easier. But we have to think about where our editions end: are we going to simply print every edition, every state of every text? This method suggests an overwhelming proliferation; but it is useful because it is capable of getting readers thinking about the authority of texts. If students begin to question the fixity of even the most rock-solid and reputable editions, that can only be a good thing. Readers schooled in the fluid online textual environment respond readily to the notion of multiple texts, even if they will not – and should not – read them comprehensively. It cannot be a bad thing when even the most casual student readers come to realize (as they will, when the digital archive exposes them to the cross-historical existence of print editions) that the text they are studying in the digital Middle English Compendium was edited in the nineteenth century by an amateur editor.

The process that Randall McLeod calls 'transformission' takes place in editing just as it does in the process of printing and in the originary act of writing down. Texts are performative, each text manifesting in individual, nearly irreproducible forms at different times, and this is especially true of texts that exist in medieval manuscript, as the EETS's editors found when they tried to re-present their originals for a Victorian readership using the existing tools of print. One of the greatest strengths of the digital edition, besides its searchability, is its ability to display and to juxtapose visual cues, not so much for 'study' as Lavagnino says (after all, unless one reads the book upside down one will always be 'reading,' even if for much bibliographical work the physical book is still the essential thing), as in support of charting the changes a page and a text undergo from edition to edition. Rather than suggest that there is some kind of aura implicit in the 'original' embodiment of a text, I want to recommend here a practice not unlike genetic editing, minus the sense of linear progress that the creation of genetic editions is sometimes made to serve. Readers inevitably develop a stronger historical sense as they engage with wider radial reading in past bibliographical forms. A sense of history is evoked when the reader recognizes differences in typography, page design, illustration, and original spelling at different times in the text's history; the digital text has more in common with the three-dimensional book than we think. The visual cues of illustration are the most obvious avenue for this kind of immersion (as, for instance, Sidney Paget's illustrations of Sherlock Holmes instantly, viscerally, evoke for us the prim, grimy, gas-lit London of the 1890s). But a different, even deeper sympathy for past social history is triggered by reading and viewing texts in their contemporary typography, spelling, and punctuation. On a related note, it is deceptive to suggest that readers need to be eased into their task by an edited text that has been utterly cleansed of accidental or even substantive alternative readings. For a generation of readers forced by the limitations of cell phone technology into adopting creative spelling and grammar, the variant spellings adopted by a Shakespeare quarto's printer to eke out his lines should pose very few problems.

Lavagnino calls this approach 'localist,' and comments that it might end up in the utter repudiation of editorial projects.[22] That criticism is valid; indeed, this is as close as I will come to arguing that, with broader access to the visual archive, books (and readers) will no longer need the interference of editors at all. But it is also true that the past necessity of scholarly editing has its origin at least in part in the fact that these works were out of print and needed to be made accessible; perfecting the text is a relatively recent innovation. Hoyt N. Duggan describes the value of the *Piers Plowman Electronic Archive* as consisting in more than its textual content:

> Fifty-four electronic transcriptions and facsimiles – perhaps none of them ever serving as a traditional reading text – will offer scholars not only new ways to study the text and the textual tradition of the poem but also possibilities for gaining fresh insight into other aspects of late medieval literary culture . . . It matters little that no one is ever likely to want to *read* all fifty-four documents. Many will want to *use* them.[23]

Remember, too, that we have another reason for wanting to preserve diverse historical versions of the works of major and even minor authors: certain editions, even with typographical or translational or editing flaws, carry a cultural weight all their own: beyond these fifty-four individual textual performances of *Piers Plowman*, I am thinking of John Dryden knowing Chaucer through Speght's edition, or John Keats knowing Dante through the Cary translation, or T.E. Lawrence's experience of Chaucer in the Kelmscott edition. A lot of interpretive latitude can be opened up or closed off by the knowledge of which particular edition of Shakespeare was considered standard by a writer like Charles Lamb. The archive is capable of capturing texts at diverse historical moments as they were known by diverse historical readers, and we are closer than ever to being able to compare, side by side, the texts that different historical readers have read, in the transformed texts in which those readers knew them. Far from representing a 'narrow documentary historicism,'[24] the interpretive possibilities of this approach are considerable.

Both the creation of archives of bibliographical images and the practice of radial reading militate against the notion of typographical fixity – when readers can compare multiple editions of texts, they rapidly come to recognize that variations are common, even in the machine-press period. The ideal of a possible definitive text is rapidly receding: the summer 2009 special issue of *Digital Humanities Quarterly* is on the theme of 'Done' – and as Matthew Kirschenbaum wryly observes in the introduction, it's very hard to know when to define a digital edition as finished, both in terms of getting the searchable text right and of providing all significant states of the text. Confusing hybridity and misleading ahistoricity lie in wait for the digital edition as well: what are we to make of the visual cues of an edition of *As You Like It* that comprises the Folio text and a modernization in

HTML, complemented by facsimiles of the play as it appeared in each of the four folios, for which the portal page is headed by a historically remote illustration from Charles and Mary Cowden Clarke's *Shakespeare's Works* of 1868?[25] We can only conclude that the Cowden Clarke illustration is purely decorative. But perhaps one of the strengths of the electronic edition is its very accretive and eclectic nature, not only because it helps readers to understand the diversity of texts and, in doing so, leads us to think about, to distrust, and even to usurp the actions of the editors whose authority we have so long taken for granted. If it is hard to tell when the process of adding texts to the archive is 'done,' then the process of editing is likewise ongoing. The EETS editors, with a daunting material archive before them, understood this, and therefore they, knee-deep in the sociology of texts, were less in awe of the authority of the scholarly print edition than we are.

The digitized image of the book, then, points beyond itself to the book in three dimensions and further to the communication circuit, to the social circumstances of the book's production, and to its reception. The sociology of texts cuts to the heart of one last uncomfortable dilemma that might undercut the practice of editing. I do not wish here to call the textual authority of authorial intention into question; but it must be acknowledged that much recent scholarship, especially in the field of the history of print culture, has been devoted to recovering the many forces that influence the printed versions of our received texts: friends and family members, amanuenses, copyeditors, compositors, publishers, bowdlerizers, reviewers, and the spectre of a fickle disapproving public. As Morris Eaves argues,

> When it becomes evident that individual authors are composing works *as* members of social groups, editors lose the great advantage of the author's individual body and especially the author's mortality in determining when the progressive movement toward 'final intentions' and 'definitive editions' ends. The relatively well-defined individual lifetime is replaced by the much more nebulous lifetimes of societies and languages. Good examples appear under our nose every time a text reminds us that authors are socialized individuals. But theories of editing have been highly reluctant to acknowledge, much less value, the shaping influence of socialization, collaboration, and historical processes on the landscape of editing.[26]

As editorial theory and a consciousness of historical textual instability filter down from scholars experienced in the tradition of editing, to scholars in the field of book history, and then on to their students – that is, as all readers of literature become editors – we might begin to re-internalize this sense of the complex sociology of texts, and to adopt it as a conscious or unconscious part of our reading strategy. This is a different kind of dead author, an author not replaced but augmented by our understanding of the way the writer's words are mediated by a circle of collaborators by turns silent and obtrusive. A bibliographical headnote acknowledging the physical circumstances of textual production is a necessity for digital editions, because it points towards the three-dimensional book; because it recognizes the material contribution of those who transmitted and transformed the text; and, most important of all, because it acknowledges that the reader has more need than ever before to access the information to make sense of the multiple textual histories that comprise or stand behind the digital archive.

I do not mean here to faithfully reiterate the seductive claims made by, for instance, George P. Landow in the early days of computer editing, for the liberating effect of hypertext, nor even to suggest that radial reading in a hypothetical digital Library of Babel will somehow make every reader into a self-conscious maker of editions. Digital archives linked by hypertext exercise their own material constraints upon the reader, as Ian Small has suggested.[27] I am more interested here in the way in which readerly engagement with the archive might serve to lead readers and editors back to the physical book, which after all is still relatively familiar territory, with traditions of display and formatting that still have a lot in common with the digital text. Many of the small practices of editing remain the same, moving from online to print: readerly annotation of digital editions is just like the traditional practice of footnoting or marginalia, while the 'exhibit' function of NINES is similar to the act of curating an exhibition of books or arranging a filing cabinet. Finally, as Gabriel Bodard and Juan Garcés maintain, the apparatus criticus and the footnote – the most important material interventions by the editor into the text – will remain essential parts of traditional textual scholarship, since 'they provide the basis and infrastructure of critical discourse and thus disclose one important feature of critical practice and open up one crucial possibility. What this reveals is, of course, that criticism is fundamentally a *communal* enterprise.'[28] Indeed, it has always been so; and it illustrates how, in a practical sense, very little changes on the social level when textual scholarship moves to the digital realm; the production of editions and archives is still carried out in conference with other editors and readers past and present, just as it was for Furnivall and Bradshaw in the nineteenth century.

Not only, then, does the editing process still have a hermeneutic face, but it also occurs in a shared space – the performative space of the material text, published in multiple print and digital forms, acted upon (and acted out) by multiple readers. As Alan Galey puts it, 'Designing an edition, digital or otherwise, is not a straightforward process of tool-building, but a creative act bound up with the cultural history of a text – something interface design shares with dramatic adaptation.'[29] This kind of melding of editorship and readership is not a new idea; when Peter Shillingsburg outlines his ideal conditions for online textual editing, interactivity is one of his central themes, and he calls for readerly annotation and comment on digital editions. If moving the reader into the performative space of the text in this way seems problematic, we have only to remember that editors have always been readers first, and that collaboration has always been inherent in textual scholarship, in the form of the social dynamic of scholarly editing, as the naturally collaborative 'weak' model of authorship, and even embedded in the complex communication circuit itself. There is no reason why the digital edition should be restricted to presenting a single text as minimally as an eclectic print edition must, just as there is no reason why we should now defer to the authority of a single editor.

The expansion of the digital record thus has many useful consequences for the study of the history of the book and of material bibliography itself. At the most basic preliminary level, the use of visual images allows for research that will adequately prepare scholars and students to interact with the physical book itself. In the long term, we can look forward to the kinds of digital textual scholarship that Peter Shillingsburg and Jerome McGann have long envisioned: a network of comprehensive, modular, peer-reviewed scholarly editions, complemented by a complete archive of images of every print edition (or at least every major edition) of every book. The medium term is equally exciting, however, as our editors can inform their theoretical approaches with recent scholarship in the sociology of material texts, creating a model of readerly engagement and a generation of reader/editors who will be neither overawed by the authority of print nor seduced by the hyperbolic claims made for the electronic edition. Our theories of editing will continue to evolve, but unlike Furnivall's *Six-Text Edition*, the archives and genetic editions that our scholarly networks are now establishing will provide solid bases for our editorial practice, because they will take material bibliography into account and allow readers to see the historical documents for themselves.

NOTES

1 http://www.blakearchive.org/blake/.
2 http://www.rc.umd.edu/.
3 http://www.nines.org/.
4 'How Literary Works Exist: Convenient Scholarly Editions,' *Digital Humanities Quarterly* 3, no. 3 (Summer 2009).
5 http://www.archive.org/index.php.
6 http://www.gutenberg.org/wiki/Main_Page.
7 http://www.scriptorium.columbia.edu/.
8 http://eebo.chadwyck.com/home.
9 http://gale.cengage.co.uk/product-highlights/history/eighteenth-century-collections-online.aspx.
10 William Morris, *The Ordination of Knighthood* [1892], ed. Yuri Cowan, in The William Morris Online Edition, http://morrisedition.lib.uiowa.edu/ordination.html.
11 William Benzie, *Dr. F.J. Furnivall: Victorian Scholar Adventurer* (Norman, OK: Pilgrim, 1983), 134.
12 Anthony Shingleton, 'The Early English Text Society in the Nineteenth Century: An Organizational History,' *Review of English Studies* 25, no. 223 (2005): 113.
13 G.W. Prothero's *Memoir of Henry Bradshaw*, qtd. in Benzie, *Dr. F.J. Furnivall*, 164.
14 Prothero, qtd. in Benzie, *Dr. F.J. Furnivall*, 165.
15 David Matthews, *The Making of Middle English, 1765–1910* (Minneapolis: University of Minnesota Press, 1999), 150.
16 Henry Bradshaw to Frederick James Furnivall. [December 1874?], MS, Correspondence of Frederick James Furnivall,The Huntington Library, San Marino, CA.
17 Jerome McGann, *The Textual Condition* (Princeton, NJ: Princeton University Press, 1991), 119.
18 http://ets.umdl.umich.edu/m/mec/.
19 Peter Robinson, 'Current Issues in Making Digital Editions of Medieval Texts – or, Do Electronic Scholarly Editions Have a Future?' *Digital Medievalist* 1, no. 1 (Spring 2005), http://www.digitalmedievalist.org/journal/1.1/robinson/.

20 When SEENET (the Society for Early English and Norse Electronic Texts; http://www.iath.virginia.edu/seenet/) or the publishers of the complete texts of Johan Daisne's novel *De trein der traagheid* (according to Edward Vanhoutte) still put out their work only in the form of CD-ROMs, that is a conscious decision on their part, made in order to maintain control over the edition and the material. They are not isolated editions, any more than any undigitized print edition is truly isolated; they are simply not linkable except in the form of bibliographical citations. Linking to them just takes a little longer, and requires more physical work. See Vanhoutte, 'Every Reader His Own Bibliographer – An Absurdity?' in *Text Editing, Print, and the Digital World*, ed. Marilyn Deegan and Kathryn Sutherland (Farnham: Ashgate, 2009).

21 John Lavagnino, 'Completeness and Adequacy in Text Encoding,' in *The Literary Text in the Digital Age*, ed. Richard J. Finneran (Ann Arbor: University of Michigan Press, 1996), 65.

22 Lavagnino, 'Completeness and Adequacy in Text Encoding,' 69.

23 Hoyt N. Duggan, 'Some Unrevolutionary Aspects of Computer Editing,' in *The Literary Text in the Digital Age*, ed. Finneran, 83.

24 Peter Shillingsburg, *Scholarly Editing in the Computer Age: Theory and Practice*, 3d. ed. (Ann Arbor: University of Michigan Press, 1996), 17.

25 William Shakespeare, *As You Like It* [1599], ed. David Bevington, Internet Shakespeare Editions, http://internetshakespeare.uvic.ca/Library/Texts/AYL/.

26 Morris Eaves, ' "Why Don't They Leave It Alone?" Speculations on the Authority of the Audience in Editorial Theory,' in *Cultural Artifacts and the Production of Meaning*, ed. Margaret J.M. Ezell and Katherine O'Brien O'Keeffe (Ann Arbor: University of Michigan Press, 1994), 88.

27 Ian Small, 'Postmodernism and the End(s) of Editing,' in *Editing the Text*, ed. Marysa Demoor, Geert Lernout, and Sylvia van Peteghem (Tilburg: Tilburg University Press, 1998), 37.

28 Gabriel Bodard and Juan Garcés, 'Open Source Critical Editions: A Rationale,' in *Text Editing, Print, and the Digital World*, ed. Marilyn Deegan and Kathryn Sutherland (Farnham, UK: Ashgate, 2009), 91.

29 Alan Galey, 'Signal to Noise: Designing a Digital Edition of *The Taming of a Shrew* (1594),' *College Literature* 36, no. 1 (2009): 42.

11 The Object and the Process; or, Take This Book and Click It!

DARCY CULLEN

What has the advent of the e-book meant for scholarly publishers and their editors? A few years ago, it seemed to hold very little promise to book publishers in the humanities and social sciences. It seemed unlikely that people would want to read full books on a computer or print them out in whole or in sections on their home printers. A journal article was one thing, but a complex intellectual argument unfolding over hundreds of pages was something completely different. Who would really buy an electronic copy of a book?

As online catalogues replaced the card files, libraries became very interested in expanding their collections digitally, limited physical space being one reason among others to do so. Scientific and other journals were being made available electronically. Mechanisms were devised to control the transmission of digitized books to respect copyright and to ensure a form of compensation to publishers and authors – royalties, for example, being paid based on the number of views, downloads, pages printed, and full book purchases, all of which would be measured. So why were book publishers so sluggish or resistant in responding to the call for digital or digitized publications? Publishers weren't jumping at the chance to do away with the printed book in order to help save shelf space, nor was it clear that there was any real demand for e-books from readers. Yet readers have become increasingly used to *accessing* any number of documents, publications, and repositories online; publishers are expected to deliver or make accessible or known via the Internet the books that they publish.

In the 1970s, philosopher Jean-François Lyotard wrote in his report to the province of Quebec on the condition of knowledge and knowledge production in the 'computerized society' that 'the nature of knowledge cannot survive unchanged within the context of general transformation. It can fit into the new channels and become operational only if learning is translated into quantities of information.'[1] Units of information are certainly the basis for book *distribution*: every detail about a book, from the number of pages to its weight, from its ISBN to its descriptive copy and table of contents, is entered into spreadsheets and exported out of and imported into databases that feed other databases, websites, and library acquisitions profiling programs. Every book is made to fit into a series of subject categories, some being good matches, others being barely adequate.[2] Computerizing the book to make it 'discoverable' also involves introducing a layer of tags to the text and images, which correspond to keywords likely to be used by searchers. As information studies professor Christine Borgman writes, 'Data have become an important form of research capital, enabling new questions to be asked. With the mass digitization of books now under way . . . [t]ext and data mining promise everything from drug discovery to cultural enlightenment.'[3] How does one choose and affix tags to the concepts and arguments of a work in the humanities and social sciences? Do we have at our disposal or within grasp flexible tools for tagging, which allow for the kind of customization that reproduces the subtleties of a well-designed book index? Who in the chain of production and distribution should be responsible for this order of text encoding?

Digital technology has altered the distributing networks for books, and with the arrival of prototypic portable devices such as Amazon's Kindle, Barnes & Nobles' Nook, Sony's Reader, and iPad tablet, the idea of reading, or at least storing and accessing, books in an electronic format is gaining appeal, while at the same time it has become more complicated rather than easier or cheaper to produce and deliver e-book editions. (The use of proprietary instead of universal software, for example, means publishers cannot deliver e-books to a variety of distributors using the same format; moreover, some of the reading devices don't yet readily accommodate illustrations.)

The question of access has taken many forms, though the Open Access model, whereby material is made available free of charge to the reader, is a predominant topic in scholarly publishing circles. The effects of the 'electronic book' were most immediately considered to have the greatest implications with respect to financial models than for book editing and production. Research publishing had found a relatively comfortable space in which to combine quality through peer review, access through university presses, journals, and scholarly societies, and financial viability in the marketplace primarily through subvention programs, subscriptions, and book sales. While electronic media have offered new means of presenting and communicating information, they have also disrupted the models and networks that enable small publishers to thrive or at least survive as not-for-profit entities with a mandate to make available specialized works for small audiences. Most university presses have little to no venture capital with which to try, fail, and try again to develop and implement technological innovations. Defining their place in a rapidly changing communications industry and commercial environment has therefore been first and foremost focused on the publishing infrastructure, and the debate about e-books in university press publishing has centred largely on financial models, copyright issues (management, protection, infringement), and the relationship between scholarly publishing and large, commercial entities.

But what of *the book?* How, if at all, is the book being transformed in the Age of New Media? How is digitization transforming the book production process? That is the question that preoccupies this chapter. As the book and the bookmaking process are digitized, what effects do we see on the roles of editors and their relationships with scholars?

What Is an Electronic Book?

In a recent discussion among acquisitions editors, one asked, 'What *are* books? Is "book" a kind of content or a kind of form?' This is a recurring question for editors, which takes on new dimensions in the debates about electronic formats. How malleable is 'the book'? Do electronic formats propose a revolutionary way of reconceptualizing it?

As textual scholar Jerome McGann neatly states in his 'Rationale of Hypertext,' the book 'has been one of our most powerful tools for developing, storing, and disseminating information,' and scholarly editions display an 'array of ingenious tools: facsimile editions, critical editions, editions with elaborate notes and contextual materials for clarifying a work's meaning. The limits of the book determined the development of the structural forms of these different mechanisms.'[4] These mechanisms are the product of the book format, which at once imposes limits on the content and affords creative solutions for weaving together different narratives, sources, illustrations, and so on. And although it has only quite recently become possible to pull together texts digitally, or hypertextually, in scholarly writing and publishing this linking of multifarious sources is *sine qua non*: books/texts/works refer to other books/texts/works and primary and secondary sources mingle in different ways, the relationship between the two varying according to the discipline. Does the ability to turn those links into forms of immediate access and ready navigation have much of an impact on what the book is?

As Yuri Cowan states in the previous chapter, 'One of the greatest strengths of the digital edition, besides its searchability, is its ability to display and to juxtapose visual cues' (232). A reader can, with considerable ease, call up and view side by side or back and forth a variety of documents whose physical embodiments are stored in different countries, in rare book collections, or in the local library. If the 'usefulness and possible uses of digital texts for criticism' are by now obvious, can the same be said about the usefulness of the same kind of interactive interoperability between texts in a research monograph? At the moment, we have only a few examples available to consider. But as the publishing community lurches forward in the digital age, it asks itself again, for the umpteenth time, whether the monograph will survive and, now, whether the 'book' as a form will survive.

In this new age of repurposing, publishers are not only looking forward but also looking back: thanks to digital printing and production, the backlist now holds a rich archive of material that can be given new life and new readerships. Beyond digitizing older collections for print-on-demand and e-book sales, presses can explore ways of enhancing editions to make them relevant in changing modes of communication and sites of intellectual exchange. University presses have published the works of great thinkers of the twentieth century, who have marked or changed the direction of their discipline. Subsequent print editions of seminal works, resituating them in current contexts, have been a mainstay of the university press, whether it's Marshall McLuhan's *The Gutenberg Galaxy* (the centennial edition was published by the University of Toronto Press in 2011), Hanna Arendt's *The Human Condition* (the anniversary edition published by the University of Chicago Press in 1998), or the translation of overseas thought for English-speaking audiences, as with Stanford University Press's publication of *Homo Sacer*, by Giorgio Agamben, translated by Daniel Heller-Roazen, to name but a few examples. It is not difficult to imagine how such scholarly books could become the hub or feature of a digital scholarly resource, an online site of comment and exchange for researchers in their respective fields.

More recent and forthcoming digital book initiatives seek to develop interactive editions of new scholarly books – or 'portal books' as UNC Press's Sylvia Miller refers to them – which are similar in many ways to the scholarly hypermedia projects and archives that have been developed in digital humanities and textual scholarship.[5] These projects see the scholarly publisher's productive role extending beyond the book to the book's online environment, in many cases to be achieved through partnerships, whether with libraries, media labs, research centres, or communities of scholars. While some of the projects are to a degree developed around the parameters of a printed book (and will be based on or adapted from the printed book, as Fordham describes its open-access edition of *Dangerous Citizens*, 'a web adaptation of the printed book'),[6] others use website features as the starting point. These projects create the host environment for the book and delineate the points of navigation and exhange in a creative and useful way.

The PDF e-Book

Several avenues have been proposed for the electronic book: some of them (whether called 'born digital,' 'web-based,' or 'portal' books) challenge the traditional book form and others (what we have come to think of as 'e-books') seem consistent with it.[7] The simplest option and the one adopted by most university presses consists of producing a book for print but then making minor adjustments to the book's text and cover files (either at the outset, to the manuscript files, or at the tail end, using the files that would be sent to the printer) to suit the requirements of the e-book vendor. The PDF format reproduces the image of each page on the computer screen. The concept of the book as a print-based technology is unchanged. The production editor's job hasn't been altered significantly by the addition of the e-book format to the production process. Manuscripts already exist as manuscript files, the design and layout process has been fully digitized since the late 1990s, and the materials sent to the printer are already almost exclusively digital. The files used for printing can quite readily be converted for online use. In this formulation, the book, from its inception as an idea through the various stages of production, is still envisioned as the traditional bound book. Towards the end of the production process, in addition to sending the book file to the printer, the editor sends it, after some manipulation to meet the different specifications, to the e-book distributor. This type of digitized book is a simulation of the bound book.

XML Formats and Born Digital Books

The alternative to developing electronic books as converted print books, or as images of the printed book, is to reconceptualize the book as an interactive experience (in the more literal, online sense), where the edges between source or research material and 'book' are softened.[8]

One of the main features of the web book (or 'born digital book' as opposed to the static e-book) is the potential for navigation. The 'book' either spins out onto or enfolds a collection of other texts, not just intertextually but also at another level that allows readers to immediately navigate to, or access, a number of intertextual sources. In chapter 4 of *My Mother Was a Computer: Digital Subjects and Literary Texts*, Katherine Hayles considers how online navigation affects the book. She asserts that 'one of the insights electronic textuality makes inescapably clear is that navigational functionalities are not merely ways to access the work but part of a work's signifying structure. An encyclopedia signifies differently than does a realistic novel in part because its navigational functionalities anticipate and structure different reading patterns.'[9] What Hayles is getting at is that form and structure cannot be separated from meaning, and ultimately she calls for a closer examination of the *materiality* of digital books, since, just as the typesetting, paper, and binding, among other things, participate in the production of meaning, so do the makeup of the electronic medium and its operation confer meaning on texts.

What meaning are we layering into a text when we produce electronic books? If we ignore the gaps and gains produced in the *translation* of a printed book into a digital medium, what inadvertent and significant changes are we introducing?[10] Throughout this volume, contributors have explored the ways in which the page, the margins, the illustrations, fonts, cover design, and scholarly apparatus signify, and they have described and questioned the conventions and processes that have been developed for the printed book. If we consider the transition from print to digital as an act of translation, it is only with a solid understanding of the methods and practices of both print publishing and the component parts of electronic media that we can anticipate and shape the electronic book. Although university presses have become expert in the production of the research monograph, their repertoire of book forms is broad and diverse; and though the one form has become predominant, copyeditors and production editors are not unfamiliar with the multifarious and often stray components that have to be brought together to give the book its final, simple form. (The chapters by Blakeley and Mahon clearly demonstrate the extent to which academic texts can confound linear reading.) Contemplating different arrangements of these elements, and new elements, is an exciting challenge for an editor.

Of course, as editors and publishers, we are struggling with the limitations and definitions of the new channels of communication as they are being developed and tested in the market. The PDF e-book of the first decade of the 2000s was a static file that was easy to produce and distribute. It can be awkward to read on a laptop or computer since it is not designed with the medium in mind – even the orientation of the standard book page, taller than it is wide, is the reverse of the computer screen's dimensions (wider than tall), something the newly released portable reading devices seek to address, thereby accommodating the traditional frame of the paperback edition. As a result of device limitations and the poor quality of print-on-demand technology, the age of 'new media' has seemed more injurious to the book and to book production than it has seemed promising.

As a production editor at UBC Press, I witnessed the growing pains of producing e-books through several stages. In 2000, as manuscript materials were being provided largely in digital form to the typesetter and the final book materials were being provided to the printer as digital files, the press decided to create a digital archiving system in-house. The cataloguing system was rudimentary but adequate. Five years later, the press became a founding partner with the Canadian Electronic Library, which distributes titles on an eBrary platform. The task of supplying, for scanning, hardcopy books from the older backlist was assigned to the Marketing Department; supplying the archived digital files for books published between 1999 and 2005, after adjusting them to meet the requirements of digital asset distribution system, was a job for the Production Department, one that was to be taken on, as new and different things often are, as a 'side project.' We knew we had a set of files in archive, a set of guidelines from the service provider, and a deadline to meet. As this was the press's first real attempt to make and distribute e-books, it was difficult to predict what the task would entail or what the scope of the project might be. Learning how to prepare the files to produce a static PDF e-book was relatively straightforward. But I also found myself in the unfamiliar world of spreadsheets. There were columns and columns of details to provide for each book. While the distribution manager might have been familiar with the term 'metadata table,' it was entirely new to editors in the early noughties; the phrase is now ubiquitous in publishing. As the press was converting the lists from over a dozen seasons, the work was time-consuming; the team assigned to the project was confronted with a wide variety of new questions and had to establish some parameters as it went along. Generally, we opted for the simplest solution, as it would have been unwise at the time for the press to invest heavily in this untested form of distribution. Identifying the permission status for every illustration simply wasn't viable so illustrated books were struck from the list of e-books. Producing even these simple, flat PDF e-books and outsourcing the other aspects of the production and distribution for backlist books proved to be more than a side project, yet the questions that the team encountered and their implications didn't immediately permeate the press. The typesetter would eventually prepare e-book–ready PDFs to the providers' basic specifications, and production editors started requesting a larger set of materials from typesetters and designers for final output (see chapter 8), but otherwise the production process was largely unaltered. The press took a leading role in electronic book initiatives nationally and provincially,[11] but manuscript and production editors experienced only small, incremental changes in their workflow during that period. It would be several years before serious, press-wide discussions about the deployment of resources for electronic publications and the larger implications of new media would introduce more radical ideas and produce deeper change.

At roughly the same time of producing its first e-books, UBC Press also experimented with newly established short-run, or print-on-demand, printers. The results at first were generally woeful. The time the press had spent to plan, create, deliberate about, and refine cover designs was time wasted, as red covers turned pink, subtle hues became stark. Carefully redrawn maps containing soft shading became murky spaces, and passable if not beautiful archival photographs offered themselves as prime examples of moiré patterns. The experiences were disheartening. The new technologies simply weren't convincing alternatives to traditional methods of printing. Recent improvements and new directions show greater potential, however, and publishers are now in a position to shape the tools for their use, as they develop online book formats and work with new systems.

The 'born digital' web book, in contrast with the PDF e-book, attempts a translation of the print book to the digital environment by both seeking out equivalencies and alternatives in electronic features that might correspond to the functions of the elements constituting a book, and maximizing the digital environment to exploit features that aren't available to print (e.g., audio) or affordable to print (e.g., lengthy or complex source documents with the potential to be appended or otherwise incorporated).

For e-reading devices, the format being proposed as a standard in the publishing industry is now based on the extended coding of XML and XHTML, in which instructions are embedded in a file to define its appearance at the destination point. Instead of a page being typeset and its image disseminated electronically to be received by the reader, like a photocopy image as is the case with the PDF, with XML the text is coded for interpretation by the reader's device.[12] What is considered advantageous in the extended coding is the versatility that it offers, for example, allowing the text to reflow to fit any screen size or dimensions of the reading device rather than mimic the printed page. But this coding can be detached from the words in the book. For example, if the codes defining the font are detached, the type will not appear in the publisher's font but in one of the device's default fonts (and the reader may even choose the font); or the style applied to chapter headings may be substituted or a single style applied to the entire text. In this formulation, the book as digital product no longer has a permanent embodiment. This is an unnerving proposition for publishers and book designers, who have held the responsibility of determining a book's appearance for its market. As Albert showed previously (chapter 8), the book designer's role is changing. Is the reader's role also being redefined? In some respects the reader is given a more limited and limiting experience, and in other respects the reader is granted a more active role. Is there a parallel to be drawn between Barthes's resituating of a text's meaning in relation to the death of the author and the suggested displacement of the designer? For the book is given up to the reader – the person and the device – in a new way, one that again places the reader in a new relationship with the elements of a text and the production of meaning.

While we still refer to 'manuscripts,' 'books,' and 'editions,' increasingly production editors and marketing staff are referring to 'content' to be 'repurposed.' By 'repurposed,' we mean placed in different containers, which range from the high-quality printed book to the low-quality print-on-demand paperback, the e-book PDF, and whichever new electronic format is adopted in the industry. The meaning of 'content' is more ambiguous. In a publisher's digital archive, 'content' includes all the files that make up the book – text files, font files, cover files, image files, and all the tags, links, and digitized instructions that bring the pieces together in reassembly. But this content isn't fixed, since the way in which these files interact and operate within different platforms varies from device to device. The 'content' may not be reassembled in the same way each time.

Currently undergirding or underlying this concept of 'repurposing' is a divorcing of the linguistic object from its expression, in favour of the former. Several of the existing portable devices are best equipped for text-only books – in that sense, trade paperbacks in particular have an easier transition from print to electronic book. Not surprisingly, things become more complicated when images are brought into the mix. So that the books can be read with the various proprietary devices, regardless of screen size or software, the text has to be able to reflow into the space of whatever screen the reader is using. The fixed nature of the book page, in this context, is found to be undesirable. Without the characteristics of the page, though, how is the relationship between the text and the images (tables, diagrams, photographs, artwork) denoted? If the text readjusts itself neatly for each type of device, where do the images go? And how does one cite a passage? Even with those reading devices designed expressly to reproduce the book 'pages', the pages aren't fixed: if the person reading the book taps a button to increase the font size, the pages reflow; the pagination therefore changes, and the table of contents cleverly adjusts itself. In scholarly publishing, where precise citations are critical, this presents an immediate problem. Does one cite a page number plus font size (e.g., 'p. 32 Large')? Does paragraph numbering present itself as the best solution? Do these remain primarily technical questions – problems to be solved or, in the case of illustrations, connections to be made, through XML or other coding? Or do we begin to plan books slightly differently (e.g., grouping images in a section instead of scattering them throughout, or vice versa, or providing links instead of images, creating new citation conventions) to accommodate the constraints of these devices?[13]

Coding cannot be dissociated from speed either, which is essential in the current era, and information moves more quickly when it is broken down into small units. The less complex the coding, the more swiftly it will travel. A book file that is filled with complex coding is going to be larger, require more memory, and take longer to load. If speed is the priority, then the file has to be pared back. The smaller reading devices make the flawed translation from print medium to digital medium glaringly obvious, and distort the definition of the book: in reducing the book to a linguistic object, they ignore the bibliographic code, denuding it of meaning. Hayles compels us to consider the implications: 'When texts are translated into electronic environments, the attempt to *define a work as an immaterial verbal construct,* already problematic for print, opens a Pandora's box of additional complexities and contradictions.'[14] Previous chapters of the present volume have discussed the materiality of text and the meaningful codification of knowledge in the book format. Hayles's work is relevant here insofar as it extends the discussion of illusory binaries to the electronic information age: in her analysis, she seizes on the uneasy relationship between information and materiality that is currently troubling the scholarly publishing industry. In the humanities and social sciences, the book has had pride of place, its form been recognized as a significant repository and vehicle for knowledge. Academic publishers and editors have been able to emphasize the value of the book as an intellectual and cultural object; with the shift to electronic media, discussions revolve around how books embody a set of processes, which are being re-examined to plan the future of scholarly publishing.

Hayles's evaluation of the transition from print to digital centres on the work of textual scholars, and she turns to Allen Renear's analysis of that community of scholars' principle of encoding – the ordered hierarchy of content objects, or OHCO. Renear divides the members into three groups representing three historical stages of the encoding principle. Reviewing the three positions, Hayles finds them all inadequate, for they 'elide from electronic texts the materiality of books and their physical differences. A more accurate perception,' she entreats, 'would focus on the editorial process of choice, which is always contextual and driven by "certain interests," although these reside not exclusively in the text but in the conjunction of text, editorial process, and cultural context.'[15] Although the type of editing she is referring to here is critical editing, her point is just as relevant for in-house editors, especially as publishers embark on web-based book projects that incorporate a wider range of archival documents, primary sources, and externally produced visual and audio material.

In his hypermedia archive project *The Rosetti Archive,* Jerome Mc-Gann sought

> to prove the correctness of a social-text approach to editing – which is to
> say, to push traditional scholarly models of editing and textuality beyond

the Masoretic wall of the linguistic object we call 'the text.' . . . We were able to build a machine that organizes for complex study and analysis, for collection and critical comparison, the entire corpus of Rosetti's documentary materials, textual as well as picturial. Critical, which is to say computational, attention was kept simultaneously on the physical features and conditions of actual objects – specific documents and picturial works – as well as on their formal and conceptual characteristics (genre, metrics, iconography).[16]

If at one end of the spectrum we have the text-only e-book of the portable e-reading devices, at the other end is the digital book that lives in the messy realm of online abundance,[17] that engages with multimedia and a new sense of materiality, and where instead of accommodating new constraints, book publishers are still trying to *define* the new constraints and creative standards. Navigation and access are the modes of electronic communication, and preparing for the translation of books from the print to electronic medium might begin with defining useful parameters for their function. Mahon's demonstration, in chapter 6 of this volume, of the effect of decentring the text took us to the heart of editors' anxiety about interactive electronic editions, which promote or suggest the displacement of the 'main text,' as supporting elements are reorganized into a new hierarchy or assembly. His analysis of the mechanisms at work in *Finnegans Wake* in this regard suggests ways of thinking about the effect of the hyperlinked environment on the book. The kinetic, citational textuality of the *Wake*, which 'open[s] up a way for the reader,' parallels the kinetic and citational textuality of the future electronic book. After all, the digital process makes it easier to produce books that 'allo[w] the reader to "enter" the text from multiple points, thus dispensing with the linear narrative, and instead allowing the reader to encounter [the] argument through images, audio, or text.'[18]

For a special issue of *The Journal of Electronic Publishing*, guest editor Phil Pochoda, director of the University of Michigan Press until his retirement in 2011, invited contributors to 'rethink from scratch what scholarly communication in the fully digital era might look like,' how it might be organized within and among universities; how scholarly texts and materials might be best recruited, organized, reviewed, edited, produced, marketed, disseminated and funded.' In her response to this invitation, contributor Kate Wittenberg focuses on the collaborative relationships between scholars and publishers in research and writing, and questions the shape of the scholarly book: 'Must narrative necessarily be presented in linear form? Are there ways to present an "authorial voice" while allowing readers to explore an interactive digital work? Can annotated archival sources become central organizing structures of a publication? Are there new kinds of scholarly arguments that are made possible through the presentation of data alongside textual narrative?'[19] Her questions are not dissimilar to Mahon's, and entwined with new forms of textuality, she asserts, are changing roles and relationships in producing these new, digital books. Developing new formats for the digital book entails some modifications to the established internal and external systems for producing books from 'manuscripts.' They may not necessarily call for a radical reconceptualization of internal structures; however, a reassessment of the production environment and the functions and roles of editors, authors, designers, and marketers is appropriate, perhaps even essential, at this time.

From Object to Process

> They are all elements, steps if you like, on the journey of making the film, which is the journey of discovering what the film is. When people say, 'Well, you must know what you're going to do' – I do and I don't. But really what I'm reporting is not news to painters and novelists and playwrights and musicians and poets – it's just that we're conditioned to the idea that films are entirely preconceived before they exist, and then they're carried out. Which is the industrial process one generally obtains with films, but my job is to *find* the film by making it.
>
> – Mike Leigh, *The Film Programme*, BBC Radio 4, 5 November 2010

As previous chapters have shown, manuscript and project editors are fascinated by the way in which the various elements of the eventual book operate and fit together – text, apparatus, styles and conventions, structure and form – and they routinely 'take apart the submitted materials to be able to identify them, sort them, and manipulate them throughout the process so that, much like taking apart a musical instrument or a piece of machinery for maintenance, the cleaned and perfected pieces can eventually be assembled into a final working whole' (Blakeley, chap. 7, 154). Now we ask ourselves, How will new media change the way in which the pieces are assembled or transform some of the pieces altogether? How do we conceive the 'working whole' of the electronic book?

What Hayles suggests is that we shift our focus away from this idea of the 'final working whole,' the *object* of the book, to the idea of *process*. That is, she draws attention to electronic text as a *process* rather than an artefact. As she explains, 'When a text is generated in an electronic environment, the data files may reside on a server hundreds of miles distant from the user's local computer . . . [the text] comes into existence as a *process* that includes the data files, the programs that call these files, and the hardware on which the programs run.'[20] She goes further to state that we must also take into account the elements that constitute the operation of those programs and the hardware ('the optical fibers, connections, switching algorithms');[21] for our purposes here, however, we can focus on the 'instantiation' of text through the electronic (HTML/XHTML/XML) edition, where the text is reconstituted over and over again, with the various elements being drawn together repeatedly though perhaps not identically, and therefore the text is continually in a physical process rather than existing as a physical object.

In a similar vein, John W. Maxwell, whose research team in Vancouver has prototyped a 'web-first' software system for an XML-based editorial and production workflow, with the aim of producing a free web-content management system for publishers, defines the book as being as much a process, or a constant state of becoming, as an object: 'If the book is to survive as a *durable and valuable cultural object*, publishers must first understand the print book as an extension of a social, fluid, digitally native text at a given moment, and not as the definitive and fixed output of a linear development process.'[22]

Digital Books and In-house Processes

Maxwell's portrait of the current editorial-production process exaggerates its linearity, but it underlines the established flow of work in a university or other book press. As the 'manuscript' moves from acquisitions editor to managing editor, copyeditor, typesetter, proofreader, and printer, there is a high level of exchange between parties, and while in the overarching structure one step follows the other, each manuscript has the potential to invite shunting between any of the stages. Nonetheless, the way in which a manuscript is shaped and reshaped to become a book is now subject to substantial change, far exceeding previous incremental adaptations to new tools made available to publishers. Different roles and relationships are emerging within the publishing and scholarly communities, and more radical departures from the familiar model are being imagined.

Internally, some of the changes may not seem dramatic though their implications may prove to be far reaching. In chapter 8, Sigrid Albert gives us a clear mapping of the evolving relationship between editor and designer as publishing is increasingly digitized. Based on recent in-house adjustments to new technologies and trends in software and hardware development, she anticipates increased reliance on templates and greater separation between the production editor and designer as their roles diverge and overlap in new ways. Production editors, she shows, have already become familiar with the technical language of designers and of desktop publishing. Beyond vocabulary, a 'fluency in digital media, file transfer, and file formats is assumed to be a basic requirement' (193), and increasingly the task of applying styles and typesetting tags is falling to editors – and in most houses, there is still debate about where in the process this step will belong, whether it's a job for the managing, production, or copy editor. The XML design supports this view, as it presents a new logic for putting styling codes and 'proofreading' ahead of typesetting.[23]

Some aspects of the managing and production editors' work are also integrated into the marketing workflow. A book's metadata is furnished by several departments, and because a book's online visibility, or 'discoverability,' determines its success, early and detailed book announcements (rich metadata), now a key form of marketing, require that this material be assembled not when the book is near completion, as we once understood it, but when the work is still in the manuscript stage, if not still in development. (And while the relationship between acquisitions' list-building and marketing's activities has always been close, a more intimate connection is being proposed by Maxwell and others, in a system where the promotion of a book and the dissemination of research results and ideas could occur during the peer review stage, as a select but large group of scholars are invited to read early versions and comment on them, making the eventual readership of the book an early collaborator.)[24]

Overlap also occurs in a new way between the acquisitions and editorial-production departments. Back-and-forth between these departments is typical, as each type of editor focuses on one aspect of the text and manuscript over others. The acquisitions editor will have attended to the text's development in peer review and will have given some comment on the use of apparatus and selection of illustrations if

included; the managing editor will need to assess the materials differently and brings a different set of skills to the project, which Rosemary
Shipton and Amy Einsohn describe in their respective chapters herein:
aspects of style will be tended to; the illustrations chosen may not be of
sufficient quality to be retained; structure and organization may even
be reworked. In short, the editorial work has been divided into steps,
and some of these steps will be moved around to facilitate the publication of digital books.

In future, the evaluation of materials by a production editor may
more routinely occur in simultaneity with the editorial review. Generally when images are needed or desired, for example, the author will
select illustrations early on but these will at a later stage be carefully
examined by the managing or production editor, who evaluates the
quality, composition, and reproducibility of the artwork, calling on the
designer's expertise as needed, before the images are approved for inclusion. The copyeditor may also be asked to comment on the suitabil-
ity of the images, their effectiveness and placement, whether they are
decorative or essential, and the like. As Camilla Blakeley explained
in her description of the editorial process for illustrated works (chapter 7), it is ideal to bring the production editor into the conversation at
a very early stage, and to discuss the design implications – or more accurately, the relationship between the text, images, and design – while
the manuscript is still with the author. It seems reasonable to assume
that electronic books containing audio-visual components, interactive
materials, online supplements, or extensive hyperlinking will similarly require early input from the production editor, and the steps from
accepting the manuscript for peer review and submitting the materials
to the editorial-production department may not be so firmly demar-
cated. We can expect that manuscript editors will become conversant
with multimedia applications and markup, in the same way that production editors have become conversant with the designer's technical
language.

The Editor as the Author's Guide

Although established mechanisms and apparatus are adapted to suit
changing needs – the *Chicago Manual of Style* and the *MLA Style Guide*,
the guides of convention and best practice, both continue to review
methods and develop others, for example, for the suddenly wide-
spread practice of citing online sources – they have been designed for

the medium of print. Furthermore, 'the dignity, weight, and authority conferred by folio production is "transdiscursive" in that the format in itself carries a residual meaning, which can be inherited by later users.'[25] That is to say, scholars are used to working with a set of familiar and recognized codes, be they conventions in their field for presenting arguments, dividing the work into parts, citing and referencing, appending documents, or applying visual markers to distinguish titles, heading, notes, and so on. Style and citation standards are maintained and revised by presses and learned societies to reflect social and other changes in academia without corrupting fundamental principles. There is thus a reciprocal relationship between the two, with the book format remaining at the centre, as decisions pertaining to editing or selecting materials for inclusion and exclusion are influenced by book and text design.

Authors generally have limited involvement in book production decisions; they format the manuscript according to the press's guidelines and respond to the press's recommendations and decisions about design, typesetting, and marketing strategies. Despite being in what one could call a responsive position, they can nonetheless predict and plan for a certain type of book.[26] They know the conventions and write within them, working with editors to shape, whittle, and refine. But with few existing models for the electronic book, how should scholars shape their research materials and arguments in preparation for publication? Since the characteristics and format that constitute a book have historical, social, and cultural value, how do we begin to think beyond the book's bookishness?[27] What will the digital book resemble? What audio and visual components can be accommodated? What design and programming are used by the publisher? What features and functionalities are in place and how do they work? The digital environment will have its own limitations, and developing digital book formats requires the collaboration of professional computer scientists and encoders, designers, editors, and indexers, who bring to the process specialized knowledge about layout, structure and organization of text, presentation of illustrated and other materials, and cataloguing of content. In other words, university presses, with their teams of experts, should be taking a leading role in shaping the future of the scholarly book.

Just as an acquisitions editor will advise an author on the number and content of appendices in a printed book, she will become adept in guiding choices for the online materials and supplements. In turn, the production editor will comment and advise on the quality of the materials for digital production and the press's requirements.

Even without considering the multimedia book, publishers are vetting research material in addition to the book manuscript, to determine where the potential lies for ancillary online material. A work may require distinct treatments for the print edition and the online edition. Or the print edition or PDF e-book may come with online ancillary materials. There are also the new pedagogical approaches that will be developed if classroom texts and recommended readings are reshaped through digitization. The University of Massachussetts Press announced the launch of 'a new series that will make available digital critical editions of classic short works in the humanities for undergraduate use. Each edition will be multifaceted but self-contained. Students will be presented with an integrated set of carefully reviewed materials, including links to audio, video, and other documentation, but not the limitless and often unreliable sources they would otherwise find on the Internet.'[28] This publisher's view of the classroom edition aims to provide a multimedia frame, exploring the permeability of the book's boundaries while insisting on the value of these new boundaries for educational purposes.

This has interesting implications for acquisitions and production editors. Currently, acquisitions editors work with the author through the peer assessment of the manuscript's scholarship, content, and organization. In the future, an additional step may consist in identifying what will constitute the core of the work and which materials, of the author and of others, will complement or buttress the central narrative in valuable ways for distinct reading and research contexts. Perhaps a new type of editor will be introduced into the chain, who brings expertise in instructional design or curriculum development and who acts as an ancillary documents editor for the projects.[29]

The Collaborative Nature of Publishing

By 2010, only a handful of university presses had obtained the resources to experiment with pushing the boundaries of the book further while still retaining its recognizable elements. Two cases that stand out are Rotunda and Gutenberg-e. The latter is the joint effort of the American Historical Association and Columbia University Press. The collection consists of monographs that not only exist on a website but also 'weav[e] traditional narrative with digitized primary sources, including maps, photographs, and oral histories.'[30] They are specially designed for the web page so that the reading is fluid: paragraph numbers are given in the equivalent of a margin space but the reader simply scrolls down to view the full chapter text.[31] Notes and illustrations are linked hypertextually; readers are also offered links to related websites. In this case, the books are presented within a defined set of interactions among complementary material, selected and arranged by the author and the publisher.

In the case of Rotunda, a digital imprint of the University of Virginia Press, the collections consist primarily of edited works – collected historical papers and literary editions.[32] These online editions are interactive and interoperable, connecting editorial annotations, facsimile pages, complete transcriptions, extant texts, illustrations, and so on. The books in Rotunda's Founding Era collection are searchable, internally cross-referenced, and can be sorted according to a variety of criteria.

Each of these university press initiatives boasts academic rigour and insists on the primacy of the scholarship and intellectual merit of the works. It is technological innovation that makes these projects unique, but what impact has that technology had on the scholarship and the publication process? According to the authors involved, the digital book production process prompted them to rethink aspects of the scholarship and writing in relationship to the primary source material.[33] In the case of Gutenberg-e, the authors were asked to think beyond the original manuscript and, with a team consisting of 'project editor, designer, information technologist, and guests from scholarly publishing and digital libraries,' they identified materials that had been left out or not considered for inclusion when the dissertation was conceived and written, materials which could potentially be added to the digital book edition. They had to figure out what would be the new criteria for inclusion in such an electronic, networked book. What would serve as useful and complementary resources to be integrated into this extension of the book form? For example, might it be useful to produce interactive maps to trace changes in settlement patterns across time, or sound and video recordings of oral histories or interviews that informed or are cited in the book? Will the three-dimensional viewing of an otherwise inaccessible sculpture or artefact be considered practically essential in the online edition?

As information scientist Clifford Lynch explains, 'Linkages between argument and underlying evidence – source documents, data, recorded testimony, etc. – can be much richer and more fluid in the electronic environment; indeed, there are questions about how much under-lying evidence should be viewed as being *incorporated into* a digital monograph.'[34] Taking the scholarly edition into a digital environment, then, requires more than technological expertise: The hypertextual or audio-visual features must be shaped by an editorial vision or goal. Gutenberg-e in fact organized workshops for its authors, who would need direction in order to understand what was possible in the particular online environment and to figure out what appropriately belonged as appended or embedded material.

When it comes to ancillary materials, who will be involved and when? How much of the material needs to be peer reviewed and in what format ought it to be presented? Would the press assemble an advisory board for its collections of digital books that are accompanied by online supplements? Digital, multimedia books bring the publishing team deeper into the amassed pile of research materials. Communications and information studies expert Christine Borgman remarks on

> the blurring of the distinction between primary sources, generally viewed as unprocessed or unanalyzed data, and secondary sources that set data in context, such as papers, articles, and books. Data sets are being listed as scholarly publications in academic vitae and cited as bibliographic references in scholarly articles. Scholarly publications may contain embedded data sets, models, moving images, and sound files, and links to other documents, data sets, and objects. Systems to manage scholarly documents must accommodate much more than text, tables, and figures.[35]

As university libraries encourage or mandate their faculty and students to post working papers, conference proceedings, pre-prints, theses, and dissertations in institutional repositories, publishers are also looking at the full life cycle of research material in a new light. Does the interest that libraries have in the preservation of and access to a research project's evolution alter the way university presses as book publishers begin to view and engage with this 'grey literature'? As Sanford Thatcher explains, 'there is value perceived by scholars themselves in having long-term access to such materials relating to the process of scholarship, not just to its final state in published form. And the new avenues scholars are able to pursue in their investigations are even beginning to blur the lines between primary and secondary sources and between informal and formal modes of communication.'[36] This observation points to the changing relationships between the library and the press and between the press and the scholar's research, while at the same time evoking a now recurring motif of the shift in concern from object to process, this time in the scholar's process of research. Like Thatcher and Borgman, Wittenberg concludes that digitization places in-house editors in a new relationship with the author's research. 'The press,' she writes, 'becomes more of a research center that plays a role in leading innovation in a scholarly discipline, in addition to serving a production and dissemination organization.'[37]

In fact, library–press collaborations are under way across the continent. They vary in complexity and in the division of resources, which reflects the period of experimentation in which we live. In July 2010, the University of Ottawa Press (UOP) launched an open-access collection of thirty-six English-language and French-language books, as a collaboration with the university library. These in-print titles have been made available in PDF format through the university's digital repository, and many will eventually be available in e-book formats for hand-held devices. It's a typical example of the first foray into library–press collaborations, where backlist titles are given new life while the press's risk and financial investments are kept to a minimum. Rebecca Ross, UOP's e-book coordinator, explains that they aimed with their selection to include 'a variety of titles in French and English, and a variety of different subject matter and dates,' and emphasizes that the project helps to market older and obscure titles to reach 'audiences all around the world.'[38] The collaboration between Penn State University Press and its campus library has resulted in a couple of projects, among them the Beaver Collection, which makes a set of historical books of regional importance available as electronic editions in a searchable collection, and the creation of the Metalmark Books joint imprint for the simultaneous publication of print-on-demand and digital formats of out-of-print works that 'that hold a significant place in Pennsylvania's rich literary and cultural past.'[39] These mark the first steps in long-term plans for digital publishing of scholarly books. The library–press collaborations also reflect a desire to build on the strengths of the parent institution and research activities that complement the press's publishing profile. In March 2010, Cornell University Press and Cornell University Library launched a German studies series. Print copies of the books in this series, titled 'Signale: Modern German Letters, Cultures, and Thought' and described as 'a new English-language book series covering the literature, culture, criticism and intellectual history of the

German-speaking world,' can be purchased on an on-demand basis, and the full text of many of the books will be available online for free, thanks to a grant from the Andrew Mellon Foundation, which provides a 'stable and sustainable forum' for these research publications. This series involves a third set of partners, as the library and the press are working in close collaboration with Cornell faculty in the departments of German Studies, Comparative Literature, History, Music, and Philosophy.[40]

Similarly, Indiana University Press, Kent State University Press, and Temple University Press have joined forces to bring their editorial, production, and marketing expertise to an ethnomusicology multimedia project, where books will be accompanied by a web-based platform for hosting audio and video materials integral to the authors' research. As with the Cornell project, this one promotes close collaboration between the publisher and research centres at its own institution; the software for the multimedia books is being developed by Indiana University's Ethnomusicological Video for Instruction and Analysis Digital Archive (EVIADA) and the Institute for Digital Arts and Humanities (IDAH).[41]

UBC Press's first project with the UBC Library consisted of joining the institutional digital repository (cIRcle) and populating its collection. The repository has the advantage of being fully indexed, catalogued, and archived, and short URLs are assigned, which are permanent (the underlying location can be changed but the assigned address will always link to the current location of the material). It has proven useful for posting materials such as lengthy appendices and other ancillary material not easily integrated into or essential to the book.[42] The press is currently undertaking a collaboration with the UBC Library and First Nations communities to produce multimedia books in Indigenous language and culture studies, which benefit from audio and visual components. These kinds of multimedia e-publishing initiatives present radical changes to 'book' production, which entail changing the relationship between scholars and presses. They also point to other changes in the organizational structure of scholarly book publishing. During the development and launching of the Gutenberg-e books, Wittenberg, then director of Electronic Publishing Initiative at Columbia, encouraged all university presses to re-evaluate their processes: 'Going forward, the conversation should add a focus on the less technical, but perhaps more intractable, issues of changing organizational cultures, creating new kinds of jobs, and incorporating innovation into a production environment. Taking that one step further, we might consider anew how we define our role as a publishing organization as a whole.'[43] The topic of press-wide and interdepartmental conversations will no doubt oscillate between the meaning of books and presses in the scholarly communication of new media and the actual way in which books are conceived and produced.

NOTES

1 Jean-François Lyotard, *The Postmodern Condition: A Report on Knowledge*, trans. Geoff Bennington and Brian Massumi, with a foreword by Fredric Jameson (Minneapolis: University of Minnesota Press, 1984 [1978]), 4.

2 For more on the roots and problematic nature of this dominant subject coding system, see Sanford Thatcher's thorough article demonstrating 'why the BISAC codes so ill-serve the academic community and the scholarly publishers that support it': 'Why I Hate the BISAC Codes,' *Against the Grain* 22, no. 2 (April 2010): 70–1, accessible at Penn State Press webpage: http://www.psupress.org/news/SandyThatchersWritings.html.

3 Christine L. Borgman, *Scholarship in the Digital Age: Information, Infrastructure, and the Internet* (Cambridge, MA: MIT Press, 2007), xvii–xviii.

4 In Jerome McGann, *Radiant Textuality: Literature after the World Wide Web* (New York: Palgrave, 2001), 55.

5 Sylvia Miller, 'Enhanced E-books and Portal Books,' 5 August 2011, in Long Civil Rights Movement Project News: 'I would like to see archiving, digitizing, and publishing happen in tandem. For example, when an author has conducted oral-history interviews and consulted archival documents during research for a book, the interviews might be ingested into an archive and made available digitally, and the archival collections that were consulted might be digitized, at a library. Simultaneously, the book would be edited and produced at the publishing house. This parallel process would make it possible to publish the book as an enhanced e-book with archival material imbedded in it and outbound links to primary-source collections included as well.' This article also includes a list of and links to enhanced e-book and 'portal book' projects: https://lcrm.lib.unc.edu/blog/index.php/2011/08/05/enhanced-e-books-and-portal-books/. See chapter 10 of this volume for a brief description of some of the pioneering projects in the digital humanities.

6 Homepage for *Dangerous Citizens: The Greek Left and the Terror of the State,* by Neni Panourgiá, http://dangerouscitizens.columbia.edu/.

7 An interesting panel on the future of the book, where Sanford Thatcher clarifies the distinction between e-books and born digital books, is available for viewing: 'Future of the Book: Can the Endangered Monograph Survive?' September 2008, http://scholcomm.columbia.edu/content/future-book-can-endangered-monograph-survive.

8 See, for example, Kate Wittenberg, 'Reimagining the University Press,' and 'Imagining a University Press System to Support Scholarship in the Digital Age,' both in *The Journal of Electronic Publishing* 3, no. 2 (Fall 2010), http://www.journalofelectronicpublishing.org.

9 N. Katherine Hayles, *My Mother Was a Computer: Digital Subjects and Literary Texts* (Chicago: University of Chicago Press, 2005), 90, my emphasis. See esp. chap. 4, 'Translating Media.'

10 Like Dene Grigar and others, Hayles likens the transition from the print edition to the electronic edition to 'translation – "media translation" – which is inevitably also an act of interpretation' (89). I hasten to add that the inadvertent and unintended are always present; what I'm asking here is whether we understand the very mechanisms we are beginning to use to make digital books.

11 Among other things, in addition to being a founding partner in the Canadian Electronic Library project, UBC Press was actively involved in the creation of 'BC Books Online,' a collaboration between British Columbia publishers and libraries that makes accessible in a digital format a collection of BC non-fiction books to the general public through school, public, and post-secondary libraries (http://books.bc.ca/bcbooksonline/).

12 Working in XML, one assigns codes to layers of text, either translating book components and textual elements (front matter, body text, bibliography and notes; chapters, subheadings, sub-subheadings; figures, maps, tables, photos, captions; quotations, epigraphs, marginalia; etc.) into the fields preassigned or predetermined by the parameters of the 'end-user's' device or forcing them into those categories. Very basic coding is done with ease, since scholarly books already do follow conventional forms. In a way, the in-house adoption of the XML workflow, wherein coding is done at an earlier stage – when the manuscript is submitted for publication or prior to or during the editing – can be considered advantageous. It could be used for its flexibility, enabling authors and editors to choose the way in which the e-book would be constructed and ultimately appear to readers. This could be seen as a natural extension into new media of what editors do in conventional/print publishing. At the same time, and

conversely, it places in the editor's purview what has been part of the designer's.

13 The features may enhance the reading experience but I refer to them in this particular case as constraints, as they present challenges to existing methods of scholarship and scholarly book publishing.

14 Hayles, *My Mother Was a Computer*, 95, my emphasis.

15 Ibid., 97.

16 Jerome McGann, 'From Text to Work: Digital Tools and the Emergence of the Social Text,' *TEXT: An Interdisciplinary Annual of Textual Studies* 16 (2006): 58–9.

17 Michael Jensen, director of strategic web communications for the National Academies, who has a wide experience with information technology in the scholarly setting, has published several essays on how dissemination models confer authority, specifically in the present era of information abundance. See, for example, his 'Authority 3.0: Friend or Foe to Scholars,' *Journal of Scholarly Publishing* 39, no. 1 (2007): 33; and 'The New Metrics of Scholarly Authority,' *The Chronicle of Higher Education Review* 53, no. 41 (15 June 2007): B6.

18 Wittenberg, 'Reimagining the University Press.'

19 Ibid.

20 Hayles, *My Mother Was a Computer*, 94.

21 Ibid., 95.

22 John W. Maxwell and Kathleen Fraser, 'Traversing The Book of MPub: An Agile, Web-First Publishing Model,' Simon Fraser University, Sept. 2010 (forthcoming in the *Journal of Electronic Publishing*), http://tkbr.ccsp.sfu.ca/research/papers/traversing-the-book-of-mpub/ (emphasis in original). The idea of the 'completed, bound book' in an online environment was tested almost a decade ago by Rotunda. As David Sewell, managing editor at Rotunda, explains, 'the Electronic Imprint of the University of Virginia Press [eventually renamed Rotunda] was established in 2001 to test the proposition that instances of digital scholarship *can* be bounded, completed, and presented for review, sale, and academic consumption in much the way journals and monographs had been for decades.' One asks, Is it a book when it has a beginning and an end? See 'It's For Sale, So It Must Be Finished: Digital Projects in the Scholarly Publishing World,' preprint of a paper submitted to *Digital Humanities Quarterly*, based on a talk given at Digital Humanities 2007, available at http://rotunda.upress.virginia.edu/docs/research/DH2007/Sewell_2007.xml.

23 For more on this, see, for example, Maxwell and Fraser, 'Traversing The Book of MPub.'

24 Maxwell's account of the Canadian Centre for Studies in Publishing's
    project, where 'the promotional process began in the editorial review
    stages of the book,' shows how the editorial review process produced a
    'promotional side effect [that] was even more important to the project. By
    the time the book launched (only four weeks after the review invitations
    went out), an interested community of some hundreds of people were
    not only aware of the project, but actively interested, many having con-
    tributed to the project themselves.' Maxwell and Fraser, 'Traversing the
    Book of MPub,' under heading 'Reconfiguring Promoting and Marketing.'
    Academic librarian Laura Cohen contemplated using the evaluative tools
    of the social web in scholarship, asking whether the time had not come
    for academia to embrace the technological parameters that are coded as
    social tools: 'Explicit evaluation might include voting, ranking, annotating
    and commenting. Implicit evaluation might include tagging, bookmark-
    ing, downloading and viewing.' 'Social scholarship' is offered here as a
    form of 'soft' evaluation and the publications she envisions resemble more
    closely grey literature than university press publishing. 'Social Software
    and New Opportunities for Peer Review,' *Library 2.0*, 27 February 2007,
    http://liblogs.albany.edu/library20/2007/02/social_software_and_new_
    opport.html. In the spring of 2011, New York University Press announced
    that it had been 'awarded a grant of $50,000 from The Andrew W. Mel-
    lon Foundation to develop and test a method of conducting open, public
    online peer-to-peer (P2P) review of scholarly monographs and journal
    articles. NYUP, which is part of the NYU Division of Libraries, will col-
    laborate on the project with MediaCommons, a digital scholarly network
    affiliated with both NYU Libraries and the Institute for the Future of the
    Book.' NYUP Press Release, 11 April 2011, http://www.nyu.edu/about/
    news-publications.html.
25 D.C. Greetham, 'What Is a Book: Some Post-Foucauldian Ruminations
    (Prolegomenon),' *Journal of Scholarly Publishing* 34 (July 2003): 195.
26 Recall Shillingsburg on the sociology of texts: 'The influence of production
    on the book does not begin when the author hands a completed manu-
    script to the publisher; it begins when the author raises his pen for the first
    word of a work intended for publication, because of a consciousness of the
    way books gets published.' In 'An Inquiry into the Social Status of Texts
    and Modes of Textual Criticism,' *Studies in Bibliography* 42 (1989): 62–3,
    cited also in chap. 1 of this volume, 10–11.
27 See, e.g., Greetham, 'What Is a Book,' 194.
28 University of Massachussetts Press director Bruce Wilcox, in Rebecca Ann
    Bartlett et al., comp., 'University Press Forum: Variations on a Digital

Theme (and Other Matters),' *Journal of Scholarly Publishing* 38, no. 4 (July 2007): 220. Several of the multimedia books in the 'Reading New England Series' are now available to the public; see http://www.readingnewen gland.org/app/?l=about.

29 My thanks to Ann Macklem for identifying and suggesting the description as a new editorial position.

30 Gutenberg-e Home Page: http://www.gutenberg-e.org/.

31 Every fifth paragraph in a chapter is numbered, following the style of the online version of the *American Historical Review*. As Kenneth Margerison explains: '(This numbering scheme remains consistent in the printed PDF version of the text.) Obviously, citations of Gutenberg-e books will require some alteration of the traditional form to accommodate this format, but Meagan Cooke, the Gutenberg-e production editor, promises a forthcoming users' guide containing suggested citation forms' ('Gutenberg-e: A Field Report,' From the Viewpoints column of *Perspectives*, October 2003).

32 The two current collections are the American Founding Era Collection and the 19th-Century Literature and Culture Collection: http://rotunda.upress.virginia.edu/.

33 See Kate Wittenberg, 'Digital Technology and Historical Scholarship: A Publishing Experiment,' *Perspectives*, Publishing History column, May 2002, available on the Gutenberg-e website: http://www.gutenberg-e.org/aboutframe.html.

34 Lynch, 'Imagining a University Press System to Support Scholarship in the Digital Age,' *Journal of Electronic Publishing* 3, no. 2 (Fall 2010), under heading 'The Intellectual Challenge of the Monograph in the Digital Age,' http://www.journalofelectronicpublishing.org.

35 Borgman, *Scholarship in the Digital Age*, 8–9.

36 Sanford Thatcher, 'How to Establish a Research Agenda for Scholarly Communication, Part II: A Sympathetic View,' *Against the Grain* 20, no. 1 (February 2008): 64–5, http://www.psupress.org/news/pdf/univ_ presses(p64).pdf.

37 Wittenberg, 'Digital Technology and Historical Scholarship.'

38 Cited in Zoe Whittall, 'University of Ottawa Press Goes Open Access,' *Quill and Quire*, 29 July 2010, http://www.quillandquire.com/google/article.cfm?article_id=11390.

39 http://www.psupress.org/books/series/book_SeriesMetalmark.html. See also http://alumni.libraries.psu.edu/digitalbooks.html.

40 http://signale.cornell.edu/.

41 http://homepages.indiana.edu/web/page/normal/12146.html; http://iupress.typepad.com/blog/2009/10/mellon-grant-

awarded-to-indiana-university-press-kent-state-university-press-and-
temple-university-p.html. For a list of collaborative e-publishing initiatives, see the Association of American University Presses website: http://
aaupnet.org/resources/collaborative.html.

42　For his monograph *Landing Native Fisheries: Indian Reserves and Fishing
Rights in British Columbia, 1849–1925,* Douglas Harris worked closely with
a cartographer to produce maps based on extensive research data that he
organized into lengthy tables. The maps were included in the book as an
appendix. The original data sets were deemed a useful resource for students and researchers, and intimately linked to the maps; the press and
the author decided that the source tables would be provided as an online
supplement. The press therefore deemed it appropriate to undertake the
editing and typesetting of the tables. In the book, a paragraph introducing
the maps section describes both the tables and the maps, and includes the
permanent library ID (with URL link).

43　Kate Wittenberg, 'Scholarly Editing in the Digital Age,' *Chronicle of Higher
Education,* 20 June 2003, available at http://www.gutenberg-e.org/
aboutframe.html.

Contributors

Sigrid Albert is principal of StepUp Communications Inc., a graphic design studio in Vancouver, BC. She has been designing books for academic and commercial publishers since 1994 and has taught several design courses, including at Vancouver Community College and Emily Carr University.

Camilla Blakeley has worked as an editor for twenty-five years, both freelance and in house. She managed editorial projects in the Toronto office of UBC Press for over a decade and is a winner of the Editors' Association of Canada (EAC) Tom Fairley Award for Editorial Excellence. She is now a partner in Blakeley Words+Pictures, an editorial/design practice with a range of corporate, government, and publishing clients. She also teaches in the Ryerson University publishing program and for the EAC.

Yuri Cowan's research as a post-doctoral fellow in the Research Project on Authorship as Performance (RAP) at Ghent University concentrates on material bibliography, textual histories, and authorship, especially with regard to the circumstances of the form, publication, and reception of nineteenth-century editions of ballads and medieval texts. His doctoral dissertation at the University of Toronto was entitled *William Morris and Medieval Material Culture*, and he has published various articles on Morris, the Aesthetic Movement, ballad literature, and the reprinting of Victorian fantasy in the 1970s.

Darcy Cullen earned an MA in French and French Canadian literature before beginning her career in scholarly publishing. She joined UBC

Press as a production editor, where she also oversaw the press's early transition to e-book production and managed the translation and production of French-English translations. Now an acquisitions editor, she acquires in the areas of Aboriginal studies, Canadian history, and gender and sexuality studies.

Amy Einsohn has worked as a freelance writer and copyeditor for more than twenty-five years. She has taught workshops in copyediting, developmental editing, and grammar, and she is the author of *The Copyeditor's Handbook: A Guide for Book Publishing and Corporate Communications* (University of California Press, 3rd ed., 2011). She earned a BA and an MA in comparative literature from the University of Michigan and a CPhil in comparative literature from the University of California, Berkeley.

Richard Hendel is a freelance designer in North Carolina. He had previously been design and production manager at the university presses of North Carolina, Yale, Texas, and Massachusetts. He is the author of *On Book Design* (Yale University Press, 1998) and the forthcoming *Aspects of Book Design*. He has received numerous awards over the course of his career, from the American Institute for Graphic Arts, the Association of American University Presses, and *Print Magazine.*

Peter Mahon teaches in the Department of English at the University of British Columbia. He is the author of *Imagining Joyce and Derrida: Between Finnegans Wake and Glas* (University of Toronto Press, 2007); *Joyce: A Guide for the Perplexed* (Continuum Books, 2009); and *Violence, Politics and Textual Interventions in Northern Ireland* (Palgrave Macmillan, 2010). He has published essays in *ELH, James Joyce Quarterly, Irish University Review,* and *Partial Answers.*

Alexander Pettit, professor of English at the University of North Texas, is general and textual editor of the *Selected Works of Eliza Haywood* (Pickering & Chatto, 2000–1); general editor of *The Works of Tobias Smollett* (University of Georgia Press, 1997–2012); and editor of *Textual Studies and the Common Reader* (University of Georgia Press, 2000) and Samuel Richardson's *Early Works* (Cambridge University Press, 2011).

Peter L. Shillingsburg, formerly director of the Centre for Textual Scholarship at De Montfort University, is currently Martin J. Svaglic

Chair of Textual Studies at Loyola University Chicago. Among his books are *Scholarly Editing in the Computer Age* (1996), *Resisting Texts* (1997), and *From Gutenberg to Google* (2006).

Rosemary Shipton is one of the founding co-coordinators of the Publishing program at Ryerson University. A partner in Shipton, McDougall Maude Associates, Publishing Consultants, she edits trade and scholarly books as well as government reports, and teaches a variety of editing and writing courses for Ryerson, corporate clients, and the Editors' Association of Canada (EAC). Many of the books she has edited have won major prizes in the United States and Canada. Rosemary has won EAC's Tom Fairley Award for Editorial Excellence as well as Excellence in Teaching Awards from both Ryerson University and the Continuing Education Students' Association of Ryerson. In 2007 she was awarded an honorary doctorate by Trinity College, University of Toronto.

John K. Young is professor of English at Marshall University, where he studies and teaches twentieth-century literatures, focusing especially on issues of material textuality. His publications include *Black Writers, White Publishers: Marketplace Politics and 20th-Century African American Literature* (University Press of Mississippi, 2006), which was awarded the Scholars Prize at the 2006 Eudora Welty Symposium, as well as published and forthcoming articles on such topics as Virginia Woolf and the Hogarth Press, Toni Morrison and Oprah's Book Club, Thomas Pynchon's publications in popular magazines, the missing last paragraph in Nella Larsen's *Passing*, and the manuscript versus Book-of-the-Month Club editions of Richard Wright's *Native Son*.

Index

Compiled by Ann Macklem

STUDIES IN BOOK AND PRINT CULTURE

Bonnie Mak, *How the Page Matters*

Eli MacLaren, *Dominion and Agency: Copyright and the Structuring of the Canadian Book Trade, 1867–1918*

Ruth Panofsky, *The Literary Legacy of the Macmillan Company of Canada: Making Books and Mapping Culture*

Archie L. Dick, *The Hidden History of South Africa's Book and Reading Cultures*

Darcy Cullen, ed., *Editors, Scholars, and the Social Text*